HOW TO DEFEND YOUR FAMILY  AND HOME

HOW TO DEFEND YOUR FAMILY AND HOME

DAVE YOUNG

WITH ALEX SEISE

OUTSMART AN INVADER,
SECURE YOUR HOME,
PREVENT A BURGLARY AND
PROTECT YOUR LOVED ONES
FROM ANY THREAT

PAGE STREET
PUBLISHING CO.

PAGE STREET
PUBLISHING CO.

First published in 2017 by
Page Street Publishing Co.
27 Congress Street, Suite 105
Salem, MA 01970
www.pagestreetpublishing.com

20 19 18 17   1 2 3 4 5

ISBN-13: 978-1-62414-363-2
ISBN-10: 1-62414-363-6

Library of Congress Control Number: 2016963762

Cover and book design by Page Street Publishing Co.
Illustrations by Robert Brandt
Written with Alex Seise

Printed and bound in the USA

"I pray for every reader who reads this book, that God gives you greater understanding and wisdom on how to protect and defend your home and family. Dave has great wisdom and understanding in the world we live in and has imparted us that wisdom. God bless you."

"Behold, I send an angel before you to keep you in the way and to bring you the place which I have prepared . . . for my angel will go before you."
(Exodus 23:20, 23)

—A BLESSING SHARED BY LUCIANO MUNIZ, PASTOR

CONTENTS

INTRODUCTION

Home invasions are scary. I know this from firsthand experience. I've survived them, rescued people from them, seen the aftermath of them and trained others around the world to survive them.

According to FBI statistics, approximately 20 percent of Americans will become victims of a home invasion at some point during their lives.[1] Official statistics such as the FBI's annual Uniform Crime Report show that casualty rates associated with home invasions continue to trend upward in recent years, while attack patterns become more and more random.

When I was fourteen, my mother, brother and I lived in Hialeah, Florida. One Saturday around three o'clock in the afternoon, two men burst into our apartment wearing ski masks with handguns drawn. My mother was asleep, and my brother was playing in his bedroom. One of the men grabbed me by the scalp and shoved me facedown onto the floor, kicking me in the head. The other dragged my mother and brother out into the living room by their hair. They told us not to move.

The two men ransacked our home, searching for money and other items of value. If it had been an action movie, I might have disarmed one of the men, shot the other and saved my family. But the home invasion didn't happen like that. After a few long minutes while we lay shaking on the floor, they ran out the door, never to be seen again.

It turns out that our apartment was mistaken for another that served as a stash house for drug money. But it didn't really matter to me; my family had been violated. After surviving that home invasion by the sheer will of God, I decided to dedicate my life to helping others survive life's dangers.

As a nationally recognized trainer for law enforcement, corrections and security forces and a former marine with deployments that took me around the world, I now know how to minimize the paralyzing grip that criminals want to hold over me and my family during a home invasion.

Throughout my career, I have seen violence up close. I understand the emotional struggles one faces when protecting their life, as well as the mental challenges, physical limitations and hardships that confront victims during a home invasion. I'm also intimately familiar with the additional obstacles that a family faces together when defending against assailants.

It's a shame that many individuals encounter difficulty reconciling being honest, law-abiding citizens with staying safe during a home invasion. These types of situations require quick thinking and fast, confident decisions. Even one moment of hesitation can get an entire family killed.

My intent in writing this book is to walk you through the dynamics of this type of violent crime and to show you ways to gain and maintain the upper hand. I'll share common strategies that attackers use, such as screening techniques, so that you are ready for almost anything that comes at you. I'll teach you to implement effective deterrents, identify the signs that you are being targeted and differentiate between chance encounters and planned attacks. I'll also teach you how to get your home off target lists. I'll list places to hide weapons of opportunity around your house and discuss the top security, surveillance and protective technologies to consider. Finally, I'll walk you through home invasions that are spontaneous and unplanned, which are some of the most dangerous attacks that occur regularly across America.

Read on to learn my expert tips on building family defense strategies that foil these vicious attacks, empowering you to survive on physical, mental and emotional levels. By the end, you should be equipped to deal with a home invasion in the safest manner. You'll have the skills needed to minimize physical injuries, reduce lasting emotional trauma and discourage attackers from going through with their devious designs.

It's important to note that throughout this book I express the idea of a home invader using the masculine pronouns he, him, himself, etc. These terms are not intended to assign gender or to minimize the female role in the topics I discuss. Rather, I feel that the use of this convention allows for simpler reading and easier transition of ideas.

You'll also notice that I primarily frame the techniques in this book for readers who do not own firearms. This is intentional. This book is designed both for those who own guns and those who do not. The strategies

> **THE BETTER YOU ARE** at making decisions to correctly manage your safety, the better prepared you will be to survive a wide range of dangerous situations.

I've laid out in these pages do not require you to use a gun, though I have noted several instances where using a traditional firearm would be beneficial to surviving specific situations. In these cases, think of the gun as an additional layer of security beyond the creative techniques I describe. You can still survive without one, but your strategy may be more effective if you have the option to reach for a firearm.

That said, it's also important to recognize that guns alone will not automatically give you the upper hand. That's why I have provided strategies to increase awareness, identify signs and develop prevention options and response tactics to home invasions. Even if you own guns, I want you to think about other ways to successfully protect your family. Remember that when homeowners use firearms, there is a 50 percent chance that the weapons will be taken and used against them.[2] The easiest way to avoid being on the wrong side of that statistic? Better planning. That planning might rely on having a gun, or on not having a gun, or it might blend the two schools of thought by making the gun optional. To me, the blended option is the best way to go since it keeps all your options available.

You must realize there is no book, video or training course that can guarantee your survival during a home invasion. However, with the right type of preparation, you can learn to be emotionally safer and set the odds in your favor. As an added bonus, you can also adapt many of my strategies to enhance your personal safety in dangerous everyday situations other than home invasions.

While reading this book, you shouldn't feel nervous or scared about the prospect of enduring a home invasion. Rather, you should feel prepared to get through the encounter successfully. Following through on your plan is up to you. You may hate what you have to do—which only means you are human—and you may dread having to do it. The aftermath may stay with you and keep you up at night. But you'll be alive to talk about it.

Take ownership of your household's safety, and plan to survive. I'll show you how to do both successfully.

1

UNDERSTAND HOME INVASIONS

On July 5, 2016, Whitney Whiteman and her husband, Gary Howard, went to sleep in their Las Vegas home.

At three o'clock in the morning on July 6, Whitney's eyes fluttered open, her retinas slowly focusing on the barrel of the gun pointed directly at her face.

"Wake up, bitch," a masked man snarled. Wondering if she was still dreaming, Whitney glanced over at Gary and immediately saw that he was tied up. The terrified couple watched helplessly as four assailants rifled through their house, pocketing money and valuables before slipping back outside.

Gary, a Vietnam War veteran, was perfectly capable of defending his family. In fact, I would say he is someone who you could consider an ideal defender. But ripped from sleep by four attackers ready to murder him and his wife, the situation immediately turned dire. Even a veteran with combat experience wouldn't necessarily be ready for that startling wake-up call.

But Whitney and Gary's story is unlike many other home invasion stories: They both survived without sustaining serious injuries. Some people might label their story a miracle or a blessing. But let me tell you, their survival was actually sheer luck right on par with winning the lottery. And that's coming from someone who has decades of experience training civilians how to best survive home invasions.[3]

SOBERING STATISTICS

In 2014, approximately 325,802 robberies occurred in the United States. Of these, 16.8 percent—or nearly 55,000 crimes—occurred in residences.[4]

Home invasions are a lot more common than you might think. Every fifteen seconds a house is burglarized in the United States.[5] In fact, residences consistently rank as the second most common location for a robbery to take place, just after the street.[6] This danger applies across the board to cities large and small, as well as mid-sized municipalities in between.

An estimated 3.7 million household burglaries occurred each year on average from 2003 to 2007 according to the U.S. Department of Justice's National Crime Victimization Survey.[7] No one is immune. Home invasions are blind to characteristics such as race, educational background, religion, gender, financial status and neighborhood. The only thing criminals care about is getting into a home and taking what they want. Because of this, they seek out the easiest targets to make fast, successful hauls that minimize their chances of getting caught.

"But I've already been the victim of a burglary! Statistically, it's very unlikely to ever happen to me again," you might say. You could not be more wrong. According to the U.S. Department of Justice, every year an average of 2 million American homes are targeted for home invasions. However, almost double that number of burglaries occur—3.8 million, in fact. Simple division means that each targeted house will experience an average of 1.9 burglaries that year. Anecdotally, the trend of multiple burglaries and home invasions occurring aligns with reality. I had my own home broken into twice within a three-year period, even though I'd lived at two different residences during that time.

In addition to the possibility that you might randomly become another perpetrator's target, there is the frightening prospect that the previous home invaders are more likely to return to your property.

This is because attackers become very comfortable with your house after having already been inside. They know your family composition, and they also remember that you unwittingly let them get inside once before. There is a good chance they will return later in the year, usually right after gift-giving holidays like Christmas, Hanukkah and Father's Day. They'll bide their time learning the neighborhood and picking out additional targets.

After all, they are looking for easy targets, and they already know the layout of your home. They also know that you were lackadaisical enough to allow such a crime to happen there before and might still be making the same mistakes.

To combat repeated offenses against your property, upgrade your security system and make it known that you've got new technology on your side with plenty of signs and stickers. Additionally, change your routines to make spying intruders feel uncomfortable. The more unpredictable you are, the less interested they will be. Upgrade your locks and deadbolts with heavy-duty hardware featuring steel pins; switch up your landscaping; and do everything you can to take them out of their comfort zone. Turn the exterior of your house into a "new" house to disorient them and reap the benefits of reduced attack likelihood.

What happens when you and your family become tangled up in a thief's plans—a chilling turn of events that happens in almost 28 percent of all burglaries?[8] Most criminals don't actually want to interact with you; spontaneous crimes such as burglaries or breaking and entering turn violent only after homeowners accidentally walk into an active crime scene. Your presence alone is one of the best deterrents. But once that initial meeting occurs, home invasions can quickly spiral into unspeakable tragedies, with 7 percent of them resulting in a form of violent victimization.[9] In fact, of all assaults reported to law enforcement, 38 percent occurred during a home invasion. And of all reported rapes, 60 percent were linked to break-ins that morphed into home invasions after the criminal discovered someone was home.[10]

Home invasions are considered by authorities to be one of the most dangerous and vicious classifications of crimes, often resulting in mutilation, rape, murder and even the indiscriminate killing of entire families. In 2014, nearly half of all robberies involved the use of a firearm, one of the most lethal weapons readily available to criminals across the United States.[11]

The surest way to survive one of these terrifying ordeals is to be prepared. Learning how these attacks take place, why specific homes are targeted, the types of tactics commonly employed by assailants and your options for fighting or fleeing can help even the odds. Though no one can guarantee survival, the strategies outlined in this book are among the best ways to emerge from a home invasion alive. The old saying applies: *If you don't have a plan, you plan to fail!*

Defending yourself during a home invasion requires you to make a stark choice. Do you fight or hang back? Your family's well-being is on the line. Family is the core unit of life and one of the most important treasures in the world. Even if you live alone, others need and want you in their lives. Can you do what needs to be done in order to succeed and, by extension, survive?

The answer is simple: you must. There is no other acceptable response.

BAD THINGS HAPPEN to good people. Horrific things happen to the unprepared.

SCREENED INTO VICTIMHOOD

No matter where you live, your home has probably already been screened by a criminal at one time or another. It's a hard pill to swallow.

Take it from an expert: Home invasions are seldom random acts of violence. They are carefully orchestrated heists designed with utmost efficiency in mind. Criminals treat home invasions with businesslike precision.

Screening is a complex process. It occurs when a criminal (or group of criminals) begin casing a neighborhood in search of their next targets. What makes one home lucrative while others fade out of mind? The answer varies from attacker to attacker, but I have captured some of the main ones here.

Advanced home invaders never just screen a property. Instead, they follow targets, observing their comings and goings, their social media posts and even their work habits. If they begin to detect a pattern of absences, they can plan an optimal strike time.

How do you know if you are being targeted? For starters, watch the happenings in your own neighborhood. Are there strange vehicles parked on the street or slowly driving by? Do you feel like you're being watched when

WITH CAREFUL PLANNING and the right type of force, home invaders can extract a tremendous profit while expending minimal effort.

you go to pick up the mail? Does your garbage look like it's been disturbed, almost as though someone opened up the bags and rifled through them?

It sounds disgusting, but garbage cans are one of the greatest sources of information about our lives. They contain discarded junk mail and important papers. They also contain pointers about who lives inside. For example, the presence of feminine hygiene products indicates a young to middle-aged woman, while male razor packaging and discarded empty cologne bottles point toward a masculine presence. Pharmaceutical bottles betray health conditions that may be exploited as weaknesses. Even food wrappers, used cleaning supply containers and magazines speak volumes about a home's occupants. You can't shape your garbage, but you can check your cans one or two times per week to see if anything looks out of order. Always peek under the lid after returning from vacation. Look for loose refuse that may have slipped from the bag. Additionally, make it a habit to shred important papers, credit offers and other documentation before throwing them away. Mix this type of paperwork with used cat litter, coffee grounds and other organic waste to deter criminals. A great way to ruin your sensitive trash is to mix a cup of bleach and half a cup of water, then pour it over checks and other sensitive information after you've shredded it. It will render the ink unreadable and ruin the paper.

It's time for a quick exercise to see just how vulnerable your home really is. Put down this book and go to your front door now. Crack it open and look outside. Count the number of windows, thick trees, shadows and unknown vehicles you spot with your naked eye. Imagine how many sets of eyes could be watching you and your family, observing every single movement you make.

Sometimes, the signs of screening are subtler. Perhaps a neighbor's gardener or service professional has been watching your property out of the corner of their eyes while they go about their work. Or perhaps you've seen the same vaguely familiar face glancing in your direction at several different locations, such as the grocery store, the gas station and the parking lot at work. Maybe the barista who serves you coffee every day before you go to work has taken a seemingly harmless, friendly interest in your affairs, inquiring about your family, vacation plans or work duties.

When screening a house, career criminals also create a profile of the family that lives there. Just think about it from the criminal's perspective. Would you rather attack a family with healthy, fit parents and several strong, teenaged children or a frail elderly couple who lives alone? In this day and age, it's almost too easy for attackers to collect this information. All they need to do is sit outside and watch from a vehicle or simply check out family photos on a social networking site from the comfort of their own home.

Flipping through the mail, trash and recycling provides confirmation of names and statuses. For instance, a house with young children will have a number of toy catalogs arriving via the mail (not to mention countless bikes and yard games scattered around the yard or porch), while houses with older children may receive letters from colleges, teen-themed magazines or trendy advertisements for mall stores. Bills and account correspondence give thieves knowledge of homeowners' service providers, providing a deceptive ruse for them to call or contact you in person while appearing legitimately associated with a reputable service you employ.

Thieves hone in on human targets as well as safeguards. They notice houses bearing the emblems of security systems, but did you know that they also take note of homes with generic, out-of-service or non-local alarm companies? Homeowners caught with fake security system signage instantly alert criminals to your abode's unprotected nature. The same goes for houses that display Beware of Dog signs. To a burglar, those slipups indicate irresistible pickings.

THE MAKINGS OF A GOOD TARGET

Though it may seem logical that attackers would pick the nicest, wealthiest looking home in a neighborhood, that criterion is rarely at the top of their lists. In fact, burglary rates typically drop as household income levels rise, with mobile homes topping the list of the most common targets.[12] Remember that a successful home invasion is one in which the attackers get in, steal quickly and get out without being detected or caught. Frequently, wealthy homeowners invest in advanced security systems and monitoring systems that silently alert authorities, making arrest a very real concern. Stolen goods are worthless when a criminal finds himself sitting in the back of a police cruiser.

Instead, a good target is one where attackers can finish their work as rapidly as possible, regardless of the perceived wealth of the occupants. Unattended homes in minor disrepair—such as those with unkempt lawns and gardens due to vacationing occupants—are prime targets. If it looks like no one is home, then there is a substantial chance that the attackers will not be caught.

Predictable shorter absences, such as homes left unattended during workdays, are also appealing to thieves. If they watch the occupants' children board the school bus every day at 7:45 a.m., followed by the parents driving away at 8:00 a.m. sharp and then they observe them returning home between 3:00 p.m. and 6:00 p.m., the attackers know there is a window of seven hours in which to break in and ravage the house before anyone will be back. What do they call this type of easy, by-the-book target? A jackpot.

Other appealing features are homes set far away from neighbors and the road, as well as those surrounded by natural hiding places and blind spots like old trees, thick shrubs, utility sheds and tall fences. These obstacles create shadows and make it hard for neighbors and locals to spot an invasion and contact the authorities. Access points are also critical for criminals. Having side and rear doors or windows that cannot be spotted from the road are optimal places for attackers to slide inside unnoticed.

Being aware of your surroundings is the first step toward managing your own safety. Shown here are suspicious signs: a new neighbor watching from a window, yard crew watching you from across the street, a stranger lurking in a parked car, damaged landscaping that indicates someone has snuck onto your property. Where else might you focus your attention for signs that something is off?

Large, leafy trees make for beautiful landscapes, but they are also cherished by criminals everywhere in the country. A thick branch accessible by climbing from the ground can provide a hidden perch for scoping out a property in near-complete secrecy. The same goes for thick, gnarled trunks that effortlessly hide snooping prowlers.

A few years ago, I conducted a safety assessment in a residential complex. I selected five homes out of the twenty in the neighborhood. One particular home was in the middle of the development, surrounded by large bushes, trees and a fence. As I approached a row of shrubs along the fence between the target house and its neighboring structure, I noticed the sides of the bushes were pulled outward while the fence was pushed in.

I crawled inside the gap, nestling between the bushes and fence. Immediately, my eyes spotted a small floor mat on the ground amid a natural, soft carpet of old pine needles that had clearly not been raked for years. There was a little lump under the mat, and when I lifted it up, I found a small bag containing marijuana blunts, a pouch containing blue Ecstasy pills and a pair of binoculars.

Sitting on the mat, I used the grimy binoculars to peer around—and would you believe it, I could see directly into the master bedroom of the home. The position of the lookout was removed from plain sight due to the poorly maintained bushes, and it gave a full visual of the homeowners' king-sized bed. Additionally, the large floor-to-ceiling mirror positioned by the bed reflected everything happening in the bathroom, including the glass shower. Whoever the perpetrator was, I'd bet he was scoping out a lot more than a robbery. The lady of the house was almost as mortified as her husband was furious.

According to the FBI, 65 percent of burglaries occur between 6:00 a.m. and 6:00 p.m., with the vast majority occurring between 10:00 a.m. and 3:00 p.m.[13] Summer is the busiest time for break-ins, thanks in part to unlocked windows as well as homeowners taking extended summer vacations. No matter when they plan to strike, getting caught in the act is a huge risk, and the smartest criminals also want to find ways to minimize their chances of being discovered long after they leave. Because of this, they appreciate features such as paved walkways and drives that extend to the asphalt of the street. This helps to dampen noise during the heist while covering footprints and tire tracks, which can be tracked from dirt paths and many types of gravel.

DETERRENTS AND OBSTACLES

Make your home as inaccessible as possible to criminals to improve your chances of avoiding home invasions altogether.

Many years ago, I conducted a training course for several neighborhood watch programs. As we walked through the neighborhood, we saw a middle-aged, well-dressed man walking from home to home. He held a clipboard and, as he approached each house, he would look at the door and front area, scribble down a few notes and walk away.

As we observed from a good way down the block behind a parked car, one of the homeowners exited his house and bumped into this person. The two talked for a few moments before the well-dressed man walked away. The homeowner got into his car and started to drive off, but I flagged him down about a block away. I introduced myself as a law enforcement trainer and explained the training course I was conducting before I asked what the two were discussing. The homeowner said the man introduced himself as a real estate consultant taking a survey of the neighborhood. He asked about the man's home, including the number of occupants residing there, their careers, the age of his kids, how he felt about the local schools and whether he owned or leased the property. The homeowner reported he was polite, calm and very well spoken with a smile that never left his face.

I asked if he'd given a business card or shared his name, and the homeowner said the well-dressed man had not. This raised a red flag in my mind as it's typical behavior for criminals who case out a residential neighborhood. They give you a lot of information in a short period of time, then transition into a series of rapid-fire questions before thanking you and leaving. This technique discourages long contact, reducing their risk of getting caught in the act while increasing their reward by simplifying the screening process.

After the homeowner drove off, I continued to watch the well-dressed man. During the span of fifteen minutes, he checked out ten more houses. I decided to test the waters and stepped into view, allowing him to see me watching. As soon as he noticed me, he pulled a cell phone out of his pants pocket and placed a hurried call. A few moments later, a car picked him up at the corner. I called the police, gave them a description of the man, told them what I had observed and provided them with the make, model and tag number of the car.

Four days later, the well-dressed man was caught inside a home in that very neighborhood. When questioned by the police, he said he picked the target because it was easy. It had no security, fences, alarms or occupants at the time. You might think the crook was mistaken in his assessment; after all, if it was such an easy house to ransack, why had he been caught?

It turns out a vigilant neighbor saw him entering the home and called the police. If that nosy individual hadn't been looking out the window at the right time, he might have gotten away with his scheme.

Hopefully, that story will help you understand the need for good deterrents!

Let's say you live in a quiet rural or suburban area far from neighbors and main roadways. All adults in the house work outside the home, and your children go to school every day. Your property is dotted with beautiful, established shade trees and landscaping, and your older house capitalizes on large, grand windows to let in plenty of sunlight. While reading this book, it hits you that you're doing everything wrong. What steps can you take to reduce the likelihood of a home invasion?

One of the most effective deterrents is the use of a loud, visible security system. This goes beyond a lawn sign, as most burglars will peek in windows to spy for operation panels, window sensors, motion detectors in the top corners of rooms and other components. Studies by major universities found that the majority of attackers looked for the presence of a security system before attempting to gain entry, and that the overwhelming majority fled immediately upon hearing an alarm. I recommend making sure the presence of an alarm system is clearly visible (such as signage), while making sure the operations panel is not visible from a window. That way, a criminal has to spend extra time figuring out where the panel is located in order to disable it. Surprisingly, despite their status as a strong deterrent, only 17 percent of American households have an alarm system.[14] I will go into greater depth about security system specifics later in this chapter, including where to place components, how to fully protect your pass code and a creative way to keep your system online even when an attacker cuts wired communication.

Like alarm systems, gardens and lawns can also serve as strong visual deterrents. Carefully plan your landscaping and prune outdoor plants often. Tall shrubs that grow close to the house should be kept as low and trim as possible. Saw off any low-lying tree branches that could make climbing to a perch easy and, if possible, install convex outdoor mirrors where you can see them from the front entry. You won't have a complete view of every blind spot, but you will be able to get quite close.

Simple changes to your landscaping and external adornments can make a huge impact. Plant spiny, spiky shrubs or foliage under first floor windows to discourage prowling. If you live in an arid climate, cactuses and thorny succulents are great options. For cooler climates, roses, barberries and scrub pines are good options. If possible, replace part of your asphalt or concrete driveway or walkway with gravel to add a loud, crunchy element to entrances. This can alert you or your neighbors if someone unexpected is trying to sneak up on your home.

A messy front yard is the first giveaway of an unoccupied home. Make arrangements to avoid these pitfalls when you're away from home: weeds in the yard and driveway, plants not taken care of, bushes and vines not landscaped, leaves and debris strewn about the yard, mail cluttering the mailbox and doorway, garbage either full or not returned to the house after trash pick up.

Set lights and lamps on erratic timers, and switch up cycles on at least a weekly basis. The goal is to make it appear that lights are being turned on and off inside as users move from room to room. Timers on televisions and radios are a great way to add depth to the illusion that someone is home.

I once knew a man who lived with his eldest son. The two went on vacation for five days, and they thought they were doing everything right. They had a neighbor pick up their mail from the mailbox, grab the newspaper off their lawn each morning and even open their curtains during the day and close them at night.

However, they slipped up with their car, which stayed in the driveway for five days.

The father and son returned to a ransacked home.

After the burglars were caught, the police asked them why they picked the man's house. The reply?

"We knew no one was home," the lead thief said, grinning proudly. "It rained for two days, but the driveway under their car stayed dry the whole time."

When going away, leave a car parked in the driveway instead of the garage and ask a neighbor to move its position slightly every day. You might wonder: Why not put the car in the garage, since it'd be safer there? It's all about making the illusion that someone is home as strong as you can muster. Alternatively, let the neighbor use your driveway to park one or more of their vehicles while you're out of town. This simple decoy makes criminals think twice about the presence of an individual in the home. If it's feasible without blocking view of the front door, pull the vehicle up to the front walkway to block an easy path in and out of the house. If a home invader is intent on stealing large objects such as designer furniture or artwork, this will make their getaway all the more difficult—dropping the chances that your home will be targeted.

To mask your whereabouts, stagger the times you come and go from the house. Create a fifteen-minute window around your normal departure or arrival time, and randomly rotate your schedule. Inject confusion by having adults leave at different times, a tactic that makes it harder for criminals to keep track of your whereabouts. Ideally, leave from different doorways or entrances.

After dark, draw the curtains around your home to block out activities that might be viewed from the outside. This still applies if you have blinds, which can cast visible shadows. Even when you go out for the afternoon, continue this pattern before you lock up. Do everything in your power to make it seem that someone is home and equipped to call for help at all times. The harder it is for criminals to spot definite absences, the less lucrative your home appears.

If you work close to home, pop in sporadically every couple of days. Avoid coming home on the same day every week if you are able to do so. Alternatively, ask neighbors, pet sitters, nearby friends or family members to stop in unannounced from time to time, ensuring that there is a constant, unpredictable stream of foot traffic to your residence. This chaotic stream closes the window of unoccupied time perceived around the property.

Take a moment to knock on your front door right now. Is it hollow, or is it solid? Is your lock and deadbolt hardware in good shape? If you have decorative glass installed, is it strong enough to withstand a heavy kick from steel-toed boots? These are important questions to answer during the early stages of preparation. If your door is hollow, replace it as soon as possible with a solid wood or steel-reinforced option. Replace the screws holding your deadbolt and lock in place with three-inch masonry screws. Most kits only include one- or two-inch screws, and these can snap if exposed to prolonged blows. I'll go into much more depth on entryway considerations when I teach you how to defend the door in Chapter 4.

Use storm panes and safety glass to protect windows. If you do not open certain panes, drill screws into the frames to keep them from being opened. Position large pieces of furniture in front of windows to create obstacles for intruders who try to break in, as well as additional evidence should they topple or break. Sharp, jagged decorations are excellent options. A great option might be a heavy die-cast model of a plane or ship, or even a geodesic glass and bronze sculpture. Plants are also great for this purpose, as they leave soil evidence and also alert animals to an invader when they shatter. Cacti and many other succulents add beauty to rooms but feature sharp, pain-inducing spines. For large windows, put a food and water bowl nearby to make it appear that a large dog lives there.

Finally, never hide spare keys near a door. I know a lot of crooks who routinely poke around under pots and statuary in search of poorly hidden spares. Instead, invest in an inexpensive key locker, which you can hide in a dark corner of a shed, under a deck or even inside a deep tree knot. Set the combination to a random grouping of digits rather than a telephone number, anniversary, birthday or other recognizable string of numbers that a savvy criminal might guess. I'll share my best tip for hiding keys in Chapter 4.

When planning out strategies, remember the golden rule of home safety: Deterrents won't work unless you use them. You need to approach them as a lifestyle change, not a temporary or occasional fix. The goal is not to make you feel paranoid or overwhelmed. Instead, the goal is to consistently and continuously bolster your safety. Once you start building most of these deterrents into your way of life, you'll find that they become second nature.

CONDUCTING A SAFETY WALK OUTSIDE

Safety walks are surveys of the exterior property conducted regularly, usually on a monthly basis. During each safety walk, patrol the perimeter of the front, side and rear yards surrounding your home. You should be on the lookout for potential threats as well as evidence that unwanted guests have been on your land.

Though they may seem trivial, safety walks are actually incredibly important. Everything we cherish resides inside our homes, including our families and much of our own lives. Safety walks enable us to see vulnerabilities we need to be aware of in order to protect against attackers who want to prey on us.

Pay particular attention to blind spots, which I refer to as "danger spots." These are areas of your property where an individual can stand outside and see inside the home without being spotted. Examples of blind spots include leafy hedges, gardens, landscaping features, thick

tree trunks, sheds, ornamental items like fountains and even shadows cast behind spotlights. Vehicles can create temporary blind spots when parked in a driveway, as an attacker can hide behind one and peer into the house.

Every property has blind spots. It's an unavoidable fact. However, you can make blind spots less attractive to home invaders by regularly checking them, keeping plants and hedges tidy and adding obstructions such as dividers and stone statues that an assailant could trip over while focusing on prowling.

Safety walks overlap slightly with interior preparation strategies, particularly in regards to windows and see-through doorway elements. Remember that simply seeing inside is a safety issue.

In my neighborhood, there is a nice house on one quiet corner. A doctor and his family lived there for several years. The family did an outstanding job keeping up their home, always boasting a neat yard, a clean driveway and nice drapes and curtains on the windows. Next to their front window, the family kept a medical mannequin that they used as a coat rack. It was a quirky piece that fit the doctor's occupation.

The mannequin never moved. Whenever the lights were on inside, it looked like there was a man sitting in their living room. Since they hung coats and outerwear like hats on it throughout the year, it always looked like someone was home. A criminal would've had to sit in front of their tidy house for hours to realize that the stationery figure was a dummy.

While walking along the front of your property, glance up and scan your windows from the road. Can you spot the glow of expensive electronics, or is treasured artwork visible hanging from the walls? Perhaps you have a clear view of a jewelry box or desktop cluttered with checks and important papers. If you can see it, so can a home invader. Remember, when they see something they like, it makes them all the more focused on getting inside and taking the property you worked so hard to earn. To put it a different way, when intruders can see inside, you become their live television.

Be alert of potential blind spots and how you approach them. Shown above, walking close to vehicles parked in your driveway gives you a limited visual and no time to respond to danger. The lower image shows how you should approach the vehicles at an angle, also called "cutting the pie," which gives you more time to see and respond to danger.

Based on the observations you collect during your property walk, invest in curtains, blinds or draperies to cover your windows when you are not home. These coverings help prevent wandering eyes from seeing any precious items, rendering your home a less lucrative target in the process. They are especially helpful for homeowners who live alone, either permanently or due to a spouse's temporary absence. Check that draperies block light to avoid casting shadows, which can quickly alert a threat to the number of individuals residing in the home.

Back outside, look in wooded or heavily planted areas around your property for signs of occupation. Indicators include empty beverage cans, cigarette butts, trash or trampled foliage. If a disturbed location is within eyeshot of a window or door, it's very likely that someone has been scoping your home for a prolonged period of time. Maintain extra vigilance to thwart any plans they may have hatched!

If you have security system signs, place them on your lawn instead of near the front door. After all, if a home invader gets close enough to your home to see inside a window and spot something they want, a protective alarm sticker will not stop them from going through with their plan. Deterring them earlier in the process, however, might be enough to keep your house secure.

The same goes for No Trespassing and Beware of Dog signs. Placing these on the house can render the fearful effect too late to stop a crook. Put these closer to the driveway and road, if used.

Remember that home invaders despise dogs. These companions are loyal to their owners. Unafraid to sink their large, sharp teeth into a leg or arm, they make formidable foes. Use the presence (or perceived presence) of a dog to your advantage when taking a safety walk.

> **IF YOU'RE A HUNGRY BURGLAR** and you've already made it halfway up the walk, do you really think a little sign is going to scare you off? At that point, it's too late to be an effective deterrent.

If employing a Beware of Dog sign, consider completing the deterrent illusion by adding a large doghouse in your backyard along with a lead line and scattered pet toys designed for larger canine breeds. Though a large, protective canine can deter thieves, you need to be careful when stretching the truth. If your property is not fenced in and you do not have a tie-up, lead or other walking device, it may seem unlikely that a dog resides there. A quick glance through a kitchen window to see if food and water bowls are out can instantly blow the cover, as can the absence of barking when knocking on a quiet afternoon. Inside, put out one or two dog toys in clear view of windows. Even if you only have one canine, this gives the illusion that the home hosts a large, protective breed as well as a smaller, loud pup whose shrill barks can alert others to trouble. Simple techniques and tricks like this raise the effort required to make a successful haul, lowering your home's position on the criminal's target list. If your illusion is not convincing, it may not force an eager attacker to take pause.

You might think it sounds extreme, but I promise that pretending to have one or more dogs works. Case in point: There used to be an elderly woman who lived a little way down the street from me. I didn't know her very well, but I noticed that she kept a dog bowl and chain on her front porch, as well as a doghouse out back. After she passed away, I saw her family struggling to move furniture out of her house. I ran over and lent a hand as they moved her belongings into a big moving truck. Curiosity got the better of me, and I asked what would happen to her dog now that she was gone. Her son smiled and said she'd never owned a dog in her entire life. He pointed at the bowl and chain, explaining that her husband of 45 years started putting out the dog equipment to deter criminals from breaking in. After he died, she continued the tradition. It worked; I lived in the neighborhood and I was none the wiser to her clever strategy!

Next, test your outside lights. If possible, convert them to photoelectric sensors that automatically turn on at dusk. Save money on your utility bills by adding a motion detector that only illuminates the bulbs when someone steps foot on your property. Look for spotlights that offer at least 240 degrees of motion detection, and use the test setting to make sure that traffic and neighbors won't set it off. Additionally, use the brightest bulbs your lights can safely handle. I recommend 60 watts or higher to fully illuminate the property.

Continue your security walk in the backyard. Are you currently employing the same deterrents in the rear yard as you are in the front? If not, you are leaving yourself massively vulnerable. The majority of thieves break into homes through back entrances to avoid detection from the road or a nosy neighbor down the street. The backyard is usually much more secluded, and as such, it's attractive to someone who wants to slip inside unnoticed. Address these issues by putting up several security system signs or stickers in the back. If you have enough of them, you can also place them alongside gardens and windows. Don't be afraid of going overboard. The more deterrents you have, the safer your family will be.

As you wrap your security walk, take note of all the vulnerabilities you uncover. Don't be ashamed if you find several deficiencies. Every home has its weaknesses. You will address these in the exercise at the end of this chapter.

Why do safety walks matter? I'm sure you're thinking that they sound a little hokey. Let me share a story that will illustrate their importance.

Back when I was a police officer, I heard a chilling story about a family who lived on the third floor of their five-story apartment building. Their unit was on the end of the structure, near the stairs. Each night, the father would look out across the street from his window, peering over an adjacent rooftop. Sometimes, he even walked along the stairwell near their front door to keep an eye out for anything out of sorts.

One afternoon, as he looked across the street, he noticed something shimmering on the rooftop. Unable to tell what it was, he called the police. That evening, when the authorities investigated the strange object, they found a pair of binoculars, a rug, a blanket, a box of latex gloves and several jars of petroleum jelly. The police placed the spot under surveillance for the evening, and around two thirty in the morning they arrested a man on the roof. The police noticed that the man could see into a number of

apartments from his vantage point, even the room where the father's young children slept, played and changed.

Safety walks make all the difference. They do not have to be formal walk-throughs; even if you don't own your property, or if you live in a small apartment, you just need to maintain constant vigilance of what's around you. The moment something slips out of place, you'll be prepared to address it.

ANALYZING THE HOME'S INTERIOR

The next step in building a plan is evaluating the interior of your home. A few key points are presented here to help you begin making preparations. On this walk-through, you will evaluate and identify escape routes, at least two places to hide out of sight, positions of cover where you can physically shield yourself from weapons and places to engage a home invader. You will also look for weapons of opportunity and identify defense positions throughout the house. That's what I like to call "the basic package" of home invasion survival strategies.

Recently, I assisted a homeowner who was conducting a safety assessment of his home and property. After we completed our review of the outside of the home, we walked through the interior. We tried to identify the key areas I noted in the previous paragraph, but we ran into some difficulty when it came to picking places for cover and concealment. The homeowner drew the conclusion that there were few places to hide, and I had to agree with him. He did have several small rooms within the home, so I pointed out a number of locations to defend from instead.

The homeowner also owned various firearms that he stored around the house. We identified angles to accompany his engagement positions. Eventually, we came up with an ingenious way to use his home's tiny size to his advantage. We placed pictures on the walls opposite specific pieces of furniture in the next room, which an intruder might bump into or jostle. This allowed him to use his firearm in the home while providing instant targeting capabilities, even without direct lines of sight. He could simply listen for the furniture that was moved in the other room while an intruder snooped and then shoot at the center of the pictures to hit the person lurking on the other side.

To conduct your own interior evaluation, start from the front door and walk through your home floor by floor. Make a list of hiding places, ranking them on a scale of zero to three. Hiding places ranked zero are not acceptable places to hide. They may be too small, too difficult to access or too hard to escape from if necessary. These locations should only be used as extreme last resorts.

Conversely, hiding places rated as three are ideal places to duck into during a siege. An example might be a closet with a weak, destructible wall that backs up to another room or one with an attic entry panel in the ceiling. This type of hiding place enables you to successfully hide while also offering a means of rapid escape. Hiding places rated between zero and three offer differing amounts of coverage and access to escape routes.

Once you finish reviewing hiding places, shift your focus to the home's layout. Are there opportune locations where you could engage an attacker to regain the upper hand? An example could be a living room or the top of a staircase. Take note of these; they will be further explored when we walk through engagement considerations.

Finally, jot down any other unique characteristics of your home that you could leverage against an attacker. Every house is different, and in the end, you will always know your layout better than any assailant. Use this information to give yourself a significant upper hand.

SCRATCHING THE TARGET OFF YOUR HOME

You established a number of deterrents and obstacles to keep criminals away from your property, a one-time step that fortifies your home. Next, you built regular safety walks into your routines to make sure deterrents are holding up and that crooks are staying away. Now, I'm going to share several ways for you to continuously keep an invisible target from creeping up onto your front door. These techniques are the types of things you can review every few months to make sure you're continuously staying safe.

First, begin with research about your neighborhood. Is there a history of home invasions? What types of crimes have occurred alongside property theft? Look for trends such as vandalism, targeted goods and even the status of the homeowners who have been victimized. Think like a criminal to determine what made those homes appealing enough to risk prison time.

Next, begin minimizing and downplaying any commonalities you share with previous victims in your area. If your neighbors suffered a home invasion while away on a vacation that they posted all over social media last summer, consider keeping your plans off of the Internet until you return. Invest in light timers, motion detectors and a security system to monitor while you are away. Ask a friend to come over and water your plants to continue foot traffic in and out of the house. Place a temporary mail hold.

Build strong connections with your neighbors. Introduce yourself when you move in, and greet new neighbors to learn about their lifestyles. Develop reciprocal watch strategies to keep an eye on each other's properties once you feel comfortable with them. As you develop a formal family action plan, consider meeting with a trusted neighbor to share your alert and alarm strategies to improve emergency response times. Though criminals will never know about this collaborative effort, it will make your escape and reporting activities more likely to succeed.

Perhaps the simplest way to make your house more secure against home invasions is making sure every door, window and other entry point is securely locked. Though 60 percent of invasions are due to forced entry, a staggering 30 percent occur due to unlocked doors or windows.[15] That's right, almost one in three attackers essentially let themselves in uninvited.

Whenever you are at home, flip through your mail to ensure that all addresses are intact. Some criminals rip the names and addresses off bulk mail while casing a property, while others take the entire piece of mail. Either act is a felony, so if you can prove that a home invader took a piece of your mail to learn more about you, you can put them away for a long time!

If you find your mailbox open or partially open, it was probably forcibly accessed by another person. The wind can only account for so much motion on the mailbox's door. Make it a habit to securely close the door every time you fetch your letters and bills.

Do everything you can to protect yourself on your own. Avoid relying on nosy neighbors, because even though they may come through for you, they are not a guarantee. Examples of looking out for yourself include illusion tactics, such as locking and securing your garage while parking your car in the driveway if you only own one vehicle. This gives the impression that there are several cars. This signifies that there are multiple people living at home, dissuading attackers from making an attempt. Additionally, never leave valuables in sight in the car, which can heighten the urge to vandalize it. Always lock your car doors even if you're only planning to be away for a few minutes!

BOLSTERING DEFENSES WITH TECHNOLOGY

While modern technology, such as Internet searches, social media and mapping software, makes criminals' jobs easier, that same technology can also be exploited to make your home defenses stronger. Alarms, cameras, signs and other technology divert attention from your house and suddenly make other targets more alluring. Intruders want quick scores with easy ways in and out. Used appropriately, technology hampers those goals. Here are a few examples of how you can turn the tables on hungry, tech-savvy burglars.

If you cannot afford a security system, try looking for non-functional decoy surveillance cameras. The best options are discontinued or broken cameras purchased online or at flea markets. Some big-box stores even sell realistic decoys. Position these outside your entrances facing toward the door. Because they will not actually capture any video or photos, they only need to appear convincing to an intruder. If possible, look for one with a blinking recording light to improve the illusion.

Set up a laptop with an inexpensive webcam programmed to record all captured motion. You can stream these to a secure, password-protected server for around-the-clock

monitoring without the cost of a pricy security system. Mount the webcam across the room from major entrances to capture full body images of criminals, as well as faces obscured by wide-brimmed hats. You can even disguise the location of the camera by placing it inside a vase, cookie jar or other container with a strategically-bored hole. Secure the camera inside with heavy-duty masking tape. Run the USB wire behind the wall to connect it with the laptop.

Outdoor trail cameras blend in with the property's surroundings. They capture photographs or video whenever their motion detectors trip. These cameras are equipped with night vision to provide around-the-clock surveillance of your entire property. Even if you're not a hunter, the cameras are a great way to bolster external monitoring.

A new trend in security systems is the use of wireless transmitters versus hard-wired cables. The transmitters contain a tiny device similar to a cell phone that connects your home to the remote monitoring station. These systems are outstanding options that eliminate the very real weakness of snipped wires. Even if a criminal cuts the communication cables to your house, or if there's a power outage, the system will continue to function normally on battery power. You'll never be left unprotected.

Monitoring technologies are excellent ways to deter attacks and capture would-be assailants. However, other technology can help reduce the potential of suffering a home invasion or identify crime information before you're attacked.

Many major search engines allow you to set up alerts for specific keywords that appear in news stories, blogs and even social media posts. Take advantage of this excellent feature to monitor happenings in your region, county, town, neighborhood or on your street. Every time a piece of content is posted online matching that keyword, you will receive an email with a link to the piece. This allows you to remain constantly connected to police reports, live social media feeds and other sources that report hyper-local information about break-ins, robberies, arson and other crimes.

Remember to ensure that your home's Internet service uses strong passwords and that they are changed on a monthly or quarterly basis. Hacking a home's security and communication system gives criminals a tremendous advantage. Not only can they monitor your whereabouts and phone calls, but they also gain access to emails, online banking details and other highly sensitive personal information. Lowering their ability to crack this system ultimately makes you safer.

If you're going to be away for more than two or three days, consider submitting a hold mail request with the postal service. Through its website, you can quickly apply a free hold for all mail received at your address, opting to pick it up later or have it delivered when you get back. For extended absences, invest in mail forwarding, an inexpensive service that routes your mail to a temporary location such as a vacation house. For larger parcels, most shipping carriers offer affordable premium tracking services via their websites that include delivery specification services. For example, you can request for packages to be dropped off only during certain hours or only on specific days, allowing you to control when parcels arrive. This is valuable for protecting your shipments, and it also cuts down on piled-up mail outside your home.

Mail indicates a home's occupancy. However you do it, make sure that your mail is accounted for while you're away, even if it means having a neighbor pick it up for you. Pile-ups of post materials indicate long absences, attracting criminals like flies to honey.

Never post anything on the Internet that could compromise your efforts to protect yourself from thieves. I know it's tempting to tell people about your upcoming cruise to the Caribbean, or a business trip to Europe, or even an afternoon shopping trip with friends. Resist! Check-ins, selfies and other location-based technologies broadcast your location to everyone—even if you think your settings are locked down.

Nothing on the Internet is ever truly private. All of the recent hacks of financial institutions, insurers' medical records, government employee data and retailers' payment transactions should tell you something about online security—and those organizations invest millions of dollars into keeping your information "safe"! Chances are that your social media feeds are not nearly as well protected as these hack victims' information. Advertising any absence from your home becomes an open invitation to burglars, a consequence-free, all-they-can-eat buffet. A whopping 78 percent of burglars use social media platforms to target properties, while 74 percent use online map street views to case homes before robberies.[16] Without even stepping foot on your street, they've managed to remotely label you as a qualified target.

These solutions are relatively high-tech for the average homeowner, I'll admit. But there are other, simpler ways to leverage technology to protect your house without investing in expensive equipment. As noted previously, set a timer on your television, stereo system and lamps so that they turn on sporadically during the day, especially around the lunch hour. This will make it seem like someone is home even when the house is empty. Talk radio is a great way to give the illusion that people are inside having a nice conversation. Crank the volume up so that muffled voices can be heard from the stoop outside each door. Take the illusion a step further by streaming a faraway radio broadcast so that the crooks don't become aware by flipping through the stations in their car.

HOME SECURITY AND CAMERA CONSIDERATIONS

Having a home security system does not automatically guarantee that attackers will turn away from your property. True, the use of a security system and its exterior signage are excellent deterrents, but when a burglar really wants to get in, they will do so at all costs.

Even though they don't guarantee your safety, I still strongly urge you to invest in a home security system. This technology synchronizes your home with the authorities, calling for backup if you are unable to do so yourself. Systems are relatively inexpensive to install. Most alarm service providers bundle monitoring with telephone, Internet and television offerings for lower rates. When seeking out a provider, look for systems that operate wirelessly, as noted in the previous section. This means that the receiver stores a communication device that operates like a cell phone, eliminating the need for a landline should a burglar cut the wires outside.

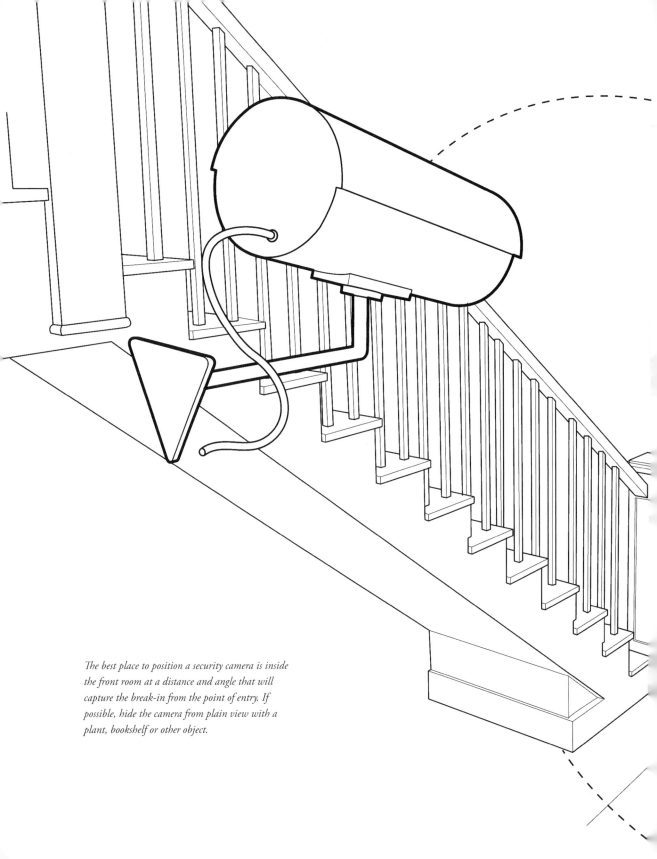

The best place to position a security camera is inside the front room at a distance and angle that will capture the break-in from the point of entry. If possible, hide the camera from plain view with a plant, bookshelf or other object.

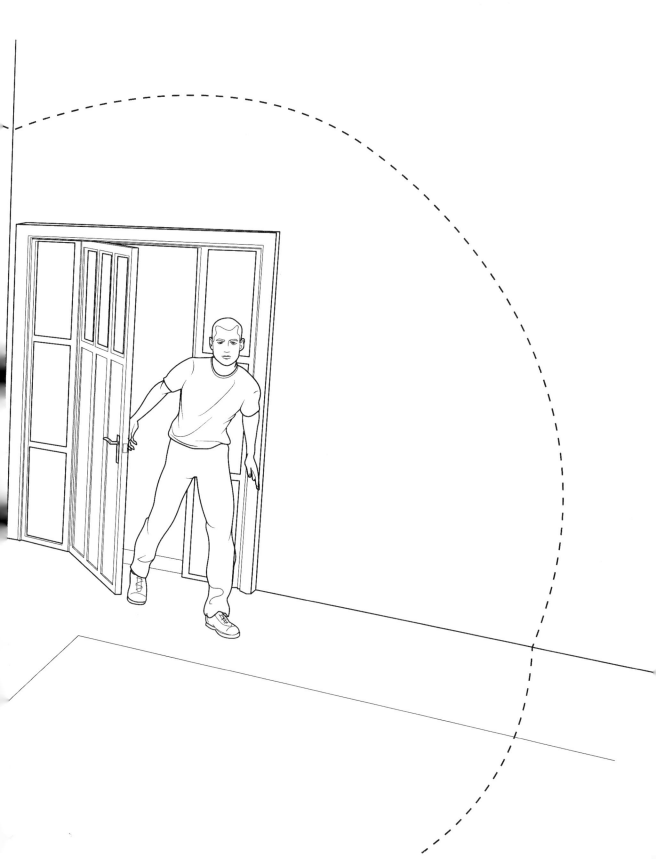

Place your system panel near the front door, but make it so you cannot see it directly from a nearby window. Attackers will look for it from the outside. Add a cover that blends with the wall or nearby décor for enhanced protection, buying more time for you. The more time the bad guys spend searching for the panel, the longer they're tied up with an obstacle they must deal with. Make them work for what they came to steal. You can also put lamination or tape over the top of the panel, improving the ability to capture fingerprints once the home invasion ends.

It goes without saying that you should NEVER leave a copy of your alarm code in or near the panel. If you must write down a copy, store it in a bank safety deposit box, in a designated book on a shelf or taped beneath a heavy piece of furniture in a room on the other side of the house. It shouldn't be anywhere near the alarm itself. Think about it: You'd much rather have a false alarm (where an operator from your alarm company calls and asks for your code word) than have an intruder pretend to be you, cutting you off from assistance. And speaking of code words, never, ever write these down. Make them something that you will always remember instantly.

When you're programming your alarm, avoid dates that are readily associated with your family. These include anniversaries, children's birthdays and phone numbers. Instead, pick a holiday—say, Christmas, which falls on the twenty-fifth day of twelfth month of the year—and translate the date to digits. A four-digit alarm based on that holiday would be 1225. You could also use childhood addresses or phone numbers that expired decades earlier, the street address of a favorite restaurant or part of the zip code for a best friend's house. These digits are all memorable but not directly associated with you. If a criminal ran a background search on you, they wouldn't turn up any of these number strings.

Position alarm system components strategically throughout the house. For example, avoid placing your only security camera outside on the front stoop. While external cameras are excellent deterrents, most entryways lack significant depth. By concentrating your capture efforts there, you will have a very limited view of someone pushing against your door. You might capture their face, but if they are masked or if they lean slightly,

even this limited visual data is lost. A much better location is diagonally across from your front door on the inside of your home. This way, when an intruder barges in, the camera will capture their height, face, posture and other key identifiers. It's also less likely to be noticed right away, helping to deter the equipment from being covered or destroyed before it can capture the intruder's likeness. To complement your interior camera, use an inexpensive decoy outside to reap the benefits of a deterrent without wasting a precious component.

In addition to wired security system components, there are also simple measures you can take to see if any part of your home has been tampered with while you are out. Put a small piece of clear tape along the top of first-floor windows, pressing down to stick it to both the sliding pane and the frame. If the pane is opened, the tape will either disconnect or break, indicating that someone accessed the window—and could potentially still be inside. Set other traps that deter and track criminals, such as placing potted plants under windows. If someone slips inside at night, they'll knock it over, making a loud commotion and leaving footprints in the soil. I've even seen people place newspapers or magazines under windows to make for slippery landing spots when someone hops inside.

Remember that booby trapping is illegal in most states. This includes setting traps that go off when a door is opened, trip wires and other types of snares. Avoid using any booby traps on your property in case someone accidentally triggers them. You don't want the neighbor being slammed by a falling brick because she accidentally opened the door without flipping a latch, or for an explosive incapacitation device to go off because your children forgot to avoid stepping on a particular floorboard of your porch. You can, however, attach items like bells and chimes to your doors and windows so that you hear anyone opening or closing them.

COMMON TELEPHONE USE MISTAKES

Telephones can save lives before and during home invasions, as long as they are used correctly. When aiming to manage first contact, avoid these common phone mistakes to keep your advantage intact.

First, do not position a phone directly next to the door. If an intruder can get their hand inside, they can push the handset off the receiver, or even snag a cordless phone and pull it outside. Without control over the landline, you will not be able to quickly call emergency services.

Let me also dispel a common myth about phones and emergency services. Until you tell the operator your location, they do not know where you are. Yes, they could find out, but the process takes additional time that is critical when your life depends on your performance. Some states require a warrant before running the trace. In many areas, calling 911 and hanging up will result in a call-back, which takes extra time and might alert the intruder of your location if you're hiding. You need to take a moment to calmly confirm that it's an emergency, then list your address and that a home invasion is occurring.

When speaking to the operator, give short, concise answers to their initial questions. These must include your first and last name, where you currently are located and the nature of the emergency, such as an intruder is breaking in. That way, if the phone gets cut off, the police still have your information and can dispatch support. Avoid rambling, whispering or stuttering. These are natural responses to a nerve-wracking situation. Practice what you would say in an emergency, and simply recite these preprogrammed responses when the time comes. The operator may ask additional questions, and you can respond if the situation allows it. But just remember that every second you spend talking to them is a second you lose for your own personal safety. If you hang up after giving them the core information, it's perfectly all right. The police will come regardless.

Never place multiple phones in one location, even cell phones. Instead, place them near a variety of exits and entrances throughout your home so you have easy access during a break-in.

Another tip is to keep the phone more than four feet away from the door but within ten feet of the entry. It may seem counterintuitive, especially since I just told you not to post a phone right next to the entry! However, you still want to be able to quickly grab the phone to place a call for help. If it's outside the reach of a home invader pounding at the front door, you can grab the cordless handset and run, phoning in help as you go into hiding. Consider putting a phone in a hallway if not in each room.

If you're like me and your cell phone is always on, use it to your advantage. When I go to sleep, I keep it on silent mode charging next to my bed, or even in the pocket of my pants. That way, if I jump out of bed and throw them on, I've got my phone at the ready without even thinking about it.

Speaking of which, keep all your phones on silent whenever feasible. Many landlines blink when a call is coming through, and cell phones use vibrate indicators. This allows you to keep phone locations hidden from intruders who might otherwise use a ringtone to find and destroy a device that could connect you to help.

Without looking, can you tell how many megahertz your cordless landline uses? Probably not! The vast majority of Americans don't pay attention to this when shopping for a landline. However, for home invasion survival, it could mean the difference between life and death. A two or three megahertz cordless might make it outside to where you keep your garbage cans before disconnecting, but a twelve megahertz model might remain connected all the way down the street.

Finally, program all of your phones the same way. That means, set the speed dial positions on all of your family's cordless, landline and cell phones to the same contacts. The first slot should be used for emergency services, while the second slot calls your home line. The third slot dials your spouse's cell phone, and the fourth dials yours. Continue until every key number is set, and instruct your family members to do the same. That way, if you grab a cell phone in the fray and it's not yours, you don't have to fumble with remembering numbers, you can press one number and get help, another family member or related assistance immediately.

PREPARING TO SURVIVE

No matter your age, gender, race, religion, ethnicity, education, income level or neighborhood, one cherished treasure is more important than anything else in the world: family.

Preparation starts with the emotional commitment to understand that you and your loved ones will need to do whatever it takes to survive. Along with the mental conditioning required to take action, you must support your body with the physical strength it needs to propel you beyond your limits toward the end of a home invasion.

No matter how much you know about home invasions or how hard you work to make your property unappealing to attackers, the unthinkable is always possible. The only way to ready yourself is with a solid, committed family action plan, which we will review in-depth during the next chapter. Though you will be preparing for planned home invasions, these strategies also work on accidental home invasions such as burglaries that morph into something much more violent.

This becomes increasingly important the moment that you walk downstairs in the middle of the night to get a glass of water from the kitchen only to find yourself face-to-face with an armed thief. Without a plan, anything could happen as events quickly slip out of your control. But with a solid strategy already in mind, you can begin the dangerous encounter with the upper hand and improve your chances for surviving unharmed.

Always keep designated escape routes free of furniture, debris and other obstacles. You need to be able to quickly sneak to a door or preselected window, open it silently and slip out undetected. Any obstacles will increase the potential for capture. You should, however, employ deterrent strategies at entry points that are not part of your predetermined escape route. Remember that hiding spots must also be maintained at all times and should not be blocked, repurposed or eliminated. Regular drills ensure that this pitfall does not ensnare you or your loved ones.

Learn your home's angles, too. What are angles? Here is an example. Just because you can see most of the yard from a particular vantage point doesn't mean that you can see everything going on outside. I often give the example of someone standing in the garage and looking out through the open door. From where they're standing, the coast may look clear. But with one or two vehicles parked, there could be as many as six or seven armed men hiding just barely out of view but within striking distance—a scary thought! Always be cautious walking in areas where angles limit your vision, and don't be afraid to verbally challenge someone as soon as you become aware of their presence.

If you're helping family or friends, particularly the sick or elderly, be sure to take as many upfront precautions as possible to preload for their safety. You may not be able to help them during a home invasion, but with the right preparations, you can give them a fighting shot.

Prepare for the unexpected. This could be as traumatic as a gunshot wound or as benign as a key member of your family being out at the movies when the attack happens. You shouldn't have one family action plan; you should have dozens of scenarios queued up in your minds, almost like the chapters on a Blu-Ray disc. The content is right there, ready to go. You're just waiting for the moment to press an invisible Play button to set things in motion. Then, you have to let yourself follow through on your preparations and training, take action and maintain confidence in your plan.

The moment you realize a home invasion is underway is chilling. It causes your mind to race, your heart to pound and your limbs to shake. Your deterrents and preventative measures have failed, but your engagement strategy is just getting started. At that very instant, you must remain calm and collected as you recall your plan. Survival for you—and your family—depends on it. Never allow your fright to cause you to freeze.

Criminals have a very simplified level of thought. The most trusted equation for criminals is easy to understand. If you raise their effort, it lowers their reward—deterring the crime. On the flip side, if you lower the effort it takes them, you raise their reward. This encourages crime against your property! Criminals crave sloppy homeowners who make their jobs easier. They want people who don't care enough to protect themselves, the same types of victims who become desperate and irrational quickly. They want easy targets to hit up over and over and over again.

PRACTICE EXERCISE 1: MASTERING A CRIMINAL'S MIND

The only way you can outsmart a home invader is by forcing yourself to be one step ahead of him. Remind yourself that you live in the real world, not a fantasy world you'd rather live in. The best technique for grabbing hold of that advantage is copious planning. Slip into the criminal mindset to make your survival strategies all the stronger.

For this exercise, conduct a safety walk around your property. Pretend you are a criminal who wants to get inside, and frame your observations like the smartest bad guy you can conjure up in your imagination. This is someone who will stop at nothing to get into your house. Don't assume that he's going to overlook anything.

Start in one corner of the perimeter and scan the entirety of your yard, driveway and house's exterior walls. While conducting your walk, make a list of the blind spots and shadows you notice. Blind spots and shadows are locations on your property that restrict your ability to see everything from a single point of view such as a window or door. Don't panic—eliminating blind spots can be as simple as trimming a bush in the front yard, adjusting the exterior lighting or moving a landscaping object to increase your visual capacity. For this exercise, you simply want to know where the problem areas exist.

Use a notebook or a smartphone app to take notes. Remember to think like a criminal who would be scanning for ways to breach your house and increase their advantage. Any opportunity they spot could become a threat against you and your loved ones, regardless of how minor it may seem. Find them now so that an attacker doesn't get to them first.

After you finish your exterior analysis, ask a family member to perform a safety walk of their own on the same property. Have them record the blind spots and shadows they see, as well as any other weaknesses that jump out at them.

After both walks conclude, sit down in your living room and compare notes. Did you find the same problem areas, or were there issues that one of you missed? Think about ways that an attacker could leverage each of those blind spots to gain entry to your home.

Finally, brainstorm ways to eliminate or reduce each problem. Make a realistic plan to neutralize each potential threat, including prioritization of the most significant issues, timelines for implementation and other threats that your solution might cause. For instance, adjusting spotlights to eliminate a shadow could create a new dark alcove elsewhere in your yard.

After you've completed the exercise, store your notes in a dedicated folder, box or secure hard drive. Keep all of your planning materials centralized to help flesh out your family action plan and encourage periodic reviews. I'll refer to this family action dossier in subsequent exercises. Build it up to make your plans stronger, and make sure everyone in your family can access it freely.

2

PLAN TO SURVIVE

On August 24, 2015, Kiewa Mason received a call from his fourteen-year-old son, Andrew.

When asked if everything was all right at their Las Vegas home, Andrew replied, "No. Someone has broken into our house."

But thanks to rigorous family planning, the nightmare turned into a carefully practiced scenario—one that the family had rehearsed many times before.

Andrew went upstairs, found his six-year-old brother and sister and told them to hide in the closet. Then, he took the cell phone his father kept on his dresser along with a loaded rifle and joined his siblings in hiding.

When the home invaders opened the closet door, they found Andrew armed, with the rifle cocked and ready to shoot. The attackers swiftly fled, snagging the family's safe in the process.

No one was harmed, and Kiewa praised his son's adherence to the family plan.

"He's excellent. He did everything perfectly," the proud father told the media.[17]

THE PURPOSE OF A FAMILY ACTION PLAN

The definition of a plan is a set of strategies and tasks that are assembled in advance for use when the time calls for it. Let's face it: If you're reading this book and you don't already have a family action plan, you're behind the eight ball. I wish I could say that you do have time to get everything ironed out and that your family is in no immediate danger. However, the fact is that anything can happen at any time. Being prepared means you are ready, and it takes you one step beyond being hopeful that nothing will happen.

But all hope is not lost. If you start assembling a plan right now—not later today, or tomorrow, or next week—and follow up with training your family and practicing regularly, you can get up to speed in just a few short days. That's right, one weekend of preparation could protect your family's lives for years to come. Creating a plan is fast and entirely painless, and once you've nailed down a strategy, you only need to practice on a monthly basis and tweak occasionally as needed.

In this chapter, I'll teach you about the contents of a good family action plan that enables you to survive a home invasion. This will include what steps to take as a family to implement the plan and stay ahead of attackers. We'll examine roles and responsibilities for each member of the family, including children, as well as practice exercises that make information stick in young minds. This will give everyone the edge they need for that moment when the front door gets kicked in and your family finds itself face-to-face with armed intruders who intend to compromise the safety of your loved ones.

I know criminals. Take it from me, though some appear disorganized or unprepared, you should NEVER underestimate your opponent. Whether they are a repeat offender or this is their first time out of the gate, it does not matter: You are protecting your family. Treat the threat like they are a well-oiled machine. The worst that happens with this type of thinking is that it takes you a little longer to win in a dangerous game where winning equates to surviving. Never lose sight of the fact that criminals are a heck of a lot scarier than coming up with a good, solid family action plan ever will be.

Family action plans are formal, rehearsed strategies that cover the entire family's roles, responsibilities and survival techniques during a home invasion. They start with passive measures (such as conducting safety walks and monthly drills), the types of activities that every prepared household should include in their schedule long before a home invasion ever occurs. Next, family action plans talk about methods for keeping would-be assailants at bay after they target your home. The bulk of the plan lays out engagement and escape tactics to use when a home invasion occurs. Communication should also be addressed. Finally, the plan ends with postattack rendezvous instructions and reporting needs that kick in once the home invasion concludes.

If you think about it, you've had other types of family action plans in place for years. When you got your first car, you planned for emergencies by having a spare tire available and certain tools in the trunk. Once you had children, you became accustomed to packing an emergency diaper bag no matter where you went—you know, just in case! In the 1950s, families made bomb shelter plans to survive nuclear attacks, and in the 1970s, we added fire drills to our cultural shift toward improved domestic safety. Now that we're in the twenty-first century, with violent home invasions rising, it's time to institute a new set of guidelines: the family action plan. Family action plans are more than just talking about staying alive, they're about rehearsing, practicing and evolving alongside new and existing threats.

The purpose of your family action plan is to arm every member of your household with the rehearsed response they need in order to survive a home invasion. Everyone, regardless of their age, has a role and set responsibilities that are clearly outlined. When a home invasion occurs, there shouldn't be any questions or doubts about what to do. Your family should instead call up the strategies and techniques they've rehearsed and act accordingly.

That's easier said than done.

I can remember one of the first marine safety talks I gave as a professional. My students and I discussed putting on personal flotation devices before boarding a boat. Heck, we even watched someone put one on in a formal group setting. I indicated a yellow plastic lever on the devices and how they needed to be pulled straight down whenever a boat started taking on water.

Well, a few days later, we conducted an open water swim. This involved entering the water at the dock, swimming 1500 meters and climbing aboard a boat. At the 900-meter mark, the person in front of me started taking on water and sank beneath the waves. He bobbed up several times, sputtering pleas for help. After the fourth submersion, I was able to reach him and yank the plastic yellow lever on his flotation device. It inflated immediately.

When we finally got to the boat, the first thing he commented on was that he never thought to pull the plastic lever while he was drowning. The idea was familiar, sure, but the action was foreign. He'd never actually practiced tugging on that little piece of yellow plastic, and the talk escaped his mind during a terrifying brush with death.

To paraphrase one of my mentors, Gary T. Klugiewicz, we had to conduct fire drills, not fire talks. After that incident, I revamped my training programs to include drills to supplement lecture-style talks. Every student ripped off a yellow tag before dipping a toe in the water. I never had another near-drowning incident occur on my watch.

Having a family action plan means you must practice the skills you will need when your life depends on it. Don't just talk about them. In order for the brain to act under stress, you need to have the physical actions stored in your memory. This is because your gross motor skills take over while your fine motor skills diminish during stressful incidents. Don't let that biological function put you at a severe disadvantage.

I'm sure you've seen home invasions in movies or television shows, so you're basically an expert and don't need a plan . . . right?

Wrong.

Acting without a plan during a home invasion—shooting from the hip, as some might say—rarely works out well for the homeowner. For one, even if some family members possess the skills and capabilities to protect themselves and fight back, not everyone in your family will be at the same level. An elderly parent or five-year-old child will not be able to fare as well as a fit, trained adult. Not only are their strengths entirely different, their emotional maturity levels span the gamut. Think about it: Could you imagine a young child using a blunt instrument on an intruder, hitting them over the head repeatedly and emerging both successful and emotionally capable of processing that decision? I can't, which is why I recommend identifying roles long beforehand.

As you prepare to build your family action plan, start by analyzing your home. Sketch out a rough blueprint of each floor, highlighting potential hiding places as well as any individual constraints. For instance, a closet connected to the attic on the second story might work very well for a fleeing child, though the opening wouldn't allow an adult to easily slip into the space. Pay particular attention to escape routes associated with each hiding place as well.

Next, note the locations of weapons of opportunity and weapons of availability. I will discuss these key terms in greater depth in Chapter 9, but essentially, a weapon of opportunity is an object that is not designed to kill, but if used properly, can inflict injuries. Weapons of opportunity belong in the environment in which they are used. An example in your office might be a heavy concrete paperweight that could be used as a bludgeoning weapon, if needed. Another example is a letter opener that could be used to stab an attacker.

Weapons of availability take the concept a step further. These are weapons with which you have practiced building up a rehearsed response. For example, you might have an umbrella near your front door. An untrained individual might take that umbrella and use it as a blunt force instrument. However, you have practiced using the tool, knowing that it will bend and give way if struck repeatedly along its length. Instead, you have a rehearsed response to use the umbrella as a sharp poking instrument thanks to its sturdy steel tip.

For now, make a list of the weapons that come to mind, leaving space for additions as you read through later chapters. Continue building your plan.

ROLES AND RESPONSIBILITIES

Once you've adequately covered the layout of your home—the battleground for an attack—you need to start strategically placing and training your family members to maximize their chances of survival. Every person residing under your roof must play a part; this is not optional.

Start strategizing roles and responsibilities according to basic strengths and limitations. Teach children survival techniques early on. These can be framed as antibullying techniques if necessary, as many of these approaches translate to home invasions as well.

In terms of weapons of opportunity, never give a child a weapon that forces them outside their emotional means. I can't provide a firm set of guidelines here; you must use your parental instincts to identify what your child can handle. Even if the youth will not be using a gun, teach them basic firearm safety starting at the age of four to prevent accidental discharges. This basic training includes how to safely hold a gun, pointing the muzzle away from others and what to do with a firearm once they find it.

As you assign roles, older children may benefit from advanced firearm and weapons training. Teach them to treat all conventional weapons as loaded or dangerous, and for guns, reiterate the importance of safely pointing a muzzle. Keeping fingers off triggers and using trigger guards are important points to drill. Bullet angles are important, too, but be sure he or she is aware of the damage they will cause by firing. Most teenagers will understand this. I've also seen kids ten and under hunting with their parents who know how to properly use a gun. It all depends on the child's maturity.

Roles and responsibilities stretch beyond weapon usage. I've outlined a few typical strengths and limitations for various demographics over the next two pages. These lists are not all-inclusive. The parameters on each of these groups are gray; know your own family's limitations to make an honest assessment. You might need to be creative, depending on the makeup of your family. This is perfectly normal and encouraged!

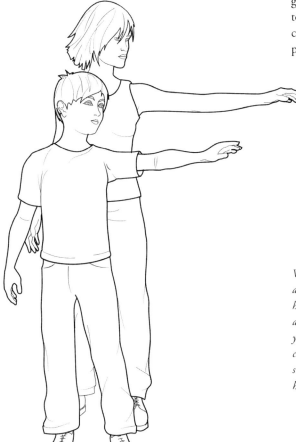

When determining roles for your family, keep in mind the distance and strength that a longer arm provides. For example, let's say you have a young son and a teenage daughter, and available weapons are a baseball bat and a pair of scissors. Give the baseball bat to your daughter as this weapon takes a greater amount of force and control to use than the sharp pair of scissors, which would be better suited for your son. Identifying each family member's attributes and how they can be effectively used can save your family's life.

DEMOGRAPHIC	STRENGTHS	LIMITATIONS
Able-bodied adult, aged 20–60.	• Of at least average strength and intellect. • Capable of wielding most weapons.	• Usually the first targeted in a family, as they possess the top strength, cunning and emotional resilience. • Difficulty accessing some tight spaces.
Fit adult, aged 20–60.	• Strong and excellent capability for physical defense. • Significant endurance. • Rapidly able to shift positions from hiding to engaging to fleeing with minimal impact on stamina.	• May draw additional attention from attackers due to physical strength/abilities. • Difficulty accessing small spaces due to increased muscle mass.
Vulnerable adult, aged 20–60.	• Often diminutive in stature, yielding greater range of hiding places. • Appears less threatening to attackers, creating advantage for non-detection.	• Physically weaker than the average adult. • Short weapons will be less impactful as attacker must be close to receive damage.
Able-bodied senior, 60+.	• Similar to able-bodied adult, with some minor lowered endurance and flexibility. • Age may be played up as an advantage to seem unthreatening or incapable.	• Similar to able-bodied adult, with some age-related mobility decline.
Disabled senior, 60+.	• Able to utilize medication needs and medical ruses to significant advantage. • May possess a walking instrument such as a cane or walker that can be used as weapon of opportunity.	• Unable to escape or hide alone. • Lowered speed, endurance and strength. • Emotionally vulnerable. • Due to lessened strength, smaller weapons require them to be physically close to attackers in order to defend.
Teenager, aged 13–20.	• Excellent stamina and size to allow them to run, hide or escape as required. • Able to fully understand and execute family action plan. • Intelligence to understand situations and adapt responses accordingly. • Well-versed in communication.	• Emotional immaturity may render them enraged or terrified, depending on their personality. • May possess over-inflated sense of strength or invulnerability. • May be targeted for sexual assaults.

(continued)

DEMOGRAPHIC	STRENGTHS	LIMITATIONS
Child, aged 7–13.	• Outstanding ability to hide, crawl and fit through tight escapes (such as casement windows). • Able to follow directions and recall major points of family action plan. • Intelligent enough to understand most situations and react appropriately. • May play a distraction role.	• Low emotional maturity that can make defensive maneuvers difficult. • Potential for whining, crying or complaining, which translates into a liability. • Lower physical strength than teenagers.
Young child, aged 4–7.	• Can fit into small areas to hide or escape. • If taught at a young age, will follow directions closely and carefully as if playing a game. • If able to escape, may be able to tell neighbor to contact authorities without being detected. • May draw sympathy.	• Easily frightened and prone to wanting parents in a terrifying situation. • May freeze up. • May also give into the attackers' demands, following their commands instead of the family action plan.
Baby/toddler, aged 0–4.	• May be able to elicit empathy from attacker, lessening severity of attacks. • Holding a baby may be a way for a family member to avoid having their arms bound.	• Crying and fussing can make hiding impossible. • Need parents or guardians to keep calm. • Easily harmed and unable to protect him or herself.
Chronically ill or disabled individual.	• Able to use medication or special needs to break up attackers. • Able to create distractions through medical ruses.	• Less able to hide or escape due to disability. • May not be allowed to access medications, causing true medical emergency. • If mentally handicapped, may have difficulty remembering or executing role.

On a sheet of paper, take a minute to write down the names of your family members. Under each, create two columns: strengths and limitations. Fill these in to fit your family's attributes and abilities. Once you are able to visualize everyone's individual strengths and limitations, begin assigning roles.

The first role involves sounding the alert and alarm. This role is perfect for a teenager, with a parent as a backup option. Everyone in the family should be trained on how to fulfill this role, even if it's not their designated specialty. This person must loudly and calmly state the **alert** phrase as soon as a potential threat is identified. If the threat intensifies into a danger, this person must then call out the **alarm**, a corresponding escalation phrase. Finally, this person must also be able to give the **all-clear** signal at the end of the home invasion. Note that alerts and alarms are not always feasible, as you saw in the story that opened this chapter. However, you should still plan on them as they will help to keep your family organized and several steps ahead of the criminal.

First, let's look at an example of an alert. Let's say you are sitting on your porch with your family and someone observes an unidentified person walking toward the home on the sidewalk. The observer might say, "Wow, has it gotten colder outside?" The rest of the family would stand and rub their arms, as if protecting against a chill. Then, everyone would calmly clear the porch area and return inside, where one person would pick up the phone and wait for the next stage of contact.

This phrase does not betray your thoughts to an attacker who could be listening through an open window. However, all of my children as well as my wife and I know what that alert means. We are instantly on guard whenever we hear it which is thankfully not frequently.

THE PERSON WHO SOUNDS THE ALERT
and alarm needs to be someone who is observant. They must be able to be loud while remaining calm and watchful.

The next example covers an alarm. Say your family is sitting inside one evening and you notice someone prowling around your backyard. You would stand up, walk toward the television and face your family, asking, "Did everyone take their showers tonight?" while placing both your hands on your stomach. Upon seeing this, your family members would go to their designated hiding places while one person calls the police to report the suspicious individual.

This phrase is our alarm, and it signals that we should brace for an attack. We'll first prepare to use escape routes, and if escape is not feasible we will get ready to assume our hiding places. The example phrase that we use is a good alarm because it immediately invokes action. If the attacker hears the phrase and sees us moving, he isn't aware that we're preparing for an assault. He thinks we are just another family going through our evening routine. An alarm can be verbal and/or nonverbal.

After the attack is over and the assailant has been subdued, arrested or has fled, the person who sounds the alert and alarm gives the all-clear phrase, something like: "All clear and safe." This signals that any hidden family members can leave their hiding places safely. If he calls out something different, such as, "Come on out," you know that he is being coerced and that it's not safe to exit yet. The exact all-clear phrase must be stated before anyone emerges.

Another important role is the door defender. This person must be the strongest in the group, and they will be backed up by one, two or more strong family members. As soon as the alert is called, this person heads to the most likely point of entry and prepares to block, barricade or defend the door. If the potential threat knocks, the door blocker must make the decision about whether or not to answer. Remember that anyone who steps on your property without your knowledge is a potential threat, even if they are performing a legally permissible or agreed-upon function. This list includes service people, delivery carriers, couriers, canvassers, religious evangelists and even unexpected friends. If you don't know why someone is on your property, they must be treated as a threat until they give you reason to trust them.

During the attack, home invaders may force someone to tie up other members of the family. This could be a teenager or parent who either volunteers or positions themselves close to the attacker. I call this role the Houdini, as the objective for this person is to make bindings escapable while still appearing sound. The Houdini has to have a basic understanding of knots, some acting skills to appear convincing while tying and testing wrist or ankle binds and the confidence to step up and work with the attackers. It's a courageous and critical role.

Everyone should be able to participate as a first aid responder. Train your family on how to treat wounds, apply tourniquets and stop bleeding. Basic first aid skills can come in handy at any point during a home invasion, and they're particularly critical at early junctures when your survival and wellness are directly connected.

Finally, the last key role is the informer. This individual could be anyone in the family, including a child or elderly person. They call the authorities and quickly relay location information after asking for assistance. This person must be good at using the phone and be able to quickly and calmly communicate under stress. The call should be placed at the earliest safe moment. The informer may make the call when the alarm is raised, or after escaping the home. Have everyone in your family practice the informer role so that they can make the call if need be.

SLOWING DOWN ATTACKERS

If you called emergency services right now, how long do you think it would take them to get to your location? According to the Bureau of Justice Statistics, the best police response time in the United States is just under five minutes. The worst response times range from an hour in some cases to within one day for others.[18]

According to *American Police Beat*, a law enforcement publication, the average interaction time between a criminal and his victim is 90 seconds. That's just one and a half lightning-fast minutes.[19]

Dwell on that for a moment. Even in the best neighborhood, you and your family could be dead almost two and a half minutes before the police ever get there to help. And that's only if a cop is on your street to begin with. The metric doesn't factor in the manpower of your local agency, equipment and vehicle availability, your town's population density or the time of day. With the response time as it is in many areas, training yourself to be the first responder can save your life!

You can understand why I tell people to start thinking about slowing down attackers the minute they begin work on a family action plan. If you are not able to slow them immediately, they might just cut you down before help arrives.

But how can you slow down an armed attacker who is desperate to barge into your home? For one, signaling the alert and alarm signals as soon as a threat begins is the best way to buy time. This requires keen vigilance and a firm commitment to knowing what's going on around your property. The moment something seems out of place, instruct your family's announcer to raise the alert.

The instant the alarm command is given, the informer should try to call emergency services and request help. It's critical that they relay the right information immediately, then hang up as quickly as possible. As long as the responder confirms it's a true emergency and receives the caller's name and address, the phone may be hung up. Your waiting period begins at that instant.

The first way to physically slow down an attacker is to hold them at the door or entry point as long as possible. Whether that involves barricading the door, bracing it or defending through the crack, keep them from getting inside. The longer they are outside, the more likely they will be to flee or be apprehended by the police on your front lawn.

If an attacker has managed to get inside, your best bet is to immediately begin following their commands. This buys you enough time to recall, set up and execute your family action plan. Maintain a relatively slow pace performing whatever they ask, wasting precious seconds without giving off the impression that you are acting deliberately slow. If you sense irritation or anger in your attackers' voices, you can begin to speed things up slightly; Just remember that your timeline still has several minutes to go.

Hiding is another way to gain one or more minutes in the midst of an attack. A good hiding place will conceal you during quick, 30- to 60-second sweeps of each room. A great hiding place will keep you safely obscured for the entirety of the attack. The best hiding place also provides cover.

Home invasion situations can turn dire on a dime. If you notice your attackers growing erratic or threatening to kill a family member, you can buy a small amount of time by engaging them. This is not ideal, but sometimes you need to build it into your plan as a last resort.

Other techniques for slowing down attackers include tossing debris or slippery cleaning chemicals on the floor as they enter into the house, interfering with their vision, sliding furniture around to block doorways (an obstruction which forces them to climb) or creating distractions such as a vase hurled against a far wall. Every one of these techniques can reduce their focus on you for a handful of seconds, making survival a bit more likely. Remember that in any critical emergency, seconds save lives. You have to become a master at managing the attackers' timeline.

NOISE DISCIPLINE AND NIGHT WHISPERING

Humans rely on five senses to interact with the world: sight, taste, smell, touch and sound. Of these, the most important sense during a home invasion is sound.

To improve your sound awareness, you must practice noise discipline and control, two vital techniques that help you communicate during a home invasion.

From the perspective of a family action plan, planning sounds is critical. After all, imagine hiding in a downstairs coat closet while three armed assailants search the adjacent living room. If hidden behind a thick row of outerwear, you are practically invisible. Your odds of being detected based on visual discovery are slim.

However, a single quiet sound can ruin the hiding place by instantly alerting intruders to your location. Even whispers can be heard from outside a closed door. Though most adults can exercise an appropriate level of noise discipline, children need some additional coaching and practice to master this important skill. Build it into your family action plan so that your family can get a jump on silent communication before a home invasion takes place.

When in doubt, the best option is to remain entirely silent. Turn phones off, remove batteries from pocketed devices, dump coins from pockets and swap day walking (heel-to-toe movement) with night walking (on tip-toes). Devise two silent communication systems to use in the event of an attack.

The first silent communication system uses hand signals for alarms. When I taught this type of communication to my children, I kept it as basic as possible to make it easy to remember. Think about the key items that need to be communicated silently:

- **IDENTIFICATIONS:** Identifications are as simple as pointing at the person who needs to accomplish a specific task. Use a single firm point toward the subject's chest coupled with unbroken eye contact to indicate that they must do something.

- **LOCATIONS:** Locations involve a mixture of pointing and directional indications. For instance, to silently communicate that children should sneak upstairs, point at the children and then at the stairs. Use a diagonal upward point in the direction of the steps

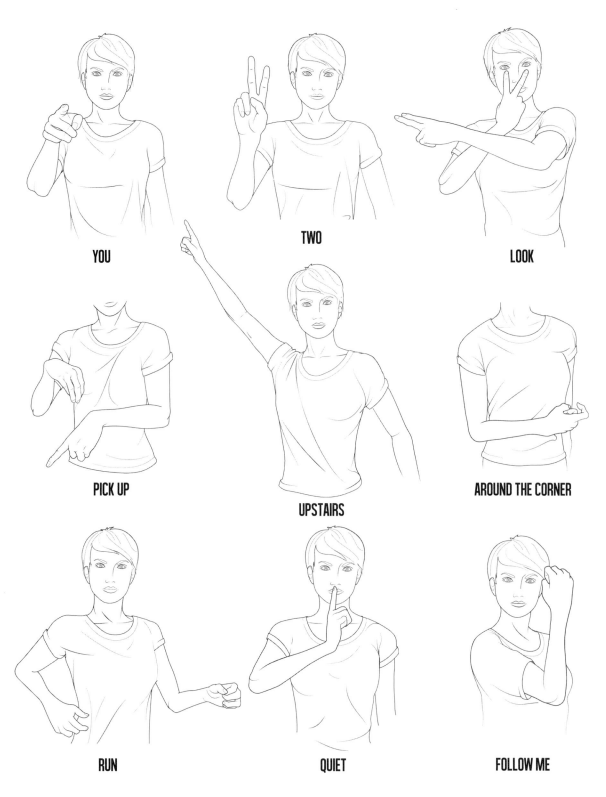

YOU

TWO

LOOK

PICK UP

UPSTAIRS

AROUND THE CORNER

RUN

QUIET

FOLLOW ME

Your five fingers and two arms can communicate thousands of commands. Choose commands with your family and rehearse them regularly. Shown here are the most common and easily understood.

to indicate motion. For locations on the other side of a wall or doorway, use a curved finger that you move forward as though going around the corner.

- **NUMBERS**: Use your fingers to silently show counts for up to ten items, objects or intruders. Exaggerate finger motions to ensure comprehension, and couple them with location indications for improved communication. For example, if you know there are two intruders downstairs and a third outside in a getaway vehicle, you could flash three fingers first. Next, point downstairs and flash two fingers on your left hand while pointing downward toward a window with one finger to indicate the outside location of the third attacker.

- **BASIC COMMANDS**: Complex communication is difficult to convey using hand motions. It's much easier to create a roster of five to seven key commands and share these within your family group. For a home invasion, these might include look (indicated by pointing two fingers at your eye and then pointing in a direction), punch (indicated by creating a fist and quietly jabbing the air), run (indicated by moving your arms in a jogging motion), freeze (indicated by raising an open palm) or retrieve an object (indicated by pinching your fingers together and pulling upward, combined with a pointing motion).

For older children, you can also mouth commands slowly to add depth to any of the silent hand signals above. Remember not to exhale while mouthing commands, and avoid accidentally smacking or clicking your lips, teeth, cheeks or tongue.

The second form of high-stress silent communication relies on touch. This is a better option for situations where your sight is also compromised, such as hiding in a dark bathroom. Though much more restrictive, there are still several touch commands that you can teach to your family. Use wrist taps, shoulder squeezes and arm pulls to convey ultraspecific commands. Once you have access to light, you can further supplement these touch commands with hand signals.

Squeeze a shoulder to indicate that your hiding partner should move in that particular direction. Tap shoulders to tell them to stay put. If you want someone to turn around, gently tap the nape of their neck twice. You can add to these with wrist taps, tugs and other silent touches.

Sometimes, hand signals and touches are not enough. I'm the first to admit that it's incredibly difficult to predict how a home invasion will play out, and without speech, most of us are rendered functionally mute. We live in a world where speech dictates communication. Even with monthly rehearsals, silent communication may not be adequate. In the event that you do need to speak, use a technique I call night whispering to do so effectively.

Night whispering requires you to speak softly by silently exhaling all of the air from your lungs and then speaking directly into the adjacent person's ear. This hyper-quiet technique is difficult to maintain for long periods of conversation, but it's extremely effective at dampening nearly all sound coming from your mouth. Use it for short bursts to get a critical point across to only the person you're speaking to. Night whispering keeps sounds from traveling far by containing the sound waves that you emit.

In the military, night whispering is used to communicate at listening posts. This enables soldiers to listen and hear everything within 100 yards or more. It works very well as part of a home invasion noise discipline routine. Note that night whispering is different from regular whispering, which can be loud enough to be heard in nearby locations and through closed interior doors.

Though you should never use light to communicate inside a dark house or other close quarters, you can use short bursts of light from a flashlight to get a neighbor's attention once you're secured in a confined space with a window or external vent. Limit the number of flashes you use to avoid being spotted by an outside intruder. Sometimes, curiosity about the flashes is enough to get someone to come outside where they can notice the situation and call for help.

CONNECTING BREATHING AND EMOTIONAL STATES

Controlling your breathing is especially important. Normally, civilians rely on pneumatic breathing in which air enters the nose and exits the mouth. Combat breathing is different. Troops are trained to breathe in through their mouths and out their noses when using gas masks, to limit fogging as well as to clean out their airways when in environments contaminated with chemical agents. This technique also grants more control over air intake, allowing you to slow your breathing down. Letting air out slowly lowers your heart rate. By forcing yourself to control your own breathing, you can better utilize night whispering and also keep your circulation going throughout a harrowing ordeal.

If you don't control your breathing, anxiety is the first sensation that will settle in. This is the fear of the unknown, and it can escalate into hyperventilation. Hyperventilation denies air to your ocular nerve, leading to blurred vision that alters sight and slows decisions. It also opens the person up to making irrational choices, escalating into blind panic or submitting to attackers to eliminate the fear of the unknown.

Left to its own devices, anxiety transforms into pure fear. I define this as confirmation of the unknown's presence in your life. Your uncontrolled breathing will be rapid, yet your circulation rates will slow down. This causes muscle cramping and makes reactions freeze up. Fearful individuals lose hope. If injured, those transitioning from anxiety to pure fear may lose consciousness and slip into shock.

Panic settles in after fear. This is complete loss of control over breathing, and it results in passing out. Panic can also leave people conscious but unaware. The saying "the lights are on upstairs but no one is home" comes to mind. Panicked individuals act like deer in headlights. They are nonresponsive, even though they can still hear and process their surroundings. I can't begin to tell you how dangerous this is.

To control your breathing and prevent these states, pick something in the room that calms you. This could be a spouse, a child, a photo on the wall or anything else that makes you feel serene and happy. Put yourself in another place with that cherished person or object. This imagined place should be where you feel safest, calming your nerves and allowing you to regain control over the situation.

When I train people on hostage situations, I regularly force them out of their comfort zones. In practical exercises, I'll blindfold people, push them into cars and take them somewhere unfamiliar. I ignore complaints and questions, letting them exist without responses for an hour. When I remove the blindfold and end the exercise, they always tell me how it felt like days—not 60 agonizing minutes. They become so focused on their inability to control the environment that they get anxiety. This helplessness causes desperation, which in turn causes people to make decisions without thinking about consequences or circumstances.

Irrationality kicks in when your emotional state transitions from anxiety to fear. People lose balance, they cannot control their tone of voice and they may kick or shout. Little things become magnified. For instance, a toy or cord brushing up against the leg can feel like a snake. As reality slips away, panic creeps in.

Panic makes people do strange things. They may leap from windows, jump in front of cars or physically challenge attackers without thinking it through. If the panicked individuals only kept a level head, they'd survive. But because of their lessened mental state they often die.

Control your breathing during stressful and dangerous moments to avoid slipping into a panic. This simple task is frequently overlooked during the chaos of a home invasion, but keeping your anxiety in check can make all the difference to your survival.

USING GAMES TO PREPARE CHILDREN

In the real-life story that opened this chapter, fourteen-year-old Andrew Mason stepped up to the plate and followed through on his family's survival plan. He protected his younger siblings and remained collected, confident and focused.

The young man is a hero. But Andrew is also among the rarest types of young home invasion survivors: He remained calm and committed to his family's plan. Children frequently become terrified when intruders burst into their home wielding weapons and threatening loved ones. They may cry, scream, hide or hit back at attackers—increasing their chances of being hurt tenfold. Worse, there is nothing that a parent can do in the moment to protect their underprepared child.

As I wrote this book, I also conducted a training exercise out on the West Coast. During one of the sessions, a woman approached me.

"Dave, everything you're talking about is very much *real*," she said, her voice a bit hesitant. "But why do I want to teach my six-year-old how to apply a tourniquet or stick his finger into a gunshot wound to stop the bleeding?"

I gave her a straight response, that she didn't have to teach her son anything. But if she didn't, she might have to live with him dying because he didn't know how to stop blood loss during an attack. It's a very harsh reality, but one that's ripped from the headlines. It seems that children are being shot in schools, on playgrounds and in their own bedrooms. Why is it okay for children to be taught that it's all right to bleed out, but that it's too grim to try to survive? Emotional courage and strength should be taught at an early age, in my opinion.

Getting children onboard with an advanced plan is the only way to mitigate this negative outcome. Part of your family action plan must also be reserved for methods to ease their young minds and reduce feelings of helplessness and violation. One of the easiest ways to accomplish both is to make the scenario into a serious type of game.

When you were young, I'll bet you played any number of games from hide-and-seek and the silent game to dominoes, cards or darts. These days, a lot of kids prefer loud smartphone apps and high-definition gaming consoles to board games and neighborhood street play, but the fun factor remains the same. Take some of the techniques used to engage and grow young minds and apply them to a survival scenario to craft an effective learning game.

One of the best games to repurpose for a home invasion survival scenario is the silent game. Players must try to remain absolutely quiet longer than their competitors. The one who stays silent for the longest period of time is deemed the winner.

Why does this work well for home invasions? For one, prolonged silence helps create the illusion of distance between the children and their attackers. The phrase "out of sight, out of mind" sums it up perfectly. If attackers forget that there are children present because they are being calm, quiet and passive, those children will stand the best chance of emerging unscathed. Additionally, during the silent game, players try to get their opponents to speak by tricking them. This increases focus on the task of remaining silent, helping children to shift their mentality away from distractions that could elicit a loud response. If a young person is trained to keep their mouth closed at all costs in order to "win," they will be better equipped to not shout or scream if they see something disturbing, such as a family member being tied up or a precious heirloom smashed. It's a lesson in restraint.

Another game that helps to calm and protect children is hide-and-seek. This is essentially the same technique that an adult uses to evade attackers, though children will see it as something a bit more fun. Unlike a normal round of the game, teach children to pick hiding spots that are better suited to home invasion scenarios. For instance, rather than hiding in a hallway coat closet without any escape points, encourage them to instead pick a first-floor pantry with a window that can be used as an escape. By practicing with strategic hiding places, they will be better equipped to replicate the "game" when assailants strike.

YOU MAY BE WONDERING what the right age is to start this training. My answer is that it can begin as young as four or when your child successfully completes his or her potty training. That's the moment when they grasp consequences for the first time in life. By putting scary situations into a game, it lessens some of the emotional trauma while still building valuable life skills.

Learning to obey strange or uncomfortable commands is another key skill that young people must master to get through a real home invasion. Picture it: a home invader enters the residence and forcefully instructs a young boy or girl to tie up an older brother, stuff a rag into his mouth and then stay in a bathroom together. None of those commands are normal instructions that a parent, sibling or friend would give them.

A game that can help reinforce the concept of following unusual commands is "Mother, may I?" During play, children ask to perform a task toward a specific goal, such as taking three steps toward the player leading the game who holds a prize. The leader either grants the request or gives the player an alternative set of instructions they must follow—such as taking two steps backward instead of three steps forward.

To prepare for a home invasion, have children work toward a substantial reward placed on one side of the room. This could be a new toy, a favorite dessert treat or a card that represents a raise in allowance. They must complete several tasks to get closer to the reward while competing with their siblings (or parents, if they are an only child). When they ask to perform a task that will get them closer to the reward, redirect them to do something different that catches them off guard, like washing the dishes, feeding the dog or moving an object from one room to another. If they obey, they are rewarded by taking one or more steps toward the reward. If they question you or perform the task inadequately, they are punished by taking a step away from the prize.

Practice games on a weekly basis to align children with the plan. For added effect, make playtimes a surprise. Even after children master remaining quiet for prolonged periods of time, hiding in the right spots or obeying strange commands, continue to drill regularly to keep their skills sharp.

LISTENING EFFECTIVELY

A major part of every family plan is listening effectively. After all, your ears are your most reliable sense during a home invasion. An attacker might blindfold you, or bind your hands, or stuff a gag in your mouth. But rendering you temporarily deaf is very tricky to pull off without alerting the neighborhood via a loud sound such as a gunshot.

Put your ears to work, and build listening strategies into your family action plan so that every family member can focus on the sounds of an attack.

Right off the bat, listen to your assailants' voices. If they use accents or inflections, take note of them. You can also hone in on the words they use to see if they sound intelligent or somewhat uneducated. Sometimes, you may even pick up on slang or other local diction that could reveal their place of birth, upbringing or current living situation. Speech issues or impediments are also important.

If an attacker stutters or struggles to get the right words out, they could be under the influence of an illegal drug or other mind-altering substance. Similarly, if they speak quickly, ramble or mix up their words, their nerves may be getting the best of them. This means they are weak, and it gives you an upper hand.

Besides the voice itself and any irregular speech patterns, hone in on what they're saying. Attackers who have a clear, defined plan are going to be harder to take down than those who are unprepared. Criminals with strategies might also have backup that you cannot see. Listen for references to other individuals and remember names.

Say that you overhear one of your attackers mutter the following command to a cohort:

"First, you're gonna check out the safe upstairs, you hear? They got wads of Jacksons in there. Joe told me 'bout it. Get the green. Bring it down here."

What's the best way to remember a detail heard during a home invasion? Simple mnemonic devices, such as word associations. In this case, you heard a reference to someone named Joe who knew about the money you keep in your safe. Create a mental image of those two ideas to remember them. The best memory devices use rhymes or feature alliteration. In this example, you could remember the phrase "coffee cash" or "Joe's Jacksons."

The word "joe" is slang for coffee, which shares the same first letter as cash. Similarly, "Joe's Jacksons" both begin with the letter "J." They are also close to the name of the Jackson family's patriarch, whose face you could associate with the phrase.

Why is it important to remember these kinds of details? First, it's next to impossible to write things down during a home invasion. Memory is the most reliable way of storing details. Second, you can use the details to figure out who your attackers are, what they want and how to get them apprehended once the home invasion ends.

In the above example, someone named Joe knew about the money-filled safe in your house. Is Joe a friend or family member? Or perhaps an attorney, banker or other professional who knows a bit more about your finances than most other outsiders? If you don't recall anyone named Joe, ask your spouse and children if they recognize the name during a family debrief before completing the police report. It's possible that a family member let the detail about the cash slip in a conversation, opening the temptation for someone to conduct an invasion.

Sometimes criminals will discuss next targets, previous hauls or other strategic details. Keep this information in mind, committing the details to memory using mnemonic devices or other similar strategies. If you can connect your criminals with past or upcoming crimes, the police may stand a better chance of catching them.

ASSESSING ASSAILANTS

A plot device in a lot of comedic movies featuring burglars or hostage situations involves a victim turning one of their attackers against his coconspirators. Usually, it's the dumbest criminal that falls for the ruse, giving the victim just enough time to sneak away while the crooks squabble.

It sounds a little crazy, but believe it or not, it can actually work if you build it into your plan.

Listen carefully to figure out the position of each of your assailants. Do they treat one another as equals, or is there a defined leadership structure in place? Sometimes this is obvious, as one attacker orders the others around and is quietly obeyed. Other times, the power structure is more subtle. You might notice an attacker showing quiet, unpronounced signs of submission—indicating that they are a follower.

Submissive body language generally involves attempts to make one appear small or quiet, as though blending in with the background. These individuals may fear the idea of leadership, completely admire the lead attacker, possess low self-esteem or simply lack motivation. Submissive individuals cringe and cower in order to appear small and less threatening, with their heads bowed and chests pushed in. Eyes may be wide or spacey, while arms may be kept crossed or in a defensive posture.

Dominant postures indicate leaders. The idea is to appear taller, larger and more imposing than those around them. Remember, though, that posturing is not always reflective of reality. It's a display of how they view themselves, which is important information on many levels that victims can leverage. Dominant poses include standing tall, spreading the arms or legs, exposing vulnerable areas and leaning back. They may place their hands on their hips, into their belt or behind their back. These are poses that intimidate while radiating an aura of self-assuredness.[20]

Let's say you're dealing with two home invaders. One displays a number of dominant postures, while the other is noticeably submissive. Which would you try to lure away from your family, and which would you rather engage? Normally, you would want to get the cocky, dominant figure far from loved ones, as his ego can cause him to act irrationally. Additionally, the weaker individual may be easier to subdue as they are not as invested in the attack.

Obviously, you'll want to make mental notes about the attacker's muscular condition, weapons, protective mechanisms and agility. These factors influence their ability to overtake you in a fight. But look beyond these surface traits to better understand how the attacker feels. If you can play the right role, you can subtly manipulate them into treating you better, fighting with their co-attackers or even abandoning the premises altogether.

The easiest form of manipulation involves priming with a small request, then following up with a larger one. For example, first ask to take your medication for a heart condition. Then, ask to go to the bathroom—a place where you can swipe a weapon of opportunity. Psychologically, if someone agrees to one request, they are more likely to agree to a second. You can use this manipulation to gradually and methodically gain the upper hand.[21]

You can also try to establish a connection with your attacker. Give them some information about yourself to remind them that you are in fact a real person. Share things like when you first moved to the city, your likes and dislikes about the area, what state and city you are originally from, when your birthday is, what you have done or what you do for a living, etc.

Listen closely to their replies. Pay attention to their tone of voice, whether they are short or chatty with you, their facial expressions, movement of their hands and feet and their body posture. Sometimes what they do not say speaks louder than what they do. For example, if they appear agitated and are mumbling or pacing back and forth and you smell cigarettes, you could suggest where they can go smoke where they won't be noticed, or you can tell them where your own cigarettes are if you have them. You can ask if they're hungry or thirsty, and suggest food or drink they might like from the kitchen. If they're injured, you can offer to treat their injury with a first aid kit in the bathroom.

Manipulation is tricky to master, and that's why I recommend planning for it. It's not something that most normal civilians can master on the fly. Plus, when death is on the line, failure can lead to disastrous consequences. Get it right during your practice sessions so you can pull it off during an actual home invasion.

THE IMPORTANCE OF PRACTICE

After making your family action plan, don't pop it in a binder and slip it away on a dusty bookshelf. That would defeat the whole purpose!

The plan goes hand in hand with practice. Every member of your family has to be involved, rehearsing their roles, actions and strategies on a monthly basis. More importantly, they need to experience a realistic scenario in which group dynamics come into play.

For instance, think about a football team. Every player has their role to play. The quarterback throws the pigskin and leads the offense. The halfback carries the ball during running plays, while fullbacks block opponents. Wide receivers and tight ends round out the team.

Each player can practice their role day in and day out. But the true magic happens when the team comes together and executes a brilliant game plan. Half the credit of a win goes to the players' skills, the other half to the strategy and dynamics between them.

Your family has to approach a family action plan with the same mindset. The announcer needs to know when to raise the alert, alarm and all-clear signals. The door blocker must be able to quickly get in position and prepare for a fight to keep the intruder out. The Houdini must be ready to perform difficult actions in a tense situation and the informer has to have one hand on the phone at all times.

Equally important, everyone needs to know what the others are doing in order for the plan to work.

Practicing the plan doesn't have to be a scary, stressful occasion. In fact, it can be transformed into a fun activity that makes remembering the plan enjoyable. Have guests such as extended family or friends show up and test your home's defenses by knocking at strange hours, or prowling around the bushes in the front yard. Reward children when they follow the right steps, and coach them when they err. Incorporate rewards when they make sense.

Practice often, and always try to rehearse various scenarios. Don't assume that a home invasion will happen one way or another. In fact, assume nothing. Prepare for more situations rather than less, and work to mitigate every possibility you can think up. If your practice sessions are repetitive and stuck in a rut, they won't do much good. Cross-train all family members when possible, and know everyone's roles!

Turn everyday events into practical scenarios that build up family members' observation and listening skills. For instance, when the kids go to the bus stop every morning, challenge them to take mental snaps of the cars they see, the friends' parents they encounter and other objects along the sidewalk. Quiz them on what they saw, and teach them to call you for help when something seems out of place, even if it makes them feel uncomfortable or silly. This gets them in the right mindset to survive.

After experiencing a home invasion firsthand, no one ever regrets having a plan. Survivors don't ever think they practiced too much. Like the Mason family in the opener, whose plan helped save three young children from an attack, those who plan for a home invasion and get through the ordeal alive say only two words: Thank God.

PRACTICE EXERCISE 2: PLANS, PLAIN AND SIMPLE

Now that you understand the importance of survival preparation and the factors that go into a good family action plan, take some time to build one for your household.

Gather all the adults who reside in your home at a convenient time. Sit down at the dining room table and determine the following plan components:

- Frequency of conducting safety walks and taking notes.

- Strategies for vacations or extended absences from the home, including mail collection, car rotations, lighting/electronics timers and friend or neighbor check-ins. Make a checklist of pre-trip duties, if it helps.

- Alert phrase to notify your family of potential first contact.

- Alarm phrase to notify your family of an active threat.

- All-clear phrase to notify your family that a threat has been neutralized.

- Where and how to hide in each section of your home, ensuring that all family members have a secure, escapable hiding place.

- The best technique for being tied up, as well as how to escape and what to do next.

- Two or three escape routes for every room.

- Rendezvous points outside of the home.

- Strategy for reporting the invasion to the authorities.

Once you finalize your plan, communicate it to all children living in your home, even those who visit on specific timetables due to divorce. In subsequent exercises, you will have an opportunity to practice and refine most elements of your preparation. Right now, the key exercise is to get the basics hashed out, jotted down and communicated properly.

You may find it helpful to read through this book in its entirety before finalizing every section of your plan. Alternatively, you can get started with basics and leave room for additions as you go. Some of the core plan areas are covered in much greater depth during later chapters. Remember that you can always add, edit or remove elements as your circumstances change. In fact, the plan should be a living strategy that grows alongside your family, and as long as you communicate changes and practice regularly, this process will only improve your odds of survival.

You shouldn't have just one plan. Prepare for contingencies and unexpected events, such as absences, various times of day and even different weather patterns. For every variable that changes, your plan must be able to adapt and your family members must be able to fill in the gaps immediately. List the core drivers that could impact the way your strategy unfolds, and for each, write down a few notes on what you could do to lessen its impact on your survival.

A quick example: Let's say that your oldest child is designated to sound the alert. However, if he or she is out at the movies with friends when an attack occurs, the next oldest child must assume that role. Run through the full contingency plan with everyone so that designations are clear. Make sure everyone knows every role and practices each, even if it's not their primary function during an invasion.

Store the latest version of your family action plan in your dedicated dossier. When replacing an older version, shred the old documents and then either burn or soak them in bleach to ruin the contents.

3

OWN FIRST CONTACT

It was a quiet summer day in June of 2016 when a resident in southwest Oklahoma City looked at his live security system feed and saw his house being burglarized.

Rather, *almost* burglarized.

Using a doorbell camera security system, the resident sat inside the home and watched the would-be attacker walk up to the door and ring. When no one answered, the man briefly disappeared off-screen before returning and attempting to kick the front door open.

At this point, the homeowner took ownership of the situation and picked up the intercom system, hollering at the suspect to stand down. The prepared man didn't even need to get up from his chair, where he sat in the safety of a locked room.

Startled by the booming voice, the failed assailant fled. He was not apprehended by the authorities.

The homeowner didn't let the escape deter him. He posted video footage of the encounter on YouTube and requested the public's assistance in apprehending the foiled criminal.[22]

Remember, every happy ending could have ended not so happily.

STOP, LOOK AND LISTEN PHILOSOPHY
Every conflict in the history of humanity opens with some form of first contact. In laymen's terms, there is always a first shot fired.

Home invasions are no exception. First contact could involve a sudden disruption at the front doorway while talking with an unidentified visitor. It could be a momentary lapse when you turn your back and the stranger breaches the entry, forcing himself inside. Or, it could be waking up to a strange noise coming from your guest bedroom as an uninvited guest slips inside the open window.

The fact of the matter is that 28 percent of burglaries—nearly one-third—occur while a homeowner is present.[23]

No matter how first contact occurs, you don't gain the upper hand by sheer chance; you own it by taking it. Otherwise, your attackers will take it from you. If you expect to look out your window in the middle of a bright, sunny day to clearly see a man with a drawn pistol approaching your front door, you're fooling yourself into a false sense of security. First contact almost never happens that way, except in the movies!

When you find yourself unexpectedly face-to-face with your attacker, what should you say? What should you do? Where should you go? These are great questions, but they'll only help you if you have the answers prepared in advance. It's like the old saying that if you don't have a plan, then you plan to fail. How you manage first contact can put you in a position of advantage, or it can drop you behind the curve.

Though first contact can take any form, three common scenarios occur in a huge majority of home invasion cases. The first is when you are overcome at the entrance to your home, or when you accidentally let your assailant enter for a seemingly legitimate reason. The second is a distraction technique where someone keeps you engaged at the door while others sneak in through side or rear entry points. The third most common scenario is that you hear a noise inside your home after the criminals have already infiltrated the premises.

Life is murky. Criminals thrive in that gray zone, blending in just enough with harmless masses to disguise their dishonest motives. They won't make it easy for you to spot them, and oftentimes, they only act outwardly threatening when it's already too late for you to proactively take first contact away from them.

I often tell civilians to adopt a "stop, look and listen" philosophy to improve their odds of wrestling the first contact advantage from an assailant. Let's walk through this technique using an example from a case I use in my safety courses.

A mother of three was in the kitchen one Friday evening after work, anxious for her husband to return from his job so she could get dinner on the table. Everything seemed normal; the kids were upstairs playing, the dog was sleeping on the couch, the television set was quietly playing one of her favorite shows as she waited. After she peeked in the oven to see if dinner was just about done, she noticed the dog had gotten up and run to the door, wagging his tail excitedly.

Her husband wasn't due home for another 30 minutes, and she hadn't heard his car pull up in the driveway. In fact, she hadn't heard anything suspicious at all.

The mother immediately stopped thinking about dinner and assessed the situation unfolding at her front door. As she watched, a shadow slipped past the large bay window overlooking the dense row of boxwoods just in front of the house.

In this example, the normalcy of a weeknight is shattered when something unexpected happens in the unnamed woman's home. No one barges in through a window or door, and there isn't a clear threat present. But the family dog's abrupt shift in activity combined with the fact that her husband was not due home for some time gave the mother reason to believe that a threat could be looming.

Let's see what happens next.

Fumbling with the remote, the woman muted her television set and stared at the front entry. Out of the corner of her eye, she'd already spied a tall shadow creeping through the front gardens, just beyond the bay window's sheer curtains.

Then, another shadow appeared.

The woman dropped to her knees and silently crawled into the living room, her heart racing. She continued to stare at the curtains where the shadows prowled. Through the open front window, she could hear muffled whispers.

She took cover behind a couch and pulled out her smartphone, bringing up their home's security app. It included a security camera hidden on the porch with a live feed of activities in the front yard and gardens. She silently watched the scene unfold as the two hooded figures quietly pointed and gestured, straining to hear what they were saying. One sported a black sweatshirt, the other a blue one bearing the symbol of a local baseball team.

- - -

The woman in this story is acting rationally and intelligently. She realizes that something is going on, and so she stops and looks to gain more information about the threats. Though she could have peered out the windows directly, this might have compromised her first contact advantage. Instead, the use of a security camera gives her a new perspective without sacrificing any possibilities.

Though the woman arguably could have taken action at this point, she knew the window was open, her children were upstairs and two likely criminals were plotting just a few feet away. Observing gave her the ability to study their heights, body language and postures, information she could use later on to identify them when speaking with the authorities. For as much as she knew, there were still many unknowns: Were they alone? What were their motives? Was someone else casing the other entrances?

That's where listening came in very handy. It's time to see how this story ends.

- - -

The whispers were barely audible from her hiding place in the living room.

"We get in, and we get out," one man told the other with a hushed voice. "If anyone gets in our way, just take 'em down."

"Yeah," the other replied. "Okay. Whatever you say."

"I'm the leader here, idiot," the first man snapped back. "Follow my lead and the two of us will have a very good day. I saw where they keep the jewelry box when I was here cleaning their pool a couple weeks ago."

Suddenly, everything clicked. The woman had heard enough. With her app, she triggered the security system's alarm, sending a siren blasting through the house. The woman watched the figures leap, tripping over the shrubs as they bolted.

A minute later, an operator called the house to report the alarm. The woman requested assistance, and five minutes later, the police arrived. Shortly after, her husband pulled in among the sea of flashing red and blue lights.

"What happened?" he asked, running from the car. "Is everyone all right?"

The woman looked up from the policemen taking her statement, nodding.

"Two men tried to break in a little while ago. It was that guy, Billy, who cleaned our pool. I have video footage, and I heard him talking about seeing my jewelry box when he was here last weekend."

Billy was apprehended on his way back home, his blue baseball team sweatshirt a match with the security camera footage.

Now, this example had a happy ending. They're rare, but they can happen if you follow your plan and maintain constant vigilance. Remember that when something seems amiss, first stop and collect preliminary details about where the risk exists. Next, look at the area and assess any threats that it contains. Finally, listen to the threats and gauge their plans before taking any action. If you thwart them appropriately, you can potentially avoid the confrontation altogether.

DIFFERENTIATING BETWEEN RISK AND THREAT ASSESSMENTS

Throughout this book, you'll notice that I reference risk and threat assessments frequently. These are common terms in the law enforcement and defense communities. If you're not familiar with them, they can be a bit confusing. Let's break them down.

A risk assessment is analysis conducted on a specific area. The area could be your front yard, living room or garage. During a risk assessment, you look for means of escape, places to cover, weapons of opportunity and immediate dangers you might face during an attack. Conversely, you should also look at dangerous advantages that an attacker might gain in a particular area. For instance, in a garage, you might notice a shovel hanging on the wall. While you could use this garden tool as a weapon of opportunity, if it's positioned closer to the garage doors than to the entry to your home, it would be easier for an intruder to get his hands on it than for you.

You can conduct a risk assessment at any time. In fact, put this book down for a moment and look around the room you're sitting in right now. Where are the entry points? Are there places where you could hide or escape? What types of furniture, decorations or tools could you fashion into a weapon of opportunity if you had to defend yourself right now? It's that simple; you can do a quick risk assessment in seconds.

Threat assessments are analyses of people in your immediate area. Watch for mannerisms, interactions with each other and direct and indirect actions they perform. I'll give you a tip: Even if you think someone knocking at your door is probably benign, treat them as a potential threat. You should opt to be safe rather than sorry. Conduct a quick threat assessment and figure out what his deal is before assuming he is harmless.

I can't tell you how many times I've traveled to communities to give classes, especially during the holidays, and found people making mistakes that compromise their ability to conduct threat assessments. The most frequent examples are people who gift wrap their front doors or cover peep holes with decorations without realizing they have compromised their own safety.

A threat assessment starts by counting the number of potential criminals. Observe each person's behaviors, actions and activities. Scope out any visible weapons or evidence of weapon paraphernalia. For instance, even though you might not see a firearm or knife, you might notice a suspiciously shaped bulge on a threat's hip, leg or chest.

Observe the target for a moment, taking in his demeanor and composure. Does he look flighty or nervous, or does he appear confident and aggressive? Is he acting as if under the influence of drugs or alcohol? Does the person exhibit any signs of mental illness, such as talking to himself, interacting with nonexistent entities or moving his limbs in a strange fashion?

Subtler clues can also yield valuable data. For example, let's say you look out your window and spot three unidentified men standing on the sidewalk in front of your house. Normally, this wouldn't worry you; after all, there is a bus stop at the corner, and the next scheduled pick up is any minute now. Two of the men are close to one another, talking and glancing over in the direction of your windows. The third, however, stands several feet away and appears to be silent. You also notice that his feet are pointing away from your house toward a neighbor's lawn across the street. Though you can't be completely certain, there is a good chance that the third man is not part of the group, as their paths would not cross if all three started walking in the direction their feet were pointed.

The better your threat assessment, the more prepared you'll be if the threat escalates. Quickly collect as much information as you possibly can before integrating it into your family action plan. Scan for backpacks, tool belts or other places where someone could hide a weapon, such as baggy shirts or cargo pockets. Keep a close eye for immediate weapons. If you spot a knife, note whether it's a tactical folding knife or if it's a fixed blade in a sheath. Also look for side-rig firearms, which can be given away by the threat patting bulges on one side of his body, even if the weapon is concealed.

During your threat assessment, pay attention to angles of contact. This way, you know where the suspicious individuals are at all times. This prevents them from orchestrating a sneak attack on you from an unobserved location.

COMMUNICATING ALERTS

Imagine that you're conducting a quick, casual risk assessment one weekend when something catches your eye or ear. A garbage can may not be where you saw it a few minutes ago, a pile of trash may have accumulated on the far side of your driveway or a strange figure may have been lurking a bit longer than you like on the neighborhood sidewalk. Whatever you've witnessed is just not quite right, you tell yourself, realizing that danger could be unfolding . . . or not. It could just be nothing.

Your family is scattered around the house doing chores, homework and other tasks. It doesn't make sense to initiate your family action plan yet. However, you still want everyone to be aware that something fishy is going on and that they should be ready to jump into action.

Sounding the alert allows you to tell your family that something is unfolding without requiring everyone to retreat to hiding places. In fact, the alert is little more than a formal heads-up announcement that the status quo is temporarily changing. If something bad does occur, the alert buys you precious seconds or minutes to get ahead of your potential attacker.

Because an alert may be the precursor to an attack, you don't want to give away too much information in case the intruder is listening (and trust me, they often are). Pick a phrase that wouldn't sound out of character echoing from one of your home's windows. It should be specific enough that it wouldn't ordinarily be used in your day-to-day life. Remember that you must be comfortable yelling the phrase you select, as you will use it to quickly tell everyone in the house that there is a possible home invasion situation brewing.

If you live in a large family home with one or more children, build your alert phrase around the specific environment in which you live. You may need one or more phrases for indoor and outdoor zones. "Put away that princess toy before I trip over it!" is a good example for a generic indoor phrase. Another alternative, specific to outside zones, might be, "Did your sister lock her bike away?" These are two options that could be used as good alerts, though remember that you should customize them to better fit your family and home's situation. After all, neither statement specifically references the potential threat. At the same time, both are feasible sentences that a parent could yell out on any given day. It sounds normal for the house.

Let's say you live in a smaller home without children. Either of the following alerts could work well for couples, elderly homeowners and people living with roommates. "Did you see my keys when you were cleaning?" is a great option as long as there is a car visible in your driveway or garage, while "Bring up an extra roll of paper towels from the basement!" can be used any time.

Let your creativity shine when devising an alert. It'll help you localize the alert to your family. Rotate alert phrases every six to twelve months, and let your family members take turns picking a phrase that they like. This makes the alert process engaging and enjoyable, and that in turn boosts children's desire to follow directions.

CALMLY SOUNDING THE ALARM

If the assailant moves in to initiate trouble, sound the alarm. As discussed in the previous chapter, the alarm is the next step after having raised an alert. Bear in mind that alarms do not require alerts, especially if a probable attacker is only just noticed. Remember that the goal is to own first contact and stop the home invasion, even if you need to skip the alert stage. Once the alarm phrase is heard in the house, everyone must calmly drop what they are doing and make their way to their designated hiding place, escape route or task post.

Hearing the alarm enables your family to rapidly realize that whatever situation caused the alert has been escalated to a clear, specific danger. This shift in understanding allows everyone to rapidly assume the position, so to speak. They can begin to prepare themselves for the attack, which may include heading to their designated location (such as the doorway) or hurrying to hiding

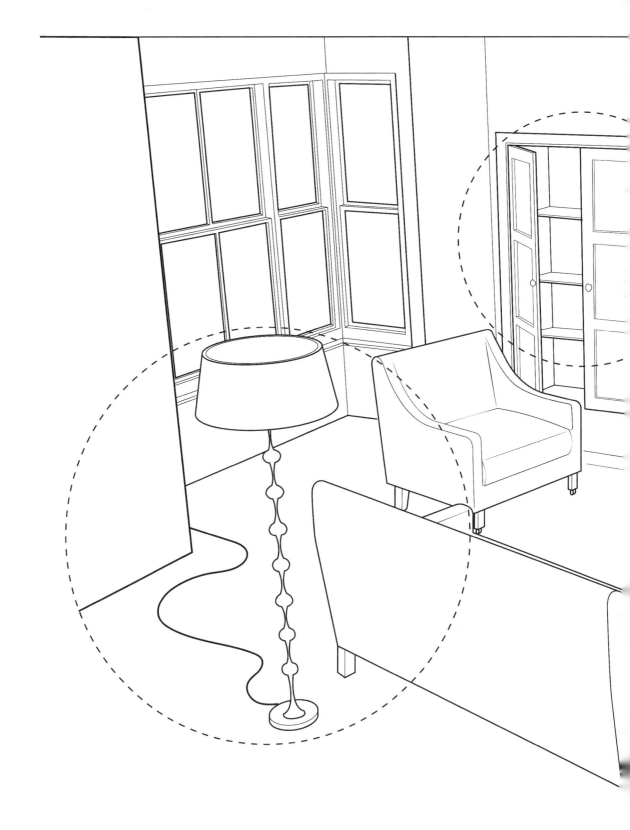

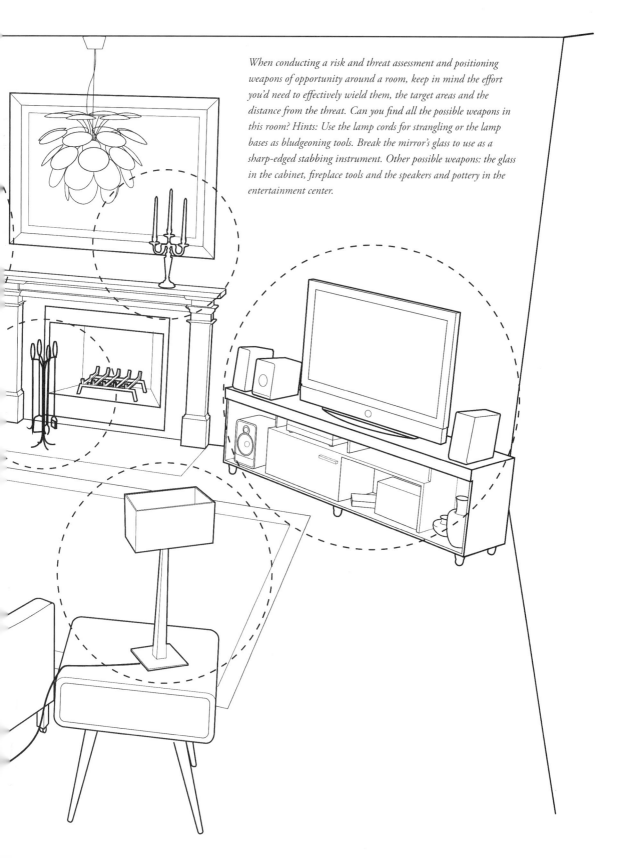

When conducting a risk and threat assessment and positioning weapons of opportunity around a room, keep in mind the effort you'd need to effectively wield them, the target areas and the distance from the threat. Can you find all the possible weapons in this room? Hints: Use the lamp cords for strangling or the lamp bases as bludgeoning tools. Break the mirror's glass to use as a sharp-edged stabbing instrument. Other possible weapons: the glass in the cabinet, fireplace tools and the speakers and pottery in the entertainment center.

places throughout the house. The alarm keeps everyone informed while encouraging order and organization, enabling a stronger, more cohesive first contact response.

The person who will answer the door must have a direct, expedient response to hearing the alarm. They should immediately clear their mind to focus on the task at hand. At the same time, they must get to the doorway, assuming the appropriate bracing stance that will be outlined in Chapter 5. Depending on how well the doorway is defended in the coming moments, the other members of the family can prepare to hide, escape or defend.

It's critical that family members remain collected during the dispersal process. Why? Home invaders may be observing or listening to activities occurring inside while they make their way toward an entry point. If they see multiple people scrambling, or lights and appliances suddenly turning off in multiple rooms, they will know that something is up. It will also clue them in to the whereabouts of individuals. Everything in the house should be left as-is; this freeze preserves the illusion of normalcy and makes it harder for attackers to quickly pinpoint where residents may or may not be hiding.

Like the alert, the alarm should be a phrase that does not imply danger. It must also be called out at a significant volume, so it should be something appropriate and consistent with the outward appearance of your home as we discussed earlier when examining alerts.

My wife and I taught our kids about alarms at an early age. I still remember a very frightening occasion when my daughter used one to get my help.

She'd been dating a young man who became aggressive. After a few dates (a lifetime for a young teenage romance!), my daughter broke it off, and a month later she came home to find him sitting in the living room. Calmly, she went to get him a drink from the kitchen, smiling and acting pleasant. She told him that she needed to call me to let me know she'd arrived home safely, and he nodded. He knew I meant business, but he also knew that I worked outside the house until early evening, so he didn't suspect a thing.

"Dad," she said on the phone, her voice calm and confident. "I made it home safe. But I really don't appreciate that you and mom threw out my butterfly collection." Then, she abruptly hung up.

Within ten minutes I was at home escorting the young man out the front door. After I made sure he wouldn't ever return to harass her again, I hugged my daughter and commended her on using her code phrase, butterfly collection, to successfully communicate distress. The moment I heard those innocent-sounding words, I got in my car and zipped straight home.

When sounding the alarm, be aware that younger children may become frightened or scared. This is natural given their immature emotional fortitude. If this happens, quickly calm their nerves while walking them to their hiding place. Assure them that they will be safe as long as they remain quiet, and quietly remind them not to come out unless they hear the designated all-clear command. Stow them with a quiet toy (such as a stuffed animal), and if at all possible, pair younger children off so that they are not left alone. This helps make them feel more at ease, which yields better survival results. For instance, if one child remembers the all-clear command but the other does not, they can help one another.

Occasionally, false alarms happen. I remember hearing a story about an elderly woman who sounded the alarm only to later find out that the perpetrator was a neighbor thoughtfully watering her front gardens! This is nothing to worry about. In fact, you should treat these mistakes as valuable learning exercises. Figure out what went wrong in determining that an alarm was warranted as well as the things that your family did well. Once in a while you can even practice by "pulling the alarm," so to speak and sending your family into their routines even when there is no danger.

SECURE THE UPPER HAND

As soon as you ensure your family is properly and safely notified about the imminent threat, it's time to take action to maintain your upper hand. I always recommend that you proactively call out to the attacker to state your awareness of his or her intrusion and their options for de-escalating the conflict.

Think back to your days on the playground. Did you ever deal with a bully? The situation with a newly discovered home invader is similar in many regards. Every person—bully, home invader or even a stranger with unknown intentions—measures another individual's level of assertiveness based on three qualities:

- **TONE OF VOICE:** An ideal tone of voice is firm, confident and steady without vocal cracks, stuttering or wild shifts in intonation or speed. Use short, direct responses that leave no room for interpretation. Speak loudly and deliberately without shouting. Remember that verbalization is a psychomotor skill and that you need to practice it to get it just right. After all, you use a different tone of voice asking your eight-year-old son to give you the television remote than you would confronting an armed intruder.

- **APPEARANCE:** Stand with your arms at your side and your hands in a defensive position. Use stern facial expressions that do not show your true emotions. Avoid hunching or standing too rigid. Though you will probably be scared, breathe softly and normally to avoid appearing flustered or flushed in the face. If you have access to a weapon of opportunity, confidently grasp it and wield it to show that you mean business.

- **ACTIONS:** Slip into a rehearsed defensive posture immediately. Avoid quick, frantic movements (such as blindly grasping for a weapon) that can betray your own unpreparedness. Stand with your back to a solid wall and walk slowly and quietly with your weapon in position.

Shouting random threats, taunts or other expressions of angst are wildly counterproductive and should be avoided. In fact, these types of outbursts could cause the attacker to call out your bluff or rush in for a preemptive assault. I get that you're angry and ready to lash out in defense of your home. But now isn't the time for blind rage. Save your revenge for the police report when you can put your attacker away for a long, long time.

Once, I was leaving a large big-box store with my wife. As we walked to our car in the parking lot, a suspicious looking man approached me with his hands in his pockets. I immediately took cover on the side of my car, pointed at him and firmly said,

"Stop right there and put your hands where I can see them."

Not only did he stop dead in his tracks, he spun on his heels and left me and my wife alone. It probably didn't hurt that I'm a former marine who still looks the part, but trust me, the tactic works for defenders of any stature, age or gender. Simply put, if you come across as tough and assertive, most would-be criminals will leave you alone in favor of a weaker target. Remember back to the first chapter: Increase their effort, lower their reward and reduce the risk!

In the case of a home invasion, make sure that you can substantiate anything you call out to the attacker with a preplanned response. For instance, don't proclaim that you have a loaded gun if it isn't in your hand with the safety off and your finger resting on the trigger. Instead, opt for a strong, general warning. My family's preferred line is:

"If you leave right now, you won't get hurt. But if you stay, there is a good chance you will die!"

Practice making these proclamations often and at different times of the day. For instance, at night, you have increased respiratory activity that can lead to stuttering. Verbalizations are psychomotor skills that can become dull without adequate use. The tone required to enact fear in an attacker is different than the voice you'd use to scold a child or pet. You can't use these voices interchangeably and expect positive results!

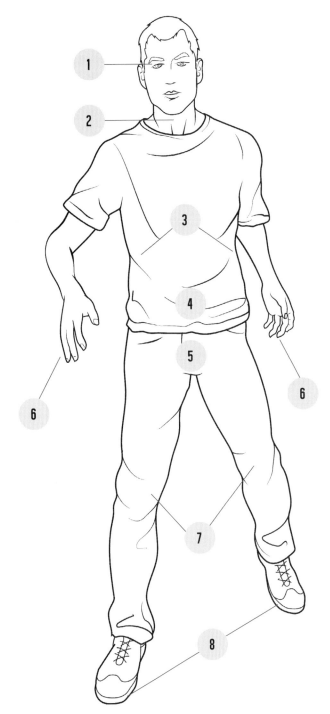

PHYSICAL DEFENSE OPTIONS

You've substantiated your threat, isolated your intruder and owned first contact, informing them that they will be hurt if they do not leave your home immediately. Instead of fleeing, the assailant continues to approach you. What next?

First contact is not the ideal time to mount a physical defense. However, sometimes it's the only option on the table, especially when an attacker is outwardly aggressive. When you find yourself face-to-face with an assailant you only just met, think quickly, think generally and think pain for your opponent.

Brace yourself and prepare to inflict as much pain as possible. That could mean lashing out at the windpipe, slamming fingers in a door or kicking the groin with extreme force. Make the attacker regret not heeding your warning to abandon the premises. If you can show enough force during your initial defense, there is even a chance that they might limp away rather than face a barrage of blows.

During first contact, you'll probably be gripping a phone. It may seem like a no-brainer that you need to use this device to call for help, but if it comes down to getting someone off your stoop or immediately phoning for assistance, weigh your options carefully. You might be able to use the phone as a bludgeoning weapon to drive them away—a more effective use than calling emergency services and waiting four or more minutes for someone to show up and save your skin! That's a prime example of successfully owning first contact.

First contact doesn't always happen while you're inside the house, though. I've heard this same story more times than I can count: Someone pulls into their driveway after a long day at work. The sun has just set, and their driveway and yard are covered in twilight shadows. Anxious to get inside to their family, the person immediately turns off their headlights, and then twists the key to turn off the car's engine. They open their door, begin gathering their things from the passenger seat and suddenly find themselves face-to-face with an armed intruder.

When physically targeting a threat, your top choices are respiratory (#2, #3, #4), vision (#1) and then pain (#5, #6, #7, #8). If the attacker cannot breathe, see or overcome his pain, you become less important.

It would've been better to keep the lights on and doors locked while they assembled their belongings. In fact, they should have turned the high beams on, clicked the engine off and waited a few seconds for their tunnel vision to dissipate before exiting the safety of the parked vehicle. But the mistake has already been made. To defend yourself, slam the car door shut or kick it out with your foot—whichever will inflict more confusion and pain onto your aggressor. Trigger the car alarm and slip your keys between your fingers, balling them into a spiked fist that you can pound into the stunned attacker. Use your briefcase or purse as a bludgeoning tool while you kick.

If the attacker waits and pounces while you're crossing your lawn, drop everything, hunch down and dive for their legs. Try to knock them down. This is a great way to even the field and defend yourself from an unexpected first contact event. It also has potential to knock the wind out of them, giving you time to pin them down and call for help.

PRACTICE EXERCISE 3:
MAKING AND TAKING FIRST CONTACT

Rev up to take control of first contact exercises, scaring off most would-be home invaders before they step over your home's threshold! In this exercise, you will practice three different techniques for managing and mitigating first contact.

First, practice answering the door correctly. Ask a neighbor or friend to surprise you with an unexpected knock at the door over the next two to three weeks. Ensure that they don't tell you when they're coming over. Train your family on the best practices for looking out the peephole or decorative side windows. When the bell rings unexpectedly, have them speak about what they see to gauge their risk and threat assessment skills.

Second, practice reacting to a possible threat. Indicate what to say aloud and what not to say, as well as alert phrases for the family to remember. Ensure that objects such as cordless phones are available to pick up for a convincing test. Treat the test event like an actual threat, and be ready for anything that may follow.

Finally, sit down with your family to review the shadows, hiding places, reflective surfaces and security system camera locations you noted in Chapter 1, pinpointing blind spots and angles. Discuss why it's important to fully scope any potential threat before deciding on how to enact your family action plan. Equally important, talk about what to do when a threat approaches from a place you cannot easily see. Be ready for anything in order to maximize your survival potential.

After completing the exercise, write a journal entry about what happened, how it was handled, who participated and other core details. Tuck this into your dossier. Add short journal entries for each practice session to track progress and mitigate deficiencies. If you see the same mistakes happening over and over again, increase family discussions on the impacted topics until you are confident that everyone is adequately equipped to survive.

4

GUARD SUCCESSFULLY

On June 8, 2010, an intruder attempted to enter a residence in Carlisle, Pennsylvania. The area had seen a number of break-ins and thefts in the weeks leading up to the incident.

In this particular case, however, the intruder failed. The resident knew how to guard his home.

The homeowner heard a knock at the door at eight o'clock in the evening. When he answered, he saw a man with a revolver in his waistband standing just outside. The assailant then rammed the door and attempted to push past the resident, but the resident stood his ground and successfully blocked the attacker from entering the property.

When his efforts proved fruitless, the would-be home invader fled, leaving the homeowner shaken but otherwise safe. The police did not apprehend the suspect.[24]

MANAGE DISTANCE AT THE DOORWAY

A lot of home invaders break in without an invitation. But get this: In almost 20 percent of reported home invasions, the homeowner accidentally let the attacker inside. You read that right. The homeowner opens the door and ushers the attacker right in. Another 12 percent opened the door before being overtaken in a forced entry.[25] And another frightening thought is that the vast majority of intruders who do not wear masks plan to kill you to avoid getting caught. Once they've tricked you or forced their way in, your life quite literally ticks away.

On most houses, the front door is the chief point of entry. I've also seen houses where homeowners use a convenient side door instead, especially if the front entry is not readily accessible. No matter which you use, your primary door is the one that sees the most daily foot traffic. It's also your first line of defense when someone tries to get inside your home.

Besides primary entries, most homes include at least one secondary access point. This could be the rear, garage or basement bulkhead door. Though many of the strategies outlined here revolve around front entries, you should be prepared to defend all exterior doors in your house.

Managing distance at the doorway is a crucial skill that you must learn in order to successfully guard your home. In this section, I'll share a few tips and pointers with you about how to keep your home adequately protected at this vulnerable spot.

Practice doorway safety whenever you answer the door. It doesn't matter if you're expecting someone or if you hear a friendly voice on the other side. Until you have visual confirmation, you can never be certain about who is waiting for you on the other side. Check the peephole by pushing your forehead to the door and looking out, and position yourself so that you can quickly block and push back if necessary. Use the instep of your foot to control the door's ability to open while leaning one side of your body against the door to brace it. A full description of the stance, including a useful illustration, is provided on page 74. Always answer with a phone in hand, and do not allow the person to see you approach. Keep curtains drawn on windows near the entry. Loudly call out to a loved one that you've got the door, even if no one else is home.

If you recognize the person as a friend or family member, go right ahead and open the door. But even if the person says they are a professional while wearing a credible outfit or sporting a convincing badge, ask them through the door to confirm their identity and the reason for their visit. You can even call their company to confirm the individual's presence at your home. If it seems paranoid, rest assured that it isn't.

Back in the early 2010s, someone rang my doorbell at around one o'clock in the afternoon. I was working in my home office, and my wife went to answer the door. She looked through the peephole and saw a well-groomed man dressed in a light blue shirt with professional looking shorts. He held a tablet computer to his chest behind his folded arms.

Unsure about who was ringing at such an odd time, my wife called for me. As soon as I opened the door, the man took a few steps back and introduced himself with a first and last name. I thought it was strange that he did not offer to shake my hand, and he did not offer me a business card. He did note that his team was conducting a survey in the neighborhood for a new type of security system that automatically connected to the phone lines. To see if I qualified for the service, he explained, he would need to walk through the home. The man was perfectly calm, though I did notice that his body remained stiff during the conversation and he never moved his tablet. We chatted about home safety and security for a few moments at the front door.

That was when I realized that his tablet was on, and it was recording both our conversation and the front entry of my home. In on his ruse, I knew he would have gotten a lot more information if I allowed him to walk through my home—just like the dozen or so neighbors he'd probably visited earlier that day. The tablet would've captured a photographic blueprint of the home's layout, our items inside as well as our family. I asked him to come back after I finished work around five o'clock in the evening, and he nodded with a smile.

As he left the area on foot, I called the police. A week or so later, the neighbors advised me that the man had visited several homes in the neighborhood that day. I also learned that he had been arrested when the police thanked me for the heads up. Scary stuff!

Criminals will go to extreme lengths to get inside your house. There is a popular Christmas movie about a young boy who is accidentally left behind when his family travels overseas for the holidays. He has to defend his house against some unruly burglars, going to extreme lengths to protect his life and property. In the very beginning of the film, one of the crooks poses as a police officer to case targets around the holidays. He uses what he learns to select prime targets for break-ins. As far-fetched as the movie was, this plot point couldn't have been more realistic.

As you speak to a visitor through the door, watch out of the peephole by putting your hands on either side of the hole and putting the top of your forehead above it. This gives you a decent cushion of space in case the door flies open from a kick. Make sure you can see the person's hands in case they are holding a weapon or throwing out visual signals. Don't be afraid to ask them to stand back if you need a better view.

Make mental notes about their behavior. If they talk to the door, that's a good sign, as it generally means they are alone. However, if they look over their shoulder while responding, or if they fidget nervously, it's a safe bet that something is amiss. If the person is delivering something, ask them to leave the package and step back off the stoop. If the delivery requires a signature, have the delivery person leave the slip or device on top of the package, then sign it and leave it on the porch while they wait a safe distance back. You can even thank them for their understanding, telling them that it's a cautious measure to protect against a home invasion attack. If on an off chance they *were* considering your house as a target, that knowledge of your preparedness could be enough to deter them.

If the situation devolves into an attack, continue to manage distance as best as you can. Use anything at your disposal to keep the attacker from getting to the door. If your car keys are nearby, press the panic button to sound a loud alarm that draws attention to your house. Frequently, this is enough to scare off most criminals. For nighttime attacks, flash your house's exterior lights for 30 seconds, then leave them illuminated. Draw as much attention as you possibly can. You want to rustle the neighbors and even tick them off with your strange behavior. After all, annoyed people take action!

If the perpetrators persist, loudly proclaim that you are calling for assistance. Pick up the phone, dial 911 and loudly tell them your name, location and the nature of your emergency. Shout if you need to so that the attacker overhears your conversation.

Sometimes, you just need to buy a little more time before the police arrive. If you have an able-bodied neighbor, call them and ask for their assistance to distract the home invader. You don't want to endanger the neighbor, you simply want to introduce enough chaos that the attacker flees. They can also activate their car's alarm, or they can shout from their own doorway. The benefit is that the rest of the neighborhood will then be alerted to the situation, communicating the threat and encouraging them to lock their doors and remain inside.

EMPLOY CONTACT-BASED COMMUNICATION EFFECTIVELY

Contact-based communication is the initial connection you make with a potential threat. Here's an example.

Say you're at home one evening when the doorbell rings. The tone shatters your resting parasympathetic nervous response, causing your muscles to tense up, your mind to race and your heart rate to elevate. You get up, place both hands on either side of the peephole, gently place your forehead to the door and peer outside, noticing a neatly composed young man standing on your stoop. As you brace the doorframe and crack the door open, he smiles and clears his throat.

"I'm sorry to bother you," he says, wringing his clean hands. "My car broke down just around the corner. Could I please borrow your phone to call for help?"

In that moment, you have a decision to make. The best choice would be to acknowledge his presence and ask him to wait outside, telling him that you will call for him. Then, close and lock the door and loudly call out to your spouse (regardless of whether or not you're actually married, or if anyone is even home), indicating the visitor's presence and purpose for ringing the bell. Get your cordless home phone or cell phone, and crack the door again. Slide it through the crack to let him borrow it, or place the call and relay the man's answers to the mechanic.

You've communicated a lot to a would-be threat in this case. By cracking the door and asking him to wait outside, he knows that you are vigilant about protecting your home. Additionally, calling out to another individual in the house indicates that you have immediate backup support waiting inside.

But it's not just what you've communicated to the would-be assailant, it's also about what you gleaned from him or her. The late hour and somewhat strange request—after all, if he broke down around the block in your neighborhood, why did he pick *your* house to call on?—alert you to the possibility of bad intentions. His clean hands and neat presentation could also signal that something is amiss.

People generally tinker under the hood when their vehicle breaks down, leading to grease smudges, stains and dirty residue on the palms and fingers.

There is always the distinct possibility that he was simply the victim of an unfortunate mechanical breakdown. Perhaps no one else answered their door on the block and you were the first to offer assistance. He could have been running late to a social function, hence the tidy appearance.

The man's true intentions are irrelevant. Only your safety matters. By effectively leveraging contact-based communication to broadcast your strengths while collecting valuable data on another potential threat, you accurately set the bar for any subsequent encounter, benign or malignant. Erring on the side of safety is both wise and recommended.

CONTROL POSITIONING

Maintaining distance at the door is critical, as is contact-based communication. But never underestimate the positive effect of maintaining control over your position. No matter what happens, remember that you are the one and only person who owns your personal defense and safety. No one can take that from you, not even an armed home invader. It's non-negotiable.

Immediately determine if the person at your door is using the conversation as a distraction, and direct anyone home with you accordingly using alarms or hand signals. If he asks you questions, turn them right back on him. This is a great way to trip him up so that you can gauge how he reacts. If he is following a script to distract you, a volley of unanticipated questions will fluster him and give you an inkling as to his true intentions. Meanwhile, peer over his shoulder to see if there's anyone out and about in the neighborhood to assist in case the situation escalates.

How can you maintain control of your positioning in a harrowing situation? First, recall your family action plan and run through your defense options in your head. Sometimes, repeating a mantra—"I am strong, and I will survive!" or "No one gets in here without my permission!"—can help you build up the mental fortitude needed to weather an attack. Mind doesn't necessarily trump matter in a home invasion, but it certainly helps to have the right mental conditioning when you prepare to face off.

As the attacker bears down, look for weapons of opportunity and plan how to use them. Umbrellas, table legs and keys placed between your knuckles are all options to consider at the doorway. Another is the phone, which you should keep near the door so that you can give the impression you are talking to someone when verifying the visitor's identity. The phone can also be used as a weapon of opportunity if the situation turns sour. If time allows, you can even grab a can of aerosol cleaner or air freshener from underneath your kitchen sink to spray in an attacker's face. You haven't lost the battle yet; in fact, you still have an opportunity to maintain your position indoors using defensive techniques that will be discussed in upcoming chapters, such as shielding, blocking, fading, evading and utilizing ruses, among others.

Right now, walk over to your front door. Look for the line on the floor where the bottom edge of the door rests when it's closed. One foot in either direction—inside and outside—is a zone called the threshold. This is the battleground for guarding successfully, and you must try your hardest not to cede it to the attacker. If you take even one or two steps back from the threshold, you've lost your position and guarding is over. Defending is instantly underway. Don't let that loss of positioning happen to you. Stand your ground.

There are no rules when it comes to surviving a home invasion. Hit below the belt whenever you need to, especially if it comes to maintaining your upper hand. Jab through the mail slot with a sharp, snapped broomstick, or shoot through the door with your own firearm. Don't just make threats, take action to keep the balance of power in your court. If you show the attacker that you mean business at the entryway, they're going to flee in terror. If you show your hand and convey weakness, it's only going to make the hunger in their greedy gut stronger.

DOORS 101

I was at the hardware store one Sunday afternoon. On my search for some masonry screws, I walked by a young couple looking at front doors with a store associate. I overheard the woman telling her husband how much she liked a trendy style with a full pane of decorative glass, while the husband said he preferred the half-pane style. He confidently stated that the extra solid material along the bottom half would make the door more secure, shifting his eyes toward the associate for confirmation. The associate only chuckled.

"With that much glass, it doesn't matter either way," he said. "It'll only keep out honest folks."

The associate was spot on. Front entry doors can either be obstructions or invitations to criminals. It's up to you to pick the right one to keep your family protected. Sure, a fancy glass door may look great to you . . . but it also looks appealing to home invaders. Think like a criminal for a moment. If a target invests in bells and whistles in their doorway, just imagine what treasures await inside the house! As an expert on the field, I'll share a few items to keep in mind when picking a front door.

Always look for a solid wood door with steel reinforcement. Mahogany and oak are the best kinds of wood, as they are solid and strong but still bend slightly under duress. If a door is too rigid or heavy, the hinges could fail.

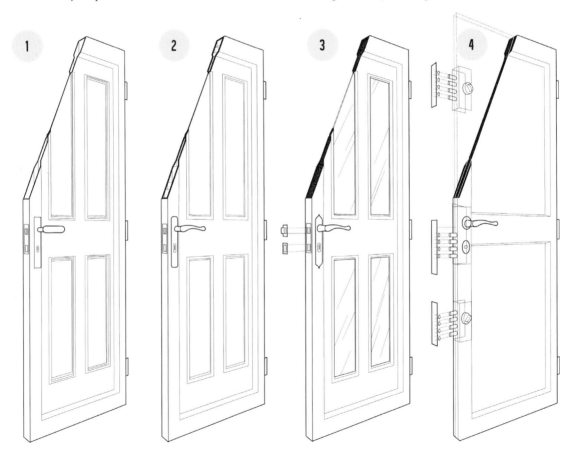

Door 1 – This hollow door with cheap aluminum hardware is the least safe. Door 2 – Even if the hardware is stronger, the doorknob and lock are still too close together to withstand a forceful kick. Door 3 – The solid wood in this door is strong, but the large decorative glass panes can be easily shattered. Door 4 – This is the ideal door, made of solid wood reinforced with steel, with two heavy metal deep-set locking mechanisms and adequate space between the knob and deadbolt.

You want that bit of flexibility. Some zoning codes today allow you to get away with a solid entry door that has some hollow spots. These types of hollow doors are security failures, and those made of lesser materials (such as particle board or pine) tend to splinter very quickly. Solid wood, however, is very hard to break. Plus, it doubles as a heavy instrument that can be used to block, slam or even break fingers when an attacker tries to get inside.

The strongest doors share a few key features. First, they have a peephole that allows you to look outside without being seen by a visitor. You'd be surprised how many homes lack this basic security device! If your door doesn't have one currently, you can have your handyman install it for a nominal fee. Better yet, install two peepholes, with one positioned at an adult's eye level and another at chest level. This allows shorter family members and children to take advantage of this safety feature, and it also gives you a secondary perspective to see more of the visitor before you open the door.

Ultimately, the fewer holes drilled into your door, the better. Optimally, the only holes should be the peepholes, the deadbolt, the knob and the hardware attachments for hinges and strike plates. Decorative glass is a major design trend in front doors these days, but I strongly discourage people from having any glass in their front door. In fact, I recently removed the glass panels surrounding my home's front door and filled them with concrete for enhanced security. The threat really is that serious.

If you really want decorative glass, opt for a quarter pane or smaller at the very top of the door. It's still permeable, but it's much less accessible. Seek out tempered storm glass with a reinforced metal frame. The glass is slightly more resistant to force, and the metalwork will keep shards from showering down on you should a criminal target it. If feasible, install sturdy metal bars over the glass to prevent intruders from reaching inside. A metal security door is a good option, too. This extra door installs over the main door and also locks from the interior, preventing intruders from getting inside even if you've opened the primary door.

Never hide your keys on or around the stoop. It's a grave tactical error that you may not realize you are making. The underside of doormats, statues, potted plants and mailboxes are the first places criminals look. I've come up with a much better solution that you should go try. It works best in warmer climates, though you can use it anywhere during warmer months. Take your spare key and loop about eighteen inches of dental floss through it. Then, go out in your yard and press the key deep into the thickest part of the lawn. The only thing that should stick out is the floss, which you can tuck away among the blades of grass. A criminal will never find it and, for added security, you can move it every time you need to use it. Just yank on the floss and the key will follow! Just be careful when mowing. In the winter, adjust the technique slightly by tying the dental floss to a statue, landscaping feature or shrub. Tuck the key under snow or beneath a small pile of leaves or mulch. The white floss should blend neatly with snow and ice, making it virtually invisible to those who don't already know where it is.

Swap keys with a trusted neighbor. This adds another layer of security. In order to get the key, the neighbor must verify the requestor's identity. There is no hiding involved, and because the key is off your property, it will be hard for any criminal to put it to use even if they come across it. If he's going away, I also have an agreement with my neighbor that I can tape a copy of my key under his mailbox, and he can do the same with mine. That way, the spare is always at hand—and it never gets out of hand, either.

Another option is an inexpensive combination key locker that you can install in a hard-to-spot location. Keep it out of view, as it could wrongly signal that your house is a vacation rental. I keep one inside my shed, which I secure with a heavy combination lock. That way, if my family or I ever get locked out, we only need two combinations to get inside. Criminals need those numbers as well as the location of the locker, making the task of finding and acquiring the key all the more difficult for them.

If you can, position your door so that there is plenty of open space along the side where it opens. This could be as simple as reorienting the hinges and strike plate when hanging it. That way, you can stand in a braced posture to open the door, interact with visitors and push back if need be. If the side of your door that swings open faces a wall, closet or tricky angle inside the home, you'll be at a disadvantage from the get-go, and that's unacceptable.

HARDWARE CONCERNS

Doors rely on hinges, locks and strike plates to function. This hardware can make the difference between letting an attacker right into your home or buying enough time to sneak out through a side exit while they pummel away. Choose the options that give you and your family the greatest potential to survive.

If you had to guess, what would you list as the most important piece of door hardware? The hinges, or the handle? Maybe the deadbolt?

Wrong. It's the doorframe itself. Most people never consider the frame when looking at doors, and yet, it's extremely important when it comes to defending against a brute force attack. Remember that the frame decides the strength of the door it's holding. Opt for a steel frame to keep your deadbolt and latch from splintering through into the home. A metal frame will also make a tampered or breached door stand out from the exterior of the home. The last thing you want is to turn your key, open the handle and walk into an active home invasion because the outside of the door was intact while the interior was splintered.

Deadbolts are fine on their own, so long as the sliding bolt enters the door frame strike plate with adequate length. That depth is directly responsible for the door's strength. One finger joint of depth is too shallow, as the bolt is liable to break or become unlocked with a few hard blows. Ensure that it slides into a depth of at least two finger joints.

Do you have twenty dollars in your checking account right now? Good for you. That means you can go online and buy a set of bump keys that will open nine out of ten standard door locks in the United States without so much as an ounce of difficulty.[26] What is a bump key? It's a special kind of door key that opens pin tumbler locks. It triggers the interior pins of the lock mechanism so that they align and open up. It takes a bit of jiggling and rattling to function, but for a little bit of effort, crooks have modern-day skeleton keys that will open 90 percent of all American doors. Invest in a high-quality lock that has security pins or one that employs shallow drilling of interior pin stacks. These locks will jam rather than open when a bump key is used.

You can also stack your traditional locking mechanism with a backup Bluetooth-enabled lock, combination lock or electronic lock. Battery-operated Bluetooth locks synchronize with your smartphone and open when the synched mobile device is nearby and the owner taps on the lock mechanism. Combination locks require you to manually insert a string of numbers to open the device. Electronic locks contain a keypad, and the appropriate pass code must be correctly entered in order to unlock the door. With any of these secondary security devices, you'll need to bypass two locks to get into your home . . . but so will a criminal. Find a local locksmith and ask them for recommendations that will best suit your family's security needs. Avoid off-the-shelf lock kits from big-box hardware stores. The best option for a backup lock is a secondary deadbolt. Consider using a one-way alternative. These types of deadbolts can be locked or unlocked from inside, but they cannot be opened or locked externally with a key. The same bolt depth minimums apply.

For added security, use a doorknob brace to provide supplemental interior pushback support. Door knob braces are heavy pieces of metal hardware that wedge under the door handle and fit against the floor at a diagonal, bracing the door beyond the capabilities of typical locking hardware. They resemble a metal table leg, with a U-shaped top that fits beneath a door handle and a pivoting rubber foot that grips the floor. In addition to their strength as a barricading mechanism, doorknob braces make excellent weapons of opportunity for bludgeoning an attacker.

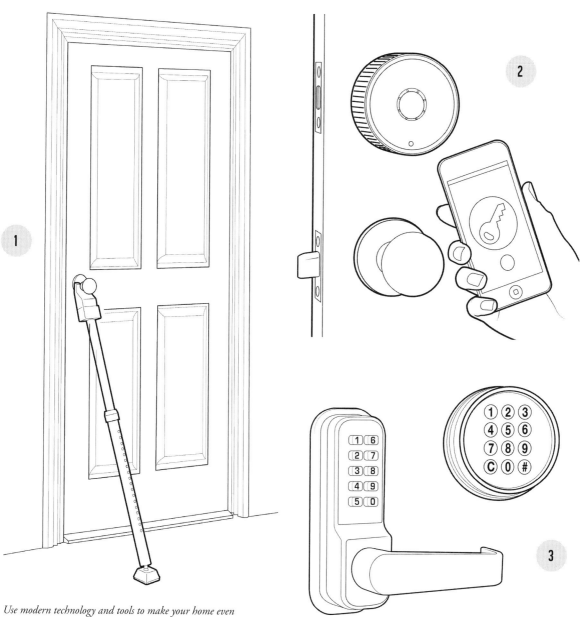

Use modern technology and tools to make your home even harder to gain entry. #1: An inexpensive, yet effective doorknob brace/jamb. #2: A Bluetooth-activated lock that syncs to a smartphone. #3: Two versions of a combination lock with an electronic keypad. Know your locks and practice your combinations regularly!

Next, shift your focus to the screws adjoining the hinges and handles to the door itself. Unscrew one and examine its length. If it's one or two inches in length, it could easily be compromised with a few shoulder blows from a strong criminal. Ensure that screws dig at least three inches deep into the frame for optimal protection.

You might think that all metal hardware is created equal, but this is not true. Aluminum locks and handles, for example, are exceptionally weak. They'll bend with minimal force. To test your hardware, try putting your two hands high on the door and push. If you feel the hardware jiggling, bending or moving, think about how it will crumble when struck by a home invader. Bronze is a bit stronger, but it can still give way. Steel is the best option that won't let you down unless the assailant has a military-grade battering ram. Even a heavy-duty tool like that will take several minutes to have any effect!

Hardware composition is only half the battle. Hardware placement matters, too. If you install the latches, handles and deadbolts too close together, they weaken the structural integrity of the door. With a well-placed strike, the entire side of the door could cleave right off, swinging wide open in the process. From your doorknob and latch, measure at least eighteen inches to install the deadbolt. The larger distance between the two drill holes reduces stress on the wood, and it also raises the weakened portion high enough that a destructive kick is difficult to execute.

SAFEGUARD STRATEGIES

It's tempting to think that a criminal will lazily only target the front door. This wishful notion just couldn't be further from the truth. Treat every exterior door with the same considerations as the front. As a former police officer, I've seen home invasions begin at any and every type of entry point. Heck, some criminals have even pulled off Christmas-style nightmares by climbing down the chimney! One of the worst offenders was an exterior side door with a hollow core—the same type of flimsy material that might be used for a bedroom or closet door. It had a deadbolt and latch, but one kick knocked it right in. The hardware couldn't save the poor construction.

Looks mean everything, and I'm not talking about fashionable runway models. If your door appears sturdy, well-lit and fitted with strong hardware, that impression makes a criminal wonder if the burglary is worth the trouble. That's a win for home defenders! Add another layer to your security blanket by placing an alarm company sticker on every door, window and entry point to the house. This safeguard strategy adds to the defensive impression of the house, further turning a crook off.

Just outside every door leading outside, install a bright exterior light controlled by an interior switch. Don't buy soft, 20- or 40-watt bulbs for these fixtures. Opt for brighter options like 75-watt bulbs that illuminate what's happening outside the door. You can use halogen bulbs as well, which are extremely bright. Avoid compact fluorescent lamp bulbs that take a few seconds to reach their advertised brightness. Another consideration is the fixture itself, which should adequately cover and protect the bulb from dust and grime. A layer of grunge can significantly dampen the light emitted by the bulb. Keep the cover clean with a weekly wipe-down. If you notice that the fixture is allowing moisture inside, replace it with something that seals. This wet environment can cause a bulb's metal base to rust, leading to a short.

Scope out the décor and landscaping that surround every entry point. If you have tall shrubbery that blocks the view or creates shadows, trim it back to improve your view. Test your lights at night, ensuring that leafy bushes or trees do not cast your lawn in dark shadows. Remember, wherever a shadow exists, danger could be lurking.

Remove items that could be used against you as bludgeoning tools from the stoop, porch or other external doorway area. It does not make sense to bolster the enemy's arsenal before they've crossed the threshold! Additionally, be sure you know the locations of all small items inside that can be used as weapons in areas such as doorways and foyers. Ensure that they are readily accessible to you in an emergency.

Just inside the door, get a nonslip mat or rug to help anchor yourself when bracing. As an added bonus, you can also flip the rug with your foot to instantly transform it into a trip obstacle or balance displacement for an intruder who suddenly bursts inside. If you don't want to keep a rug there, that's fine, but consider laying out an open magazine or two by the door at night just before you turn in. They'll make entering slippery, and the sound of rustling papers can be enough to spook the home invader while alerting you to his presence. Another option is a chair or other piece of furniture for inward-opening doors, which you could use to barricade the doorway before going to bed. An intrusion would be slowed, and the noise of crashing furniture would be helpful in waking you up. For doors that open outwards, an easily removable tie-off is a good option for making sure the door remains closed. Just make certain you can remove the tie-off easily in case of an emergency.

BRACE THE FLOOR

Triangles are the strongest shape in nature. Structural engineers use them all the time to reinforce construction materials when building. In fact, their superior strength makes them the basis for one of the strongest man-made structures, the tetrahedral truss. The three-sided truss is used in industrial construction, bridges, vehicle design and other areas of engineering.[27] As polygons go, triangles mean serious business.

Why the geometry lesson in a section about bracing the floor? I'm glad you asked! A right triangle consists of three sides: two legs and a long diagonal hypotenuse. When you brace the entry, the door itself serves as one leg. Your body transforms into the diagonal hypotenuse. The final leg is the floor, which completes your entry safety triangle. Combined, this makes for the strongest natural defense position.

In order to brace successfully, you must have enough friction to keep from sliding. Keep a pair of sturdy shoes or boots near the door at all times that you can quickly slip on when pushing against the door. Rubber rain boots are the best option because you can pull them on in less than a second, and their thick soles will grip the entryway's floor.

Between the boots and a nonslip mat, you should be in good shape. You can supplement with a sturdy rubber wedge or doorknob brace as well. Though most front doors seal quite tightly to keep moisture and pests outside, you can also stuff sturdy objects like shoes into the crack between the door and frame to make it harder to open. Use the floor to your advantage!

Another great way to brace the floor involves using a steel kickstand with a rubber tip. These hinged devices mount at the bottom of the door and create a small triangle between the door and floor. You simply need to kick it free, let it fall and then leave it be. Bear in mind that they won't entirely prevent an intruder from pushing the door open, but they will add another layer of resistance that sources its strength from the floor—not your muscles. That will free you up to fight the home invader off should they make it inside.

DEFEND THE DOOR

A committed home invader wants to get into your home. They will fight through alarms, threats and physical barriers to capture their trophy, which is your hard-earned property, and oftentimes, your family's life. Defend the door with everything you have to give yourself the best chance of escaping unscathed. I sometimes refer to this as the "Custer's Last Stand" of your home. If the attacker gets in here, there's a good chance it'll all be over soon. And I don't mean that a happy ending awaits.

The first defensive element to consider is your stance. There is a myth that when you're getting ready to defend a closed entry, you should place your foot with your toe to the door and lean into it with your hips. This is completely wrong! It comes down to basic physics. The door uses its hinges as a fulcrum. By consolidating your energy anywhere other than at the lock's level, you're giving the attacker a prime position to blow the door open and get inside. On top of that, you're putting your fragile body into harm's way.

Let me teach you the right way to defend a door. Imagine that the door in our scenario opens with its lock on the left side and its hinges on the right. Position your left

foot at an angle along the bottom of the door, with your toes pointed toward the hinges. Take your right hand and push it against the door above the locks with all of your weight. Stand toward the lock side of the door. Then, take your left hand and grab onto the door knob, bracing your arm against the door frame, wall or some other element of the house's structure. This position is strong, and it also shields you from initial gunfire that an attacker might unleash into the door. If the attacker attempts to gain entry, you'll be better able to hold the door and prevent him from entering. Even if he is successful in barging inside, the door won't slam into your face and disable you. This position will give you a chance to recover and regroup.

Assume that the assailant is successful and that he has started entering the doorway. Once the attacker has his body halfway inside, line up your heel along the bottom of the door if it's not there already, continue to lean your body's core weight into the door and bring your right hand around to push, strike or grasp a weapon. Your left arm and leg remain pushed up against the door. This posture allows you to multitask. Your body weight holds the door, while your free right hand functions as a weapon. You can also slam into the door to inflict damage. Fight until you break the attacker's arm or he retreats, then revert to the bracing position.

As your mind grapples with your defense, recall four words: Brace, Heave, Strike, Repeat.

- **Brace** the door in the correct position, resetting your foot, arms, torso and hips as necessary to account for pushback or slippage. Remember to protect your body from blows or bullets.

- **Heave** against the door to counter the attacker's thrusts. Timed to the same rhythm, the equal thrusts will cancel out and prevent the door's hardware from giving way.

- **Strike** out with your free hand whenever the opportunity presents itself. Examples include the attacker getting partially inside, or wielding a long weapon of opportunity that you can jab through the door's crack to push him back.

Use a strong, yet protected position when bracing the door. Position your head to the side of the doorway to avoid a concussive strike if the door swings open. Position your front foot along the bottom of the door to prevent it from swinging open. Use your front hand and arm to strongly brace the door just above the handle, and use your back arm to brace yourself against the doorframe. Overall, keep yourself toward the lock-side of the door to avoid possible gunfire shot into the middle of the door.

- **Repeat** the process, getting back into position as needed. Even if the threat relents, stand ready until the moment the police pull up.

Repeat these four words under your breath. That way, you won't forget your mission or lose courage. Continue using them until the threat abandons his cause or manages to force his way inside. Maintain your balance at all costs, and keep your wits about you. Even if there's a break in the action, the threat is not yet neutralized. Continue to remain vigilant and ready to fight for when he comes back up for the next round.

BARRICADE THE ENTRANCE

I get that sometimes, the odds are stacked against you and you're fighting a losing battle. If the criminal is slowly gaining entry by overwhelming you at the door, it's time to shift strategies and move on to the next phase of your plan. But that doesn't mean you should abandon the entry altogether. Just because the home invader is strong doesn't mean he should be rewarded with an open invitation to your home and family!

Call out to get the attention of a family member inside the house. With their help, start pushing furniture toward the door while one person continues to brace the door itself. Heavy, solid wood or metal pieces are far better than particle board pieces, aluminum lounge chairs or inexpensive items you assembled yourself from a certain Swedish home goods chain. Slide them up against the door, allowing their weight to replace your pushing motion. Realize that they won't hold forever, but they will buy you some time to hide or (better yet) escape through another exit point.

When barricading, the item's center of gravity plays a key role. If you select something too tall, such as a curio cabinet, it can easily be tipped by a hit to the upper half of the piece. This could cause the furniture to topple. Stand back, and keep far away—especially if there is glass involved. The heavy weight of the piece and the sharp shards it can produce have the potential to kill defenders. Furniture with a lower center of gravity is better because it will remain upright. Examples include solid wood desks, heavy rocking or reclining chairs, credenzas and coffee tables. Drag them rapidly and avoid stopping, which will cause you to lose momentum. Even if the piece drags easily, when used as a barricade, friction will make it much harder to push out of the way.

This might sound great if you're a young, fit person, but what if you're elderly or unable to move heavy furniture? Or what if you have carpets on your first floor, making quick dragging motions nearly impossible? The good news is that there are other ways to barricade the door. The easiest is a doorknob brace, which anyone can set up in a matter of seconds. Another is a kickstand. If you have a few heavy items nearby and the door seems to be holding, you can also stack pieces rather than moving one single heavy piece. Dump a pile in front of the door if need be, since even if it won't fully barricade the entrance it will make it harder for someone to get inside. They could slip and fall while climbing. It's all about layers of security; chaos is a great way to build some additional security into what you're doing to protect yourself.

Along the same lines, set a trap before you make your exit from the entryway. Shatter a glass light bulb, vase or picture frame, leaving sharp shards that can puncture shoes and the soles of feet. You can also make the entrance slippery by quickly spraying it with furniture wax, non-stick cooking spray or water in a pinch. Make certain your attacker does not have an easy time getting inside your home to steal what belongs to you, including you and your family's lives.

PRACTICE EXERCISE 4:
SLAM YOUR DOOR'S WEAKNESSES

Before home invaders can get into your home, they need to get past the front door. Don't let that happen on your watch. During this practice exercise, you will check your home's exterior doors to see if they meet the minimum safety criteria to withstand most intrusions.

Examine your front, side and rear doors for each item listed here. If you spot any deficiencies, come up with a realistic plan to address them, including cost, timelines and prioritization. Remember that you can easily mitigate some of these deficiencies by simply moving furniture around within your house—no purchase necessary!

Choose items suited to barricading a door BEFORE the attack and pre-set the item(s) close by. In this illustrated example, as someone is about to break in the woman can push the nearby cabinet with her shoulder and arms just enough that it inches over the hardwood floor and blocks the door, barricading it closed. She can conceal herself behind the cabinet, which is angled slightly against the wall and door, allowing her to observe, defend herself or escape.

- Is your front door made of solid wood with steel reinforcement?

- Do you have a peephole, security camera or nearby window to see outside?

- Do you have a deadbolt?

- Are your strike plates at least 2½ to 3 inches deep?

- Have you placed an entry mat with a nonskid bottom inside?

- Do you have enough space on the side of the door that opens that you can successfully brace and defend the entry?

- Are there options available to barricade the door, such as a knob brace, a sturdy kitchen chair or another heavy piece of furniture?

- Have you stored at least one weapon of opportunity near the entry for emergency use?

- Have you limited the number of potential weapons available to an intruder on your stoop, porch or exterior walk-up?

- Is there a phone within close proximity of the entrance, but not within four feet of the door frame?

Tuck your findings, plans and any drawings you made into your family action plan dossier. If you wind up purchasing hardware or other equipment, staple the receipts to your notes so that you have a record of safety improvements. If you ever need to replace any components, you can quickly find duplicate items thanks to the handy receipts.

I've also found that it helps to make a task or checklist to keep implementation running according to plan. Print a copy and revisit the document on a monthly basis to make sure you are not overlooking any important pieces of the strategy.

5

SHIELD CONTACT

On August 25, 2016, in Battle Creek, Michigan, a woman and her two sons were winding down in their home shortly after ten o'clock in the evening. Suddenly, the evening's peace was broken by their dog barking. Something stirred in front of their home.

The younger son went to the front door, cracked it open and discovered a masked man standing outside.

The boy immediately pushed against the door and yelled for his mother and brother. The three rushed at the door, pushing with all their might, but they couldn't quite get the door to close. The assailant sprayed an aerosol substance inside, adding further chaos to the moment. Fortunately, the older son grabbed a decorative machete kept in the living room and shielded the attacker's attempts to harm the family. He also swung it at the intruder, pushing him away just enough that the door could be closed and latched.

The attacker continued to kick, breaking the door while the three huddled inside. They called the police and held the door firmly closed. When the authorities arrived, the assailant finally fled. He was not apprehended, and none of the family members recognized him.[28]

BLOCKING AND SHIELDING OVERVIEW

Did the mother and sons in the attempted home invasion in Battle Creek do everything right? No. Actually, opening the front door could have been a death sentence. But do they deserve praise for their quick thinking, impressive team effort and successful shielding against a late-night attacker armed with an aerosol spray? Absolutely!

Blocking and shielding are risky, scary maneuvers. They force you to either absorb or intercept blows from an attacker as they worm their way into your home. You might suffer broken bones, lacerations or other horrific wounds, but you cannot let hesitation, fear or pain deter you. Use your adrenaline to summon up the strength to protect yourself at all costs.

Many injuries can occur during a home invasion. Blunt force trauma results from repeated blows from heavy objects, rendering you unable to defend or protect yourself. Slash and stab wounds cut into your skin when edged weapons are wielded by criminals. Bullet holes dig deep into flesh, causing tremendous damage while incapacitating victims. The good news is that these are all types of injuries that can be minimized when shielding and blocking are used effectively. By protectively covering yourself with even a small item like a book, pillow or other household object, you can greatly reduce trauma and associated injuries stemming from attacks.

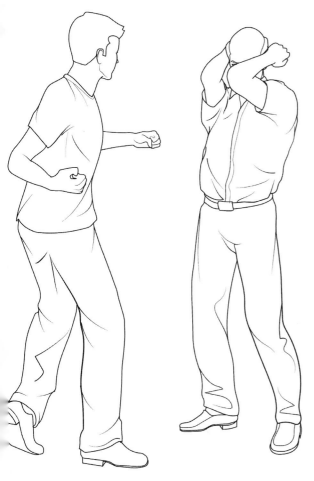

Shield blows from an attacker by protecting your head and neck with your hands and crouching down if possible to divert the fists away from your face and torso.

Blocking is an active technique in which you physically meet the attacker's blows and deflect them. Remain relaxed when being hit, not tense, exhaling as they are striking you and you are blocking. This enables you to wrestle control from their hits, turning their own strength against them. While blocking is more likely to be effective for fit, strong individuals, anyone can initiate and conduct a successful block with adequate practice and training.

Take my family, for instance. My sons and I are very big on physical training. We are veterans of the military and have experienced combat. We train in some capacity regularly, building up the muscles in our arms and legs. When it comes to blocking, we could easily go head-to-head with the vast majority of home invaders and come out on top using just our limbs. However, the same doesn't necessarily apply to my wife and daughter, whose smaller statures and reduced muscle masses are not conducive to hand-to-hand blocks. But that fact would never stop either of them from successfully blocking a home invader's blows. Rather than using their arms or legs, they would instead grab an item off the decorative end table located next to our front door and thrust it at the attacker as he thrashed his way inside, deflecting his strikes and pushing him back. In between blocks, they have trained to grab the end table and use the table's legs as jabbing instruments to target the attacker's soft tissues. They've identified similar blocking strategies throughout our home.

Shielding is a passive technique that places an inanimate object between you and the weapon the criminal is using, preventing the assailant's blows from causing maximum harm. An example of shielding would be grabbing a book and placing it between your body and an attacker's foot if they were kicking you while you were on the ground. The technique helps prevent fractures and muscular injuries.

By shielding, you essentially take control and dictate the places where the attacker's blows will not hit. That is because their punches, kicks or weapon strikes hit the object instead of you. Protect your head, chest and neck at all costs. If a shielding device is not readily available, use your hands and arms to block and cover your chest, belly and head from being hit. Hold your head slightly back

You can either be the punching bag or the one giving the punches. In this position, a defender can successfully shield a blow and counterattack. First protect your head and neck with your hands, curl down and exhale when hit. Then propel yourself forward and drive your elbows into the attacker's vulnerable abdomen.

from your hand and arm to shield it, though be careful to not cover your eyes. Recall that the arms, hands, legs and feet lack critical organs that could be damaged, rendering them more expendable. This means they rarely have a life-threatening response to injury. Whenever possible, force your extremities (such as a fist or thrashing foot) into harm's way to lessen the impact against soft tissue like your belly, neck and face. You can also incorporate ducking and dodging into your shielding approaches.

Should you focus your training on shielding or blocking? My answer is both. You can never be too prepared for a home invasion, and by knowing when to shield and when to block, you will always have a trick up your sleeve to keep your own body from sustaining serious injuries. Prepare for every situation, then respond accordingly.

Tactically speaking, prioritize blocking over shielding. This technique is more aggressive, and even if your blocks fall short, you can swiftly shift gears to shield instead. On the flip side, it's hard to ramp up to blocking if your shielding efforts have already gone awry.

Simple actions can make a big difference when it comes to the success of shielding. Exhaling upon impact from an object or during a fall greatly reduces the potential for sustaining internal injuries. Similarly, forcing your body to relax during a pummeling helps limit injuries.

In fact, you can use this perceived weakness to your favor by feigning injury to force the attacker off guard. While shielding, pretend to become knocked out. Let your body fall limp. Watch as your attacker instantly relents. Believing that any threat you previously posed is now neutralized, he will divert his attention elsewhere—buying you enough time to enact your defense strategies.

This technique is not perfect. Yes, he will probably enter your home if you were shielding at the door, and yes you will have to sacrifice your controlling positioning as you lie motionless. However, if you plan for this fallback approach, these weaknesses do not have to be negatives. In fact, they can even become part of a trap that you set and control, eventually regaining an even stronger controlling position when the timing is right for you.

ENVIRONMENTAL BARRIERS

When you're shielding, you might instinctively want to grab an object and wield it. This mentality puts space and another object between you and your assailant. However, remember that just about any object that you're holding with your own two hands is relatively weak, barring metal tools and solid wood decorations. If you can lift an object easily, there is a good chance that someone else can break it or use it against you.

Instead of shielding with a handheld object, look for stationary environmental barriers to shield the strikes leveled at your head and chest. These types of objects are heavy, immobile and generally able to withstand quite a thrashing. Their rigidity makes them extremely effective at protecting you. Examples of good environmental barriers include sofas, solid wood dining room tables, solid wood support columns and kitchen appliances.

If you've watched any recent action movies, you've seen environmental barriers being used. Generally, the action hero ducks behind a large object—such as a stone outcrop, a concrete wall, a thick crate or another set piece—while enemies attack him or her from multiple angles. The hero takes a moment to collect his or her thoughts before emerging with a solid tactical strategy, taking down everyone who has been firing on the protected position. It makes for exciting and dramatic cinema, but more importantly, it's effective in real life.

Using environmental barriers in home invasion defense works. The key is finding large objects that are sturdy enough to withstand a barrage of slams, kicks and punches. I'll walk you through a number of potential candidates that most of us have around our houses.

Starting at the curb, look for objects that you can use to put any distance between you and your attacker while struggling outside. This could be a tree trunk, lamp post or even your mailbox. Though these options may not provide optimal cover, they put a sturdy object between you and a strike—that's worth keeping in mind. If you have cars in your driveway, they can also serve this function, though bear in mind that their exceptionally large sizes can be challenging to maneuver around. You don't want to become winded trying to force yourself into temporary cover.

Working toward the entry, think about the features of your front stoop, porch or doorway. Do you have columns on the front of your house, or perhaps even porch struts? In a bind, you can use the corner of the house as cover, crouching close and deflecting blows directly into the siding. Gutter downspouts are options as well, though their flimsy construction and small size must be considered as potential negatives. The best they could do is add chaos to the attacker's plan, buying you a few precious seconds to find a better place to hide or engage from.

Now, let's head inside. In the front entry, most homeowners keep a piece of furniture such as a desk, table or coat rack. You can use any of these large items to shield and duck behind. The same goes for living or family room furniture, which is generally located very close to the entry. Your best bet is to rush into one of these rooms, grab a piece of heavy furniture and push it askew. This creates an angular safe spot where you can crouch and deflect strikes. If the attacker forces an advantage, you can crawl around the piece to escape or grab a weapon of opportunity. Angle the furniture so that it comes to an acute angle against the wall. That way, it will prevent the attacker from running directly at you; they will have to go over or around it to get at you.

The kitchen is full of great environmental barriers. Hinged appliance doors, like those on stoves and refrigerators, are of the ideal size and shape to shield you. Countertops (especially breakfast bars) and kitchen tables and chairs offer good overhead shelter, while cabinetry can be used for quick shielding.

Bedrooms have similar advantages to living rooms. Heavy furniture such as bed frames and dressers are good for angled defenses, while closet doors add additional mobile barriers. If you have a smaller stature, you can also pull yourself under the bed to use it as a shield. However, avoid two pitfalls: First, if you are not nimble enough to hide yourself immediately, an attacker can stomp your limbs and cause great pain. Second, make sure you can rapidly slide out on the other side once under the bed in case the attacker pulls a firearm. You don't want to trap yourself for the sake of concealment.

Bathrooms, hallways and closets offer limited shielding potential other than door frames. If you can avoid shielding in these places, you will be better off. In addition to containing fewer environmental barriers, they also have limited space and few escape routes. Stick to areas with heavy furniture and appliances. If you have to rely on small, empty spaces, make sure you can quickly move from one space to another in multiple directions, using wall corners to shield as needed.

BLOCKING WITH HANDHELD INSTRUMENTS

Environmental barriers make great options for shielding, but sometimes you're in a space that lacks such large, effective coverage objects. That's when you must consider blocking with instruments instead.

Ideal blocking instruments are rigid, strong pieces that will not bend. They should be able to withstand significant force before breaking. An example of a perfect blocking instrument is a sturdy metal wine rack that's empty or whose contents you've quickly removed. Why? For one, it's light enough that you can easily lift it and brandish it defensively. The curved wine slots provide excellent handholds that you can grip while swinging, pushing and shielding. Because it's made of sturdy metal, it won't easily break or bend. Finally, the design will catch punches, kicks and other attacks, deflecting them from hitting your body. You might even catch an attacker's wrist in a curved wine slot, giving you an opportunity to snap the bone with a quick jerk. The bottles themselves can be smashed and brandished, or they can be rolled toward an attacker to create a tripping hazard.

Think about other objects around your house that could be used in a similar capacity. A magazine holder is a great example, as is a small ottoman. Barstools and tray tables can be used for blocking purposes as well. When selecting an object with which to shield, remember your own strength and the distance you want to maintain between yourself and the attacker. Let these two factors guide your decision.

When blocking, remember: In addition to protecting yourself, always try to discourage the attacker in the process. In this position, the woman can block the attacker's blow with the stool, and then also use the stool's legs to jab back at him, aiming for vulnerable places such as the face and abdomen.

It can be tempting to try to block with a straight instrument such as a baseball bat, umbrella, fireplace poker or standalone coat rack. They can work as handheld blocking tools in a pinch. However, realize that these objects offer limited shielding potential. If an attacker recovers from the block and rapidly shifts their attack, your defense options will be limited. Additionally, these instruments require a lot of upper body strength to wield successfully, making them unsuitable for elderly defenders and those with limited upper body strength.

If your blocking instrument does shatter or break, do not panic. That's why I always tell people to make backup plans for their backup plans; anything can happen during a home invasion. Sometimes, sharp edges and splintered wood can be quickly repurposed into a weapon, giving you an unexpected edge (both literally and figuratively). Use the shards to jab your attacker away. If they're too small or blunt, you can also throw the pieces at the attacker and grab another item to replace it.

USING THE DOORWAY

We've extensively explored using the front door and entry as a way to keep attackers outside. But did you know that if they've gained entry to your home, you can still use these areas as tools to further your advantage? Doorways are unique facets of the home in that they provide ample coverage to hide, a swinging weapon and a protective barrier in one convenient location. In a lot of ways, they are the closest thing to a perfect weapon during a home invasion! Use them to segregate attackers and take them on one-by-one while shielding yourself.

You can use any door in your house as a shield, but always consider its limitations. It will fail under extensive duress, and even solid wood doors with steel reinforcement will allow bullets to pass through. However, working within the door's limitations, it's an excellent way to block bludgeoning attacks and fist throws. It can also catch knives and wrench them from a criminal's hand, reducing the capacity for stabbing or slashing offenses.

Standing behind a door that you can swing shut with a quick maneuver, pounce toward your enemy after they've entered the room or hall. Block the door with your weight or a barricade, and then neutralize the attacker on your side with punches, kicks and other protective techniques, which we will explore later in this chapter. The key is to knock one assailant down while the others are out of reach.

After neutralizing the lone attacker, continue to use the door to shield blows and to trap limbs, immobilizing the second home invader. If he continues to swing, slash or fight with his other hand, use the door frame for cover, shielding away from the direction of the blows. In case you trapped a hand inside, kick or bite at the fingers to break them, inducing pain and panic in the intruder.

Timed perfectly, you can also use the door to land a hard, firm blow to an attacker's body. While hiding behind a door, wait for an attacker to step onto the threshold of the frame. Before he can put one foot into the next space, quickly slam the door with all of your force. The blow could result in a concussion if executed against the head,

or it could knock him off balance. Either way, the door becomes a great protective measure that packs one heck of a punch.

COVERING BLOWS WITH YOUR HANDS

Your hands are the most important assets you possess during a home invasion. They are your tools for escaping, your primary shielding mechanisms and your links to rescue when you punch numbers into a phone. They are incredibly important for survival. You don't want to risk damaging them during a home invasion scenario, even if you do need to shield with them out of sheer necessity. I'll share a few tips to minimize injury to these versatile body parts.

The first technique for covering blows with your hands is a direct overhead block. This is used when your assailant looms over you and rains down attacks. Overhead attacks can occur if you're shorter than your attacker, or if you've fallen to the floor. To use this technique, reach up into the strike and stop it with your forearm, allowing enough space for your arm to slightly fall. You shouldn't be trying to fully halt the punch; you just want to slow it down before it reaches your head, neck, chest or other exposed area. Keep in mind that your forearm will still bear the strike, so there is potential for injury there. The most common injuries are bruises and fractures.

Another overhead blocking technique involves using both hands to push the striking arm away from your body, then grabbing it with your free hand. This doesn't stop the attacker from expending force on the blow, but it does misdirect the target so that his hand or fist does not strike you.[29] It also stuns the attacker for a moment, buying a valuable instant for you to counter with a breathing disruption, vision impairment or pain overload, which we'll discuss in Chapter 6.

You might not be trapped underneath an attacker's blows. If they are striking directly at you, use a combination of ducking, blocking with your forearms, deflecting and using open-palm pushes to divert blows and increase distance between you and the assailant. They can only strike you as far as their arms can reach, so the greater the distance between you, the better off you will be.

Always use open palms and forearms to counter blows. The palm is muscular and cushioned, enabling it to take a good deal of force before suffering damage. If you use the back of your hands, however, you stand a good chance of breaking one or more bones and losing functionality. Look at your hands right now; you can see the difference. The palms are thick and fleshy, while the undersides are ribbed with delicate bones. Similarly, avoid using your fists to block or counter, as you can crack all of your fingers or knuckles with a single collision. An added benefit to using your palms is the increased surface area, making your shielding efforts all the more effective.

THE FADE AND EVADE TECHNIQUE

Fading and evading is crucial to learn. I often explain it using a coordinate system, with you and the attacker positioned along a straight line. In this system, every step equals one unit. Between you and the home invader, there may be five units. If you take two steps forward, that decreases the distance to three units. But if you take two steps back, and he takes four steps forward, he's managed to gain distance on you while also closing the distance gap. This analogy will help you understand the ways you can use both fading and evading to your benefit.

Fading involves walking along that line between you and the attacker. Specifically, it refers to adding distance between the two of you. Say you open the door and there's a suspicious person standing two steps off the threshold. You, however, are directly atop the threshold. After telling the assailant to back off or leave, say he takes two steps away from you, beginning to fade away in a positive direction. Tension reduces, and the threat of attack significantly diminishes. There is no side to side motion, he simply steps away from where you are.

On the other hand, fading also works in reverse. If you open the door and take two steps back, you're fading away from the visitor. This negative fading creates enough space for them to dash into your house and begin their assault—a very bad situation that you have got to avoid at all costs! Prevent negative fading by maintaining your position at the doorway and blocking, shielding and bracing the door rather than stepping backward.

Evading involves lateral movement from side to side. More often than not, it's combined with fading to create complex maneuvers. An attacker may back up and then run along one side of your house toward another entry point. If you fell into the trap of negative fading, they can even run inside and then immediately evade in a lateral position along the front wall to get further into the home.

I'm sure that fading and evading sounds scary to most readers. But rest assured that you can block entry evading using a really easy technique that you could set up right now. Simply position a tall piece of furniture two to three steps away from your doorway. This could be anything from a bookshelf to a china cabinet. Make sure it's steady and that it can withstand a significant amount of force rushing at it. When the home invader dashes inside and instantly evades toward the side of the house away from the door, he'll slam into the furniture and stun himself. It might sound like something out of a cartoon, but it happens a lot. Criminals experience tunnel vision when focusing on a heist, losing sight of their surroundings. Combined with an intense adrenaline rush while aiming their eyes toward the homeowner, they can be tricked quite easily. This buys you enough time to throw him outside, draw your weapon or otherwise disable him. The best part? He won't know what hit him, causing a delayed recovery response.

At other points during an active home invasion, evading can also be used by an attacker as he shifts from cover to cover. This commonly occurs while he is still outside scoping the property. He may be attempting to hide while taking in information from multiple vantage points, or he may be inching closer and closer to a particular entry point of the house. Use your knowledge of the property to determine where he will likely evade to next, and prepare yourself accordingly. For instance, if you spot someone hiding behind a large tree in your front yard, and then you see him dashing for cover behind another tree closer to your shed, you can connect the dots to figure out his plan. The shed is a logical place for him to gain significant coverage, and that's where he's headed. Cut him off or confront him before he can use it to his advantage.

Home invaders aren't the only ones who can use fading and evading to their advantage. Victims can also use this technique to fight back. Some tips for evading:

- Take two or three steps backward, then immediately move laterally to the right or left. This move is called the "tactical L."

- If there is no space to create distance, then right at the last moment before making physical contact, move off the line by taking three or four steps to one side as the attacker closes distance.

- If you cannot move backward or initially to the side, at the last moment possible, take the line and move forward toward the attacker. Run directly at their shoulder to knock them off guard.

DISCOURAGING ATTACKERS' STRIKES

What's the best way to avoid getting hit by a punch or kick? Keep the attacker from striking in the first place! Home invaders are rough, ruthless criminals who have no qualms about beating you senseless. But at the end of the day, they'd rather get in, get their loot and get out with minimal fuss or danger to themselves. You give them what they want, and nine times out of ten, they'll leave you be.

Of course, don't rest on your laurels. Situations may not play out so fortuitously. Be ready to shield and block.

A surefire way to discourage strikes is to make them painful for attackers. If he slaps at your face, then lower your head with a quick jerk just before he strikes. His hand slamming into the top of your thick skull can break finger bones and incite massive pain, giving you a moment to seize the position of advantage. Though you cannot force him to stop hitting you, you can change the attacker's target area with quick movements. If the attacker is brutish, however, make a split-second decision. Will your efforts likely stop him, or are they simply going to prolong your own whipping?

Shielding isn't just about physical blocking and protective measures, it's also about emotional and social boundaries. If you plan ahead, you can use these techniques to lessen or eliminate multiple classes of strikes from your attackers.

Now, I wouldn't necessary recommend these techniques as a first line of defense. You need to be confident and pushy with your defensive strategy to show attackers that you are a formidable target. Rolling over and letting them inside is a really bad idea that can feed their egos and prompt them to cook up horrific plots as they go. Submissive behaviors feed into sexual assaults, potentially morphing a home invasion into a burglary, rape and murder crime scene. No one wants that to happen to their family.

That said, you sometimes don't have another alternative. Let's say you are a diminutive homeowner facing off against a beefy, six-foot-tall invader with bulging arm muscles. You know that he could take you down, and you also know that shielding with your hands will be futile. What could you do in this situation to discourage strikes?

If you are a woman, one of the quickest ways to stop strikes is to yell out that you are pregnant while pushing out your belly and gingerly cradling your stomach. The vast majority of home invaders will take pause and lay off striking a woman carrying a child. If they continue to attack, you know that they are psychotic and warrant extreme measures. Men, children and older women can try using similar ruses of a medical nature, such as pleading not to hit where you recently had surgery, where you currently have a cardiac port or where your diabetic insulin pump connects to your bloodstream. I'll cover medical ruses in greater depth in Chapter 8.

If the attacker stops their striking, they will expect something in return for their "kindness." I say this because it's how the criminal mind works. If they do you a favor, they expect something bigger in return. And trust me, they will hold you to it. This could be allowing them to enter the home without resistance, giving them a hidden wad of cash or offering up no fight once inside. You can break these promises, but be aware that the consequences will be extreme. A few examples include:

- "Please stop! Our valuables are upstairs in the top dresser drawer."

- "Okay, okay. Our jewelry is under the bed in a shoe box."

- "I can't take anymore . . . we hid money in the top kitchen cabinet."

TIES AND GAGS

Quite frequently, criminals will bind their victims' hands and ankles to prevent them from moving. It can be a panic-inducing moment when you feel hopeless. Without any range of motion, you're trapped . . . or so it may seem.

Don't despair. You can fight ties and gags successfully without appearing to resist! Usually, criminals will do the tying. However, if they ask for one family member to tie up the others, this is a fantastic opportunity to plant the seeds of escape. Family members can tie looser knots that still appear solid, and they can also encourage others to be bound the right way.

Regardless who's on the tying end, what is the right way to be tied up, anyway? Place your palms facing one another. Then, slip one hand slightly forward onto your adjacent palm. This will create enough slack to escape a knot while preventing circulation from being cut off to your extremities. The technique works for twine as well as plastic wrist binds. Never struggle when being tied up, as this will cause the individual binding you to tie a tighter knot. Cooperation yields valuable slack, and that can be your key to freedom.

If you're placed on the floor after your hands or feet are tied, try to lie on your side instead of your stomach. This position opens your airway, keeps you more alert, provides a better view of your surroundings and makes it far more comfortable for you overall. If they place you on your stomach, cough and gag until you are allowed to move to your side, bringing your knees up to keep your airway open. Avoid "turtling," as I call it. This happens when your hands or feet are bound and you become trapped on either your stomach or back, unable to move.

Some attackers do not care where you sit, as long as you stay out of their way. In this case, aim for a spot next to a window where you can roll to safety should police arrive early to rescue you. Avoid sitting by doors, halls or entryways where you could be trampled. When the police do arrive, lay on the floor as close to the wall as possible to shield your body from debris, stamping feet and gunfire.

Let's say you're tied up and dumped in a bedroom. You hear gunshots from another part of the house a short while later, and you want to pick the best spot to hide from rogue bullets. Get onto your knees and crawl to the wall closest to where the shots were fired. You're much more likely to be hit from other points in the room as the bullets fan out. Stay curled up to decrease the exposed surface area of your body.

When having your feet tied, do not cross your ankles or put the feet firmly together. Offset your ankles to create distance between them. This mirrors the wrist-tying technique we just reviewed. Adopting this posture can enable you to wiggle free later on.

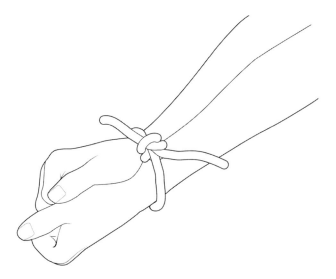

If your hands are being tied, always offset your hands and wrists with one higher than the other. This will create some slack in the knot when the hands are tied, giving you an opportunity to later slip free. Practice illusions like this often, as they can save your life in a real-life situation.

If you're the one doing the tying, make sure the victim's hands are extended in front of the body, not behind. The victim can feign an injury such as a bad shoulder or dislocated joint, or even a chronic condition like asthma to get this request honored. Wrap the wrists twice, and then tie a simple half hitch (which is the same knot you use to start tying your shoes every morning). Wrap once more and tie a final knot to give it the illusion of being tight and secure. The attacker can even check your work, if he likes.

Gags should be approached similarly. Whether the attacker stuffs a rag in your mouth, duct tapes over your lips or inserts a rope across your mouth, the same mitigation technique works. Force your tongue to the front of your mouth to provide false resistance, which limits how far the gag can be inserted. That way, your airway will remain open. When tape is used, puff out your cheeks to gain some added movement space and breathability after the adhesive attaches to your skin.

If you are blindfolded, do everything you can to remain calm. Tell yourself that you can still breathe and hear what's going on, and force yourself to believe that everything will be all right. Keep anxiety, fear and panic at bay. If you can stand, push yourself against a wall for support. When you talk, continue to speak firmly to hide any fear in your voice. If you show that you're frightened, they will use this against you and put you into a riskier situation. Attackers may punch or kick you. Exhale and relax so that you manage how your body responds to physical hits. You're not superhuman, so don't act like you are. And never slip into a blind panic or rage. This will never do you any good.

PRACTICE EXERCISE 5:
BLOCKING OUT A SHIELDING STRATEGY

Shielding can be frightening to think about, as it means that you are being physically attacked. However, it's very important to run through protective techniques so that you are ready in the case of a home invasion. Very few of us shield on a regular basis, and without practice you will likely leave yourself open to novice mistakes that could cost you your life.

First, practice defending yourself. Imagine that an attacker is thrusting blows at you from various directions. Test maneuvers to successfully divert blows aimed at your head, neck, arms, chest, groin and legs. If you feel comfortable practicing with a family member, try shielding simulated blows by having them pretend to attack you from various positions, slowly and without making contact. Speed up the exercise as you become more comfortable with the pretend attacks and your responses. Then, switch positions so that your family member can get a feel for shielding, too.

Next, practice blocking. You can use your body or objects you have around your house. Make a mental note of how you could use each item you see to put distance between you and the attacker's blows, ultimately forcing them to concede the position of advantage. Try practicing in several rooms of the house, placing particular emphasis on the front entry. If you want to go one step further, sign up for classes at a reputable local self-defense school, or work on strength training at the gym.

Make a quick journal entry to track progress for you and each member of your family. Tuck it away in your dossier. Read these annually to see just how far you've come! If you notice that someone is having difficulty in a particular area or technique over the course of several months, consider visiting a self-defense expert to learn techniques. Similarly, look for areas of shielding strength in your family and incorporate them into your family action plan. Perhaps one child is a blocking pro and might be a good candidate for defending at the door since they exhibit strengths related to keeping an invader at bay.

Once you feel confident in your abilities to shield and block, continue to the next section to learn tips for working beyond your limitations. This is quite possibly the most important chapter in this whole book, and I think it will really change your perspective on how you see yourself, your defenses and your ability to survive a home invasion.

6

WORK BEYOND LIMITATIONS

"Melinda," Donnie Herman told his wife over the phone, "If he opens that door, you shoot him. You understand?"

Melinda Herman didn't need to be told twice. She chose to survive a harrowing ordeal with a home invader at her Loganville, Georgia, house on January 10, 2013. After using a crowbar to break into the residence, the 32-year-old attacker shifted his focus from stealing belongings to terrorizing Melinda and her nine-year-old twins.

But Melinda worked beyond her fear, one of the most crippling emotional limitations, to protect her family—all while her husband was away from the house. He talked her through the incident over the phone, relaying messages to an emergency operator as his wife and family searched for an escape.

After hiding in several spaces, Melinda and her children were finally cornered by the assailant in a crawlspace. The phone went eerily quiet for several seconds.

Then, Donnie heard shots ring out.

"She shot him. She's shooting him, she's shooting him," Donnie told the operator. The bullets continued to fly.

"Shoot him again! Shoot him!" The shots rang out one after another, punctuated by screams. "She shot him, a lot."

Melinda fired off her handgun until it was out of bullets, striking the intruder five times. Then, while he was stunned, she grabbed her family and fled to a neighbor's home.

Capt. Greg Hall with the Walton County Sheriff's Office spoke with the frightened family—who survived without sustaining injuries—before addressing the media about the intruder's capture.

"Just like I told her that night," the captain said, "You know there's right and there's wrong, and then there's not natural, and it's not natural for people to have to shoot people. So it's going to bother you."[30] Even though the harrowing ordeal may have bothered or haunted her, Melinda and her children escaped with their lives because they overcame limitations that might have cost them dearly.

DEFENDING VERSUS PROTECTING

Limitations are real roadblocks to surviving a home invasion. The most visible kinds are physical limitations such as muscular weakness, small stature, disability and even temporary illness. But never discount emotional and mental limitations, as these can be even more fatal to you and your family during a home invasion.

Defending and protecting are two related concepts that perfectly illustrate the gap that can be caused by the three primary types of limitations. Anyone can defend themselves. Only those who are ready and willing to overcome their limitations can successfully protect.

Melinda Herman is one hell of a defender, and she is an even better protector. She fought past any limitations that might have lingered in her mind, emerging victorious with her twins safe and sound. The woman is a bona fide hero, and she is an excellent example of what you need to do during a home invasion if you want to survive.

Defending is the act of deterring attacks against you and your family during a crisis. It's defined by the immediate action you take. Defensive strategies incorporate tactical reasoning, rational thinking and goal-oriented actions. The primary objective of defending is keeping your loved ones safe and secure. When you're defending, you're focused exclusively on blocking, putting up barriers, barricading the door and managing the safe zone around yourself so as to deter a direct attack.

Unlike defending, protecting is classified as an offensive strategy. It's defined by the consequences that come into play after you've taken an initial defensive action. Though similar, there are subtle nuances that differentiate defending from protecting. The most obvious is intent, which is something that only you can truly know in your heart.

Let's say someone grabs you, but it's not a life-threatening situation. You may want to put him into an arm bind to defend yourself. However, if the person pulls a punch and you can no longer restrain him, you need to block and strike back. The situation shifts from defending to protecting with that minor perspective adjustment.

Defending and protecting extend to family members as well. Pretend you're walking in a public place with your child, holding hands as you stroll along. Suddenly, a stranger grabs your child's arm and tries to yank them away into a crowd. As you try desperately to hang on and hit the person's arm to cause them to lose their grip, you're defending the child. But if you start to lose your grip, or your ability to defend, you need to escalate the situation. Examples include striking the abductor's face or eyes, actions that qualify as protecting.

The idea of defending comes natural to most. It's an innate human quality. However, protecting requires more fortitude and a detailed understanding of consequences. Your family action plan should cover both techniques in detail with a number of what-if scenarios practiced during monthly drills to build up courage and preprogrammed responses.

You might be thinking: But it's a home invasion! The perpetrator is on my property, threatening my family, possibly thinking about assaulting or killing all of us. The rules don't apply!

They do, however. You need to think quickly and respond appropriately, and electing whether to defend or protect is a big decision. If you hear someone breaking into your home and grab a weapon, you have two options: defend your family, or lash out and protect them. But what if the "break-in" is actually your son or daughter slipping in through a window late at night because they forgot their keys? If you decided to blindly protect yourself, you'd have shot, stabbed or slammed your own child.

Another thing to consider is the criminal's intentions, especially if you discover them inside the house without defending at the door. It may sound counterintuitive, but not all home invaders are out to burglarize, sexually assault or kill innocent family members. There's a big difference between someone who broke into your kitchen for bread, cold cuts and a glass of milk because they were literally starving on the streets and someone who's lurking around your hallway with an outstretched knife. Both characters are criminals—they've trespassed on your property—but only one has the direct intention of hurting you.

When it comes to deciding whether to initially defend or protect during a home invasion, the best advice I can give you is that if you cannot escape, you will more than likely have to defend yourself. This will mean acting out of your own personal character and taking action whether you like it or not.

If you choose to verbally challenge your assailant, set the context immediately. Loudly and clearly state that police have been notified and are en route. Never state that you have a firearm, even if you are armed. That intimidation technique only works in the movies! If they think you are lying, they may challenge you with a firearm of their own. Alternatively, if you are unarmed and they discover your bluff, the message you are sending is not in your favor.

Move around to adjust your angles so that you can observe the intruder safely. You don't have to tell them you have a weapon, all you have to say is that they should leave. If they do not heed your warning and you have to use your weapon to defend yourself, then you have verbally laid the foundation for self-defense. This strategy will help you weigh whether or not you should risk a human life, and it gives you the information you need to use deadly force if necessary.

DISRUPT ATTACKERS' BREATHING

Now, it's time for a quick quiz. What is the one thing that every single living person on Earth does an average of fifteen times per minute, around the clock, from the moment they are born until the moment they die? As you might have guessed from this section's title: They breathe.

If an attacker isn't breathing, that means he is already dead—and, therefore, no longer poses a threat to you or your family. This rarely happens on its own. Disrupting an attacker's ability to inhale is critical to disabling their offensive strategy, and it's a surprisingly easy thing to do. Have you ever slipped and fallen into a countertop or chair, knocking the breath out of you? It's a scary experience that induces panic in even the strongest grown men. I've seen military men's eyes go wide after a firm smack to the gut that made them struggle to catch a gulp of air!

Knowing what to do with your hands and body when attackers are grabbing for you is key. Strike for the face and kick furiously as they attempt to force their way inside. Your immediate response should consist of two steps: protecting your body and discouraging them from sticking around. The easiest way to do this is by restricting breathing, followed by impairing vision and triggering pain, which we'll dive into later.

To target an attacker's respiratory system, you don't need great strength. The throat is a very soft target, and the human fist or forearm can serve as a hard, firm weapon. This physiology feeds into an important phrase: hard weapon, soft target. When the two collide, the home invader's breath will be swiftly taken away. His primal instinct will be to increase distance between himself and your fist. That survival urge becomes his top priority, and he will stop worrying about burglarizing your home. Instead, he will be entirely consumed by a profound lust for mouthfuls of air.

Defense expert Tony Schiena recommends striking the throat of the attacker first with as much force as you can muster. Not only is it often exposed and unprotected by both equipment and bone, but it takes minimal strength to do damage. Damaging the Adam's apple on a male attacker can cause suffocation, while lighter blows initiate enough shock to allow escape. Schiena also notes that fingernails, high heels and other weapons of opportunity are excellent ways to target this area. I agree entirely with Schiena's assessment.[31]

Another way to disrupt breathing is a sharp, sudden jerk of your palm into the attacker's nose and mouth. This can cause a momentary loss of breath as well as a painful broken nose and loss of teeth. With enough force, a palm heel can also cause concussion, loss of consciousness or other neurological effects.

Perhaps your attacker is wearing a jacket or other equipment that prevents you from directly hitting the throat, or maybe you simply can't reach it. There are other ways to disrupt an assailant's breathing. One of the most ingenious is a strong head butt to the solar plexus. The solar plexus is located in the dead center of the chest. It's a cluster of abdominal nerves tucked away behind the breastbone. A swift, strong blow to the upper stomach can cause the diaphragm to spasm. This makes it hard to catch one's breath, and it can cause an attacker to drop their weapons in fear as they attempt to recover. These nerves also connect to the internal digestive organs, causing great discomfort and creating potential for the attacker to lose control of his bowels.

INDUCE VISION IMPAIRMENTS

If you cannot disrupt your attacker's breathing, or if your strike fails, then go for the next logical soft target: his eyes. Of the five senses, sight is the most treasured for home invaders. They use their eyes to survey the situation, find their way around your house and locate the loot they crave. Without sight, they are sitting ducks in an unfamiliar environment.

People get squeamish around eyes. I've even heard of people passing out when the subject of poking an attacker's eyes comes up. But this is not the time to think about his comfort and long-term well-being, this is about your life and your potential to die. Drop your preconceived notions and have at it.

An effective visual impairment that does not involve direct contact with the eyes is the use of spray chemicals. If feasible, opt for aerosol containers such as disinfectants, furniture wax or even cooking sprays. These irritants will cause temporary blindness in a target, and the containers are easy to control and spray. Additionally, you can use the hard aluminum can as a weapon between sprays. Glass cleaners in pump-style containers can work, though be wary of pump failure in a chaotic situation.

Avoid pepper spray and mace. I can't tell you how many times I've heard about people releasing these weapons and stopping their attackers . . . as well as themselves. These sprays have a significant area of effect, causing temporary blindness, increased tear production and irritation of the eyelids for all living creatures in a significant radius. True, you might be able to take down your attacker, but you might wind up disabling all of your defenses at the same time. The one exception would be if the front door

is cracked. Only use self-defense sprays if you can release the weapon and then slam the door shut to neutralize most effects inside the house.

Another visual impairment strategy that doesn't involve direct contact with the eyes is covering the criminal's face with a heavy material, such as a thick microfleece blanket or a bucket. I don't recommend this approach as an end-all strategy because it buys such a small amount of time, but if it's the best you can do, it's something. At the very least, have the next step in your plan ready to go before you cover the attacker's face and impair his vision. He will become enraged after reorienting himself, and if you haven't escaped or aren't ready to attack back, you may be hurt or killed.

The least gory technique to impair vision while still going for the eyes is a punch to the orbital socket. By aiming directly for the eye, you can stun the optical nerve and induce a tremendous amount of pain. The blindness will be fleeting, but it will be sharp enough that it forces your attacker to pause and tend to his injury. If you believe you are too physically weak to use your fist effectively, you can swing an object (such as a baseball bat, broomstick or heavy fireplace poker, as appropriate for the distance between you and the attacker) toward the bridge of his nose instead.

The next section is graphic, but I strongly encourage you to read it even if you find the subject matter uncomfortable. It could save your life.

If you are a female with long nails, jab them into the attackers face and wiggle them to increase the damage radius in a short span of time. Avoid two-fingered pokes, which result in an instinctive flinching motion away from the approaching fingers. Instead, use a full, open-palmed strike, which impacts a larger surface area and has strong potential to create fractures in the nose and eye sockets as well as scratch the skin or eye. Focus the force onto the base of your palm near the wrist, but keep your fingers relaxed. After making contact with your palm, scratch your fingers in from the sides of the attacker's face, along the temples, or up over the cheekbones. Withdraw, then repeat until the attacker is disabled. Avoid using closed fists, which could result in you breaking your hand. If you are sensitive, close your own eyes and recite your plan as you do the deed. You are protecting your family, yourself and your home, and this person is trying to take all three of those things away from you. He would be lucky to escape with only ocular injuries!

Shift to gouging as a very last resort. Gouging is a jab combined with a scooping motion designed to crush or damage the eyeballs by removing organic material from the socket, leading to permanent vision impairment or loss.[32] Do not let that deter you. Your life is more important than this evil person's sight. Drive your thumb deeply into the socket and push, scooping the pad of your finger along the firm socket behind the retina.

Gouging is extreme, but bear in mind that an attacker under the influence of adrenaline will not be deterred by simple jabs or light scratches. They will only incense him and make him want to hurt you more. You need to fight to win, and shielding contact with a visual impairment calls for incredible force. If you need to tell yourself something to gain the necessary emotional edge, let it be this: You didn't choose to be attacked. He chose to attack you. Because of that, he deserves everything coming to him as you rightfully defend yourself, including blindness, permanent injury or even death.

TRIGGER PAIN OVERLOADS

It makes us flinch, it makes us pause, it makes us fearful. Pain is the great equalizer, a driving biological force that causes us to become quiet, cautious and uncharacteristically scared. During a home invasion, you'll certainly be thinking about the pain that you might endure if you are not successful. But turn that frame of thought around. If you induce enough pain in your attacker while defending yourself, you might just get him to change his mind and retreat.

Aim for specific muscle groups. The lower abdominal muscles, biceps, triceps and pectoral muscles are great places to strike, as they are packed with nerves. You can also aim for specific blood vessels such as the carotid artery in the neck or the femoral artery in the leg. In addition to being painful, blunt trauma to these regions can cause internal bleeding that leads to unconsciousness.

The majority of home invaders are men, and as such, their groins are especially susceptible to blackout levels of pain. Use this weakness to your advantage! The extremely soft tissue of the male genitals is highly sensitive, making it an optimal place to land an elbow jab, kick, head butt or punch. Because of its sensitivity, most men will flinch to cover this area the second they suspect a blow. Use the momentary slip of the hands to aim for the face and neck, if feasible.

Knuckles and other joints are great targets as well. Try to snap fingers, twist elbows or kick at knees, which can debilitate an assailant instantly. If I had to rank these extremities, I'd recommend you go for the knees and legs first, followed by the elbows and then fingers. If you break the assailant's knees, you'll hinder their ability to stand. Imagine a threatening figure crawling after you, pulling themselves by the sheer force of their arms alone—it's not that frightening! To target elbows, grab the wrist or forearm and twist the joint until it pops or cracks. You may need to pull it behind the assailant's back to build up enough force.

When targeting fingers, try to bend them back toward the back of their hand or snap them to the side. Broken thumb and index fingers can disable the entire hand, as none of the other fingers will function normally without causing excruciating levels of pain.

The next section is also quite graphic, but it may help save your life. You can use your teeth to further disable your attacker's digits. Think of the finger joints like thick rubber bands. If you bite firmly at the knuckle closest to the palm and push down with the full force of your jaw, wiggling as necessary, you can easily detach the finger from the hand. Break the cartilage and pull backward with your teeth clenched until the finger detaches. Spit it out under a piece of furniture or down a drain, which may cause the perpetrator to panic trying to retrieve it for reattachment.

Another pain trigger is the instep of the foot. If an attacker grabs you and restrains you from behind, you will still have the use of your legs. Bending at the knee, bring your stronger leg up and smash it down on the inner side of the attacker's foot. If he is wearing heavy boots, slam your heel back into his upper shin instead. Whether you hit his instep or shin, target a pain point in his lower legs that causes him to flinch and let go of your arms.

Let's say the attacker has you pinned down and only your head is mobile. Fling your mouth toward any exposed skin and bite down, grasping a small piece of skin and flesh between your teeth. Twist, rip and tear until the flesh comes loose, creating a sizable surface wound. Don't mash your teeth as though you're eating; tear like you're ripping meat off a tough pork rib. If you happen to catch a hand, bite the back of the hand where it's more sensitive and softer, greatly improving your ability to inflict more damage. The attacker can't grab you if they lose use of their hands, after all!

At the risk of sounding morbid, never forget the potential for death or grievous injury during a home invasion. By biting, you mark the attacker for injuries in the future while gathering unique deoxyribonucleic acid (DNA) in your mouth. Should you succumb during the attack, the authorities will be able to collect this DNA evidence from your teeth and track your attacker down, bringing them to justice for all of their crimes, including your murder. But I'm not mentioning this so you lose hope. Rather, I want to encourage you to do all you can to deliver justice, even if you face impossible odds. Plus, by following the techniques in this book, you'll be best equipped to survive the encounter while landing the bad guys in jail.

SURPASSING YOUR EMOTIONAL AND PHYSICAL LIMITS

The protective measures we discussed in the last three sections were probably pretty brutal to most civilians. Yet, I think you can understand the necessity of employing these painful techniques in order to survive a home invasion.

You could argue that every human attribute—physical, mental, emotional—qualifies as a limitation. Even our strengths double as weaknesses. Think about it: A strong, muscular man may have the brute force necessary to beat up an attacker, but could he crawl through a tight, narrow space to escape a flurry of bullets? Possibly, but it's not likely. Similarly, an elderly person might lack the

strength to succeed in hand-to-hand defense, but they are capable of creating convincing ruses that can tip the upper hand.

What I'm getting at is that every strength can become a limitation. And reversely, even physical limitations can be used to your benefit. It's all in how you look at things. Limitations are purely mental, and true strength emerges when you successfully play the hand you're dealt.

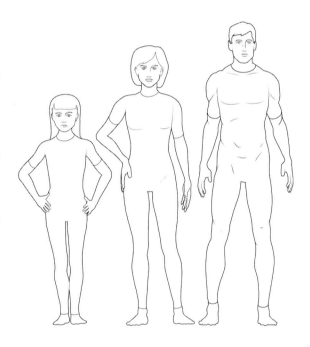

Know what your strengths and limitations are BEFORE you need them! In the illustrated example, a child, though weak and vulnerable, can fit into small hiding places and escape to a neighbor's house to call 911. A woman of average build can effectively hide next to a doorway and use a weapon of opportunity to surprise and injure an invader. An able-bodied male adult, though unable to hide in small places, may be able to physically defend himself while the rest of the family escapes.

In home invasions, limitations sit atop the line between living and dying. Recently, I led a program on school shooting survival techniques for teachers and staff. During the program, an actor posing as a masked assailant burst into the room. Holding a prop handgun, he asked one teacher what she would do as he lifted the fake gun to a student's head. She exclaimed that she would push the child out of the way and cover him with her own body, as she would never be able to kill another person.

The assailant coolly replied:

"Wrong."

He then proceeded to tell her that he'd kill her first. Then, he would shoot every single student in the head. As the prop gun pointed at each young child's forehead, the teacher finally understood the stakes. Overcoming her limitation—killing the would-be killer—would be the only way to protect a handful of innocent lives.

When we ran the simulation a second time, she lunged at the attacker and wrestled the firearm from his fingers, clicking it several times once she had the barrel pointed at his chest.

The story proves my point that limitations are in our heads. Some may have an anchor in physical disabilities or difficulties, but everything can be overcome.

Some of the most common limitations I encounter when training people to survive home invasions are listed below. After each limitation, I describe ways to mentally overcome them. As you read through the list, think about the things that limit you. Write them down. Ask yourself: How can you rise above them? We'll talk more about mental conditioning strategies a bit later on, so keep your notes handy.

- **I CANNOT KILL ANOTHER PERSON.** Do not think of this intruder like you would a grocery clerk, a neighbor, a doctor or anyone else you encounter in your daily life. This person is not your friend. They are ready to kill you and your family if you do not act. You did not ask them to attack you, and you've done all you can do to get them out of your life without taking theirs. If you still struggle, think about what this person wants from you. You are not killing a person, you are stopping a monster who is prepared to murder you, your loved ones and countless other people after they escape. Your limitation becomes their fuel to cause more terror.

- **I CANNOT INJURE ANOTHER PERSON.** This is not the time to be squeamish or afraid. You have to incapacitate the threat before they take you down, or before the situation becomes so dire that you must kill them. Injuries can be fixed, and by stopping the attackers now, you expedite the time that they will be transported for treatment and then incarceration. By protecting yourself, you can also protect the other families on his target list. Your goal is not to hurt someone, it's to protect your family, and injuring another is the only path you can take to achieve that outcome.

- **MY LIFE IS MORE IMPORTANT THAN PROTECTING MY FAMILY AND HOME.** Never fear death. Rail against it at all costs. That said, everyone is going to die at some point, and cowering during a home invasion is not going to save you or those around you. Sure, you may survive five or six more minutes. But what comes next? Will you be bound up, shoved in a closet and shot in the head? Or your face dunked in a bucket of water until you drown? Take ownership of the situation now so that no one dies that day. Take an opportunity to escape so you can call for help.

- **I AM AFRAID OF BEING HURT.** Pain sucks, plain and simple. But no physical distress is worse than watching your loved ones suffer or die. Don't think about the lacerations, or broken bones, or bruises you might endure if you engage your attacker. Think only about surviving. You can get your injuries treated at the hospital after you escape. Healing times have vastly improved in recent years, and chances are, the injuries you fear are far worse than the ones you might actually sustain.

- **I FREEZE UP WHEN I'M IN A DIFFICULT SITUATION OR I AM INDECISIVE.** Plan, plan, plan! If you have a plan, there is no reason to freeze up. Practice often, and if you find yourself stumbling, plan some more. If it helps, develop a short mantra that you can repeat during the event to ground yourself. When you feel yourself locking up, wriggle your fingers and conduct a threat assessment. Then, act.

- **I WOULD SACRIFICE MY LIFE TO PROTECT MY FAMILY.** Many people feel this way and it's only natural. A lot of people find the notion heroic and even honorable. But if you die now, who will protect them the moment you're gone? You are worth more to them alive, especially during a home invasion. Corpses cannot defend, protect, hide, escape or call for the authorities. Instead of sacrificing yourself to take a bullet, or to redirect an assailant's rage away from a child, quickly think of ways to take the bad guy down immediately. After all, it's better to go down fighting, especially when there is a good chance you might come out on top. The hard reality is that no matter your ego or courage, no matter what you do, how much you practiced or how many times you rehearsed in your head, you might lose a loved one during a home invasion. But if you stand up and take action, whether it be fighting or fleeing, you give everyone the best chance possible of escaping alive.

- **GIVEN THE CHOICE, I WILL ALWAYS LET MY ATTACKERS HAVE ANYTHING THEY WANT, SO LONG AS THEY LEAVE US ALONE.** Do you take criminals to be honest, promise-keeping types? They're not. If you give an inch, they will take a mile. Do not let them walk all over you, as the consequences will be far worse. True, there may be times when concessions make sense, especially if you think you can use the situation to quickly end an incident. But in general, here's my advice. Be confident, but not overly confident. Be strong, but not driven by your ego. Most importantly, be ready.

CARE, OR SURVIVE?

In a home invasion, which instinct wins out: your humanity or your drive to survive?

If you had to think about that question, you are not prepared enough. It may sound callous, but it's true. During a home invasion, you need to work beyond your limitations so that you can survive and see another day. Being a so-called decent person is off the table for the time being. It's the ultimate limitation that gets good people slaughtered.

As a former police officer, I recognize that I am jaded on this front. I know all about human nature, and having a suspicious mind has saved my skin more times than I care to count. But for normal citizens like you, it's tempting to look at a criminal and try to humanize them. You may wonder what led them down the path of crime or what abuses they faced as a child. That scar you see above the attacker's temple, perhaps that was from a home invasion when he lost everything he held dear, or perhaps it was from a drunken stepfather slamming a glass into his head. Was he bullied because of his lisp? Does he have children at home who need him to survive?

None of it matters to you in the moment. Their history, their motives and their values are dust to you. The instant this person decided to cross the threshold of your living space to wrongfully take what was rightfully yours, they gave up their claims to decent treatment and humanization.

Let me take a step back to flesh out the perspective with some legal background, however. The fact that they victimized you does not permit you to recklessly murder an intruder for trespassing or turn the tables and hold them hostage out of revenge. Those types of reactions turn you into a criminal as well. The threat to your life does, however, provide you the leeway necessary to go above and beyond normal social interactions. Though legal protections vary from state to state, the vast majority of jurisdictions will protect someone who defends against an extraordinary threat, even if they must resort to deadly force.

Recognize that choosing to survive is not incompatible with a certain degree of compassion. You can build your family action plan in such a way that it heavily favors incapacitating a home invader rather than ending his life. For instance, a sharp, blunt blow to the temple is a good way to knock someone out cold without killing them. But in order to accomplish that, you need to have the right strategy, weapons of opportunity and physical strength to back up your plan. You also need to reconcile the fact that an attacker may react so violently that ending their life is the only option available to you. Never let your emotions prevent you from doing what you need to do to survive.

In the next sections, I will share my tips for building up your emotional strength and improving your mental conditioning. With practice, you can manage the anxiety, fear and panic that flood the mind during a home invasion. By keeping these factors in check, you will enable yourself to defend correctly during times of true danger.

FORTIFY EMOTIONAL STRENGTH

I could spend twenty pages talking about how to jumpstart your physical fitness routines so that you're ready to outrun, outmaneuver and outlast an in-shape intruder. Throughout this book, I'm pouring out strategies to top up your knowledge of how to survive a home invasion. But hands down, the hardest thing to build up prior to a home invasion is emotional strength. Emotional strength is the courage required to rise above the results of the actions you must take in order to stay alive. This strength has to sustain you during the invasion and afterward. Your life depends on your emotional performance and resilience. Without an established emotional foundation, you will lag behind and hand your advantage to your attacker.

The FBI shared the story of a violent home invasion in Lakewood, Washington, in which three attackers forced their way into an elderly couple's home. They pistol whipped the husband, tying his hands and covering him with a blanket. Then, they dragged the wife from her hiding spot in the bathroom and stabbed her, bound her hands and forced her under the same blanket as her husband. The man regained consciousness while the assailants were carting belongings out to their vehicle. Quietly, he got to his handgun and shot one of the intruders, who fled and later died after being dumped on the side of the road by his accomplices.

Despite the significant injuries sustained during the attack, the couple survived and recovered from their physical wounds. However, according to Jeff Martin, the police detective assigned to the case, the emotional impact was far worse.

"There are definitely lasting effects from the attack," Martin said. "Maybe effects that will last the rest of their lives."[33]

Emotions are raw, deep feelings that slip in and out of our control based on external stimuli. They can be manipulated by internal thoughts and instincts as well as outside forces such as the media, conversations with friends and events observed in daily life. Emotions are not rational, and they are not compatible with tactical strategies. They form instantaneously, they bubble up and muddle our thought processes and they hold us back with greater restraint than steel handcuffs. It'd be dramatic to say that emotions are your worst enemy during a home invasion, but they do reside in the enemy's court. They are a weapon that can be used against you unless you have the strength to keep them in check.

Start building your emotional resilience today. In the following paragraphs, I've provided a few tried-and-true techniques for you to apply right now. Work these into your daily routines, and every time you conduct a practice scenario, take a few seconds to recall your emotional strategies. If you find a technique that works better for you, use it!

First, look deep inside yourself to figure out your core values. These could be family, faith or other common beliefs. It may sound cheesy, but these values drive your emotional responses. Think of them as the skeletal structure of your mental well-being. Once you've prioritized what is most important to you, I want you to shuffle the list until survival is at the very top. Everything else must fit below that level, and you must be comfortable with this arrangement.

Why? Without survival, you have nothing. You are dead, unable to pursue any other values that matter in your life. If you fail to survive, you cannot protect those around you. Your stability disappears, and your legacy slips away from your grasp. By putting you and your family's safety at the center of your emotions, you will notice subtle changes in the way you live your life. You will still treat others with dignity and respect, but you will do so without compromising your survival in the process. It's fine to maintain and uphold other values, too. However, avoid compromising your security in the process in order to continue leading healthy, happy lives.

The next technique requires you to separate out the things that serve your core goal—surviving—and rooting out those behaviors and reactions that hamper it. This is a bit tricky. For instance, think about the objects you keep in your home. A lot of people want to make their house into a comfortable abode in which they can host gatherings, celebrate family achievements and grow old peacefully. These are nice milestones to think about, but in reality, they will not help you survive a home invasion. You need to reconcile survival with daily comfort to find a workable balance that services all of your emotional desires. Yes, you may need to store a firearm in your living room sofa table drawer for protective purposes, but you can still have a framed photo of your wedding day resting atop that piece of furniture. You can stow a heavy weapon of opportunity at the door, but it can be propped in an upright position behind the nearby loveseat so that it remains accessible without being visible. During a home invasion, you might need to sacrifice a treasured family heirloom to distract or disable an intruder, but in doing so, you will give your family the opportunity to make new memories in the future.

The third technique is critical: Think about outcomes before taking actions. Look, it's never fun or comfortable being forced into a home invasion situation. I will never try to sell that line. However, if you focus on your negative circumstances—watching your family's terror unfold, seeing someone you love being hurt, grappling with killing another person—your fortitude will never grow. It's like planting a seed in sand and expecting it to thrive. Without the right support, your fortitude will always wallow, and it can even shrink. Instead, think about the need to do certain deeds now so that you can open doors in the future.

Thinking productively is not the same as thinking happily. Pondering positively and productively means that you are focused on the potential for growth and future benefits stemming from an action. Thinking happily, on the other hand, means that there is immediate joy associated with what you are doing. Consider these events. You're not slamming an intruder's knuckles in the door to harm them, you're doing it so that you can be present at your grandchild's sixth birthday party next weekend. You aren't binding your spouse's hands so that they are an easier target to hurt, you're tying them in such a manner that they have a much better opportunity to escape. You're not taking a menacing attacker's life for the thrill of it, you're being forced to trade their life for yours so that you can continue to do good deeds in the world.

Before and during a home invasion, repeat these three short words: I will survive. Repeat them until you are entirely convinced that they are true. Then, continue saying them over and over again in your head up until the moment the authorities arrive. Never let that primary goal slip from your mind or actions.

Finally, practice taking one step at a time toward becoming a more confident, assertive survivor. This means stepping outside your comfort zone one inch at a time. Emotional fortitude grows over time, and you can't expect an instant, overnight or week-long transformation. This investment in yourself will develop over the course of months. Do things in life that you may not be comfortable with but which will benefit you during a home invasion. Sign up for a free self-defense seminar offered by a local organization, tag along with your spouse to the rifle range and fire a few rounds, watch upsetting videos about home invasions on the Internet to learn from other's mistakes. I don't think you'll find all of these exercises pleasant, but this isn't about leisure. It's about living. And after a few repetitions, you'll find yourself becoming more and more confident in your mindset, actions and emotional state.

DEVELOP MENTAL CONDITIONING

Go ahead and pat yourself on the back right now. By reading this book, you're taking the first step toward positive mental conditioning to survive a home invasion! But don't celebrate too much yet. It's a long road, so don't get cocky. You still have quite a ways to go before you'll be ready to survive an encounter with an armed attacker.

Dr. Lauren Tashman of Inspire Performance Consulting defines mental conditioning as the dynamic process of self-awareness and mental skills training that works to help people optimize their thinking in order to optimize their performance. She adds that mental skills affect performance whether we want them to or not. Under intense pressure situations, confidence is key for success—and by properly mentally conditioning ourselves, we can ensure that we are better able to manage and maintain that critical confidence.[34]

Dr. Tashman's definition is spot-on. It reflects another cornerstone of surpassing your limitations, which is having the right knowledge of both the situation and your own skills to effectively act. If your emotional fortitude is strong and your mental capability is adequately maintained, you have almost everything you need to thwart and overcome an attacker. It's that simple. Physical well-being is important, but it pales in comparison to these critical components.

The first step to developing good mental conditioning is absorbing as much knowledge and training as feasible. Read this book cover to cover, and be sure to try every practice exercise at least once. Take notes and apply the techniques to your home, family and situation. But don't stop there. Go to your library and check out as many self-defense, home improvement and survival planning books as you can. Read them, adding to your notes as you go. Keep all the information you collect in your centralized folder.

After that, start conducting regular Internet searches on the topic of home invasions. Follow relevant blogs, social media feeds and news publications like the American Police Beat to stay on top of current home defense trends. Check out online videos from how-to websites to see techniques in motion. Know what tricks home invaders are using and exploiting, then figure out how to counteract those weaknesses in your own strategies. When you feel confident, you can even join conversations on forums and chat rooms to share your expertise and experiences. Exercise good judgment in what you share to avoid enticing criminals posing as fellow homeowners.

The second step is applying your knowledge. The Internet is a great forum for this type of training. Look for professional electronic learning (e-learning) courseware available from government agencies, local police organizations and home defense websites. A lot of excellent courseware is free to use! Tying in with improved emotional fortitude, you can also sign up for self-defense courses or a martial arts discipline such as taekwondo or karate to apply physical defense techniques. The added benefit is that you will find your emotional fortitude growing while your mental conditioning blossoms. It's a two-for-one deal.

The goal of the second phase is to go beyond information absorption to actually engage with what you've learned. You need to be challenged in order to fully understand information, and by seeking out these types of exercises, you can start to better recall and adjust what you know to fit unfamiliar situations.

Run through what-if scenarios in your head to test your mental readiness. Think through the ways you'd approach a scenario, as well as the consequences you might need to endure. This allows you to make mistakes in your head, not the kind that affect your body, life and future. I call the mental mistakes "lessons learned," since they will stick around for a long time.

The third and final step is actually using those skills in a realistic scenario. That doesn't mean that you can shelve your training once you've utilized the skills one time. Rather, it's a cycle that you need to continuously repeat and build into your daily routines.

Throughout this book, I've included a number of practical scenarios that will ask you to run through tasks with family and friends in order to try techniques in the comfort of your own home. Use these as a starting point for phase three of the mental conditioning process. Once you've run through each of these exercises, the third step is to contact local police organizations for upcoming seminars and training classes that will put you into the center of the action. Unlike courseware, these practical exercises force you to actually perform what you've learned with an expert who can fairly assess and critique your abilities.

If you have a group of like-minded friends who are also intent on surviving home invasions and you're having trouble finding a program that fits what you're looking for, why not start one yourself? Like a neighborhood watch, this group can meet two or three times per month to practice techniques with one another. Invite guest speakers such as local police officers, self-defense experts, locksmiths, security system sales representatives and private investigators to share their knowledge with the group. These professionals can walk the group through members' homes to show you what you're doing right and areas where you're faltering.

With the right mental conditioning, lack of knowledge no longer acts as a limitation. Instead, you gain a tremendous new tool in the fight against home invaders: your brain.

PHYSICAL READINESS

My goal in writing this book isn't to offer fitness advice so that you can moonlight as an Olympian. You're not going to find tips on becoming a bodybuilder here, this section is about hardening your physique enough to survive and mitigate an attacker's actions. Plus, physical abilities vary from person to person. It'd be impossible to create a one-size-fits-all regimen.

Physical readiness means that your body is in its best shape to counter threats. It has nothing to do with looks, muscle tone or bench press capacities. It's a state that exists solely in your heart. Someone who runs ten miles a day with rippling muscles may feel they are in top physical readiness, while someone who is overweight but who recently started taking half-mile walks after dinner may feel the same way. And they're both absolutely right.

Think about the types of actions you have to master to survive a home invasion. You need to have the upper body strength to push against a door as an attacker forces his way in. You also need to be able to crawl and sneak into hiding places and escape routes. It's advantageous to be able to run once you leave the house, but it's not absolutely essential. You also have to have enough blocking strength to shield blows to your chest and face.

Improve your readiness by implementing a daily exercise program into your life. This doesn't have to be incredibly intensive. Keep it within your current limitations so that you can stretch your limits a bit further tomorrow and the day after that. Every day, get a little better. Even if this is simply stretching on your bed for seven minutes, or taking a half-hour walk, you are improving your physical capabilities.

To improve your agility and flexibility, try yoga classes led by a certified yoga professional. You don't need fancy mats, workout clothes or studio classes. If you want to try it before joining a class, look on the Internet for free courses or YouTube videos showing basic techniques. Yoga is ideal for stretching, and it also teaches controlled breathing. Other benefits include better balance, holistic body toning and improved mindfulness, mental control and fortitude. These are very important skill sets to have in your home invasion survival toolkit.

If solo exercise is difficult, make it into a fun family activity. When my kids were young, they used to ride bikes behind me as I ran six miles each day. Now that they're grown, they do the running while my wife and I push them forward from the comfort of our bicycles! We've promoted this routine into a fun family response that helps us stay in top shape.

If you've started a neighborhood group, consider doing joint visits to the local gym or YMCA. Making exercise into a social activity takes a lot of the edge off it, and you can kill two birds with one stone by catching up with friends while you sweat. Have you seen those portable fitness monitors that people wear on their wrists? Hold a neighborhood challenge to see who can get the most steps in over the course of a month. The winner gets dinner out, paid for by the other participants.

While you're going through the workout motions, don't lose sight of why you're doing what you're doing. It's about more than numbers or social contests. It's about improving your physical strength and fitness to push past limitations that encroach upon your own safety. You can feel good about your newfound fitness as well as the boon it'll give your survival efforts!

RESPONDING VERSUS REACTING

One time, I was out hiking with friends. We were heading up the side of a medium-sized hill covered with tall grasses and stones. One of my friends at the front of the pack reached down to lift himself up over a rock, then quickly yanked his hand up, flinging something long and vine-like through the air behind him.

That thing was a rattlesnake that had just bitten his hand. His immediate reaction was to jerk upward and throw the animal as far as he could muster. Was it the smartest course of action? No, it certainly was not. The snake could've landed in someone else's face, or it could have wrapped around his hand and sunk its fangs in for round two. It could've been a non-lethal garter snake instead of a rattlesnake, one whose bite didn't warrant immediate hospitalization. But the distinction would have been impossible to tell with the snake halfway down the mountain.

Flinging the hissing aggressor up and out of the danger zone was the guy's natural human behavior. He wasn't expecting to encounter a snake on the trail, and he didn't have any actions planned for that moment. He followed his gut and reacted in a less-than-stellar manner.

For the rest of us on the trail with him, I'm proud to say that our response was a lot more organized. We called for help and followed snakebite protocols, keeping him calm and restricting his movement. One of my friends removed the guy's watch. We held his bitten hand low, underneath the level of his heart, to slow the spread of venom. Then, we got him back down the trail to waiting emergency medical technicians. A few days later, he was out of the hospital and back to his normal self, save for two gnarly puncture scars and some minor swelling.

That story is a perfect way to encapsulate the difference between responding and reacting. Responding to danger means that your actions are planned, practiced and rehearsed. Instead of coming up with a strategy, you can spend the precious few seconds before a strike making adjustments to your existing technique. Responding is sequential and non-emotional existing purely in the realm of logic. There is no anger or frustration when you respond. Instead, you're moving forward in the manner you've trained.

Reacting, on the other hand, occurs when your actions are not planned in advance. Without practice or rehearsal, you'll find your efforts poisoned by emotions like rage. These emotions cloud your judgment and lead to poor decisions, and as I've told you several times throughout this book, bad decisions lead to injury and death. Sometimes, reactions result in you doing the right actions but in the wrong order, a flaw that lessens their impact and drops survivability rates at the same time.

The moment a home invasion begins, switch your mind from reaction mode to response mode. You, as the defender, must be firmly in the response stage long before physical contact occurs. The goal is to push the attackers into the reaction stage.

Achieving that goal comes down to tactical thinking. If you're busy reacting to everything happening around you, you will lose sight of the mid- and long-term survival objectives. Sure, you might avoid getting punched by following an attacker's command to get inside a closet, but what happens after he locks the door and sexually assaults your child? Or, even worse, when he lights the house on fire and takes off through the back door? If you'd responded instead of reacting, you could have incapacitated him or escaped. Instead you sealed your fate and the fates of your family members.

Author and business expert Jon Mertz highlights some of the differences between reacting and responding in an outstanding blog post on Thin Difference.[35] I've summarized them here.

Reactions:
- Reactions are defensive in nature, and they imply a disadvantage.

- Reactions also highlight discomforts.

- They place emotions in a central role, and our bodies quickly follow suit with racing pulses and flushed faces.

- Control dissipates as emotions propel you forward.

Responses:
- Responses are thoughtful actions driven by reasoning.

- They are guided by logic.

- Responses are more passive and inactive, but these qualities enable them to change an interaction's direction.

So, in the heat of the moment, how can you force yourself to rely on responses instead of reactions? The short answer is practice. The longer answer is more complex. Keep your breathing controlled, and take a moment to release stress as soon as you feel it building. Then, focus on the most important aspect or aspects that require your immediate attention, as well as the consequences of your actions. A preprogrammed response will come together much more quickly.

PREPROGRAMMING DIRECT PHYSICAL RESPONSES

Imagine that late one evening you're sitting at home watching television. It's your favorite show, and you're completely engrossed in the drama unfolding on the screen. Your favorite character quietly reaches for their beloved's hand, when suddenly, you hear a crash followed by the sound of shattered glass raining down on a hard surface.

You immediately realize it's not coming from your television. The noise is coming from down the hallway, possibly in your kitchen. Unsure what you'll find, you grab your rolled up copy of the morning's newspaper, charge down the corridor and spy an attacker climbing over your

sink, which is now filled with shards of broken glass. You look at your hand and immediately start striking him with the newspaper, trying to get him to leave.

It wouldn't matter if you hit him with the rolled up daily rag, a pair of shoes, a collapsible umbrella or a wooden spoon. None of these objects would make a significant difference. Because you didn't have a programmed direct physical response, you would have succeeded only in letting the intruder know you were home and aware of his presence and in making him mad by pelting him with an ineffective, annoying weapon.

In this situation, I'd place your odds of survival at one to twenty.

We'll examine weapons of opportunity in Chapter 9, but right now, I want to give you some tips and pointers on preparing, selecting and employing the most effective direct physical response possible. In that example with the newspaper, the defender knew they needed to take immediate action, but the appropriate response was not programmed or rehearsed in their mind. It meant that they were playing a life-or-death game without a full deck of cards. And let's face it, you can't make a full house without a queen or king.

A direct physical response is the specific set of actions you take without even thinking about them the instant that a specific event occurs. It includes an exact order of events. All humans have some of these responses in their brains, either from instinct, nurture or experience. When we taste something bitter, we instinctively spit it out because our body believes it could be poison. This is a strictly biological reaction. Then, we examine it by poking it and staring at it, trying to figure out what went wrong. We analyze the half-chewed blob to better understand exactly what was in our mouth and if there will be any lasting consequences. When we touch something blisteringly hot, we quickly yank our fingers away because of the pain response. After that, we cool the burned area and apply first aid. And when a mother hears her baby crying, she quickly comes to differentiate between cries of hunger, discomfort and pain, reacting separately to each with the right set of assurances and follow-up tasks.

Though defensive actions such as raising one's hands to protect the face and chest are instinctive, working through a home invasion plan is not innate. Police and military personnel such as myself know how to evaluate options and understand the right decision in these types of deadly force situations. We also know that these decisions aren't formed out of thin air. Without programming, you can wind up yelling or freezing instead of taking that critical action needed to survive. Worse, you might employ the wrong action—drawing your pepper spray or Taser instead of a firearm, for example—and wind up incapacitating yourself or angering your attacker. Attackers are a bit like wasps in that sense; if you ignore them, they'll generally go about their business and leave you alone. But if you swat at them and they survive, they'll attack with the harshest sting they can deliver, even if it puts them at a disadvantage.

Choosing to do the wrong action for the right reasons when your life is in danger can compromise your safety more than most people realize. Criminals want you to get to the point of desperation faster so that you slip up, make mistakes and fall into their traps. Thinking back to my days on the force, I remember an occasion when I got a call over my radio that a break-in suspect had just fled a man's property. I headed over in my cruiser and learned that the attacker had been trying to break into the man's car, but the victim managed to fend him off. Later, with the help of our K-9 force, we caught him running across the neighbor's yard.

The man who fended him off was slapping at him with a flimsy pair of evening slippers. The would-be car thief we arrested had a .38 on him. If this was a high-stakes game of rock, paper, scissors the gun would have beat out the slippers ten times out of ten. The victim would have been dead. In fact, it was a miracle that the assailant fled. I'm still not sure why the homeowner got so lucky, but I hope he bought a lottery ticket that night.

I can't stress the importance of programming direct physical responses to use under stress enough. You can't afford to muck things up when your life is in immediate danger. On the flip side, you have to make sure you don't stab someone for something inconsequential like a push or shove when retreating would be a better option.

In moments of desperation, people will grab whatever is closest to defend against an assailant. But just because it's close does not mean that it's a good option. Baseball bats are a prime example. Everyone seems to think that just because it's big, heavy and associated with tremendous force that they will be able to successfully wield it against a bad guy. In reality, few people are physically capable of holding it upright, let alone swinging it in such a manner that delivers optimal force without losing it to their foe—who could possibly turn it against them.

Certain situations force you into an inescapable corner. An example is when someone is choking you but you can't physically get away. If you don't program a response to that situation, you might not come up with striking at their throat, the right decision in the moment. Instead, you might waste your dwindling energy on slapping at the attacker's face or kicking at their boots, gestures that do not fit the magnitude of your dire situation.

Calling for help is not an acceptable rehearsed response! Years ago, I worked security at a bar. Two guys got into a fight, and one needed to be escorted out. The other left. Anyway, last call rolled around, and by two o'clock in the morning the whole place was cleared out. After locking up, we heard a scuffle coming from the parking lot. The security team rushed outside to see what was going on.

The two men who'd been fighting were going at it in the parking lot, with lots of pushing and shoving. The guy who had started the fight was trapped in a headlock while the other pounded his skull repeatedly. The trapped man was not blocking or protecting himself but instead was trying to reach into his pocket to call the police. If we hadn't intervened and broken it up, he probably would have suffered some really tremendous brain injuries.

The point is that if you don't preprogram, you probably won't get the response that you need in an emergency.

MAINTAIN TACTICAL RATIONALITY IN AN IRRATIONAL SITUATION

Let's start assembling some of the elements we've been discussing up until now. In order to overcome limitations, you need to decide when to defend and when to protect. You have to understand your limitations and how to overcome them long before an attack starts. Over time, it's critical to build up emotional fortitude, mental conditioning and preprogrammed direct physical responses. Your mental toolbox is just about complete.

Now, you need to be able to quickly recall all of the components and apply them to an unfamiliar, frightening situation.

Avoid asking for things you do not need unless they feed into a ruse. It may seem tactically advantageous to relieve yourself in the bathroom, but remember that the crooks will want something in return. For every inch they give, they expect a mile in return. Even if you are setting up an elaborate ruse, be prepared to balance any kindness received with a hard trade-off such as car keys or computer passwords. Give them what they want to maintain your tactical advantage as long as it makes sense in the scope of your survival plan.

Many untrained people miscalculate the needed response to danger. I've seen it a thousand times over. They do not take into consideration their attacker's current physical state or the injuries that a particular weapon will inflict. I use the following scenario in my training classes to illustrate the grip that irrational thinking holds over untrained minds.

You're standing in the hallway of your home, and an attacker is charging directly at you with the clear intent to kill you. They've yelled that they're coming to take your life, and they have fire in their eyes. You can see a drawn weapon resting in their hand. Little doubt exists in your mind that they are playing around.

To your right, a loaded shotgun leans against the wall. All you need to do is point the barrel, aim at the raging attacker and pull the trigger, three simple physical movements that will end the altercation. You'll walk away from it, though your assailant will not be so lucky.

To your left, a wooden baseball bat leans against the opposite wall. With this weapon, you just need to pick it up, hold it in both hands and swing, executing three different simple movements.

What's the difference between the two weapons? Limitations caused by irrational thinking.

Sure, both weapons will do significant damage. However, the shotgun is going to cause lasting damage that very likely may kill the intruder with one shot. The baseball bat will maim him, but he may not be incapacitated. It could also catch on the tight hallway walls when you swing, ending your defensive strike before it lands. If he has a firearm and the ability to wiggle just one finger, you'll undoubtedly be staring down the barrel of a pistol within seconds.

Getting back to the scenario, which weapon do you think most untrained civilians pick? If you guessed the baseball bat, you're right. They make this selection due to their untrained response to understanding true danger. In their minds, the limitation of killing another human being outweighs their own drive to survive. They become irrational at a time where they need tactical rationality to continue breathing.

Keep your wits about you during a home invasion and maintain tactical rationality, no matter what unspeakable events befall you and your loved ones. Any other option is a recipe for disaster.

PRACTICE EXERCISE 6: REGULARLY UNSCHEDULED PROGRAMMING

To survive a home invasion, you must think quickly and act even faster. There is no other option if you hope to survive the ordeal. In order to be ready, preprogram yourself with at least one direct physical response to several of the most common forms of attack. If you prepare for the most common types of assault, you can readily call up the most pertinent responses when the time calls for it.

Jot down several bullet points outlining your own direct physical responses for eight of the most common home invasion milestones listed here:

- Guarding the Entry
- Blocking the Entry
- Hiding
- Tying/Binding Limbs
- Selecting a Weapon of Opportunity
- Using a Weapon of Opportunity
- Defending/Attacking
- Escaping

Once you've finished your list, hand it over to a trusted friend. Then, ask that same person to come up with a mock attack that will catch you off guard. This could be as simple as a knock at the door while you're busy preparing dinner, followed by a barge-in, or ambushing you when you're leaving for work in the morning. The mock attack must be a surprise, as you are going to be testing your ability to recall one or more of your direct physical responses. A good tip is to ask your friend to wait at least two weeks after planning your responses to initiate the attack, as you will be less likely to expect it after some time passes.

Make sure your friend is not masked or unidentifiable. The goal is to shock you, not to endanger them!

As soon as your friend initiates the exercise, begin executing your prepared response. Do not perform any physical actions that could harm you, your friend or your property. Instead, perform safe motions such as looking through the front door's peephole, bracing the door or hiding while talking through defense techniques, actions you would take and analysis of your tactical reasoning. Have your friend evaluate your responses against the list you provided to see if you successfully recalled and performed each. Then, reverse roles to help your friend practice at their home.

Keep your lists in your family action plan dossier, and if your friend does not yet have one set up, make it a point to help them build one. You can even share some of your blueprints and journal entries so that they can use them as models for their own strategies.

7

IDENTIFY ESCAPES

In Winter Haven Oaks, a serene retirement community tucked away in Winter Haven, Florida, residents have difficulty recalling anything bad ever happening in the quiet neighborhood. Aside from some minor car break-ins, life in this corner of the Sunshine State has always been peaceful.

But that changed on July 9, 2016, when Paul and Mary McLees' home was brutally invaded in broad daylight.

The precise details are scarce due to the rapid, unexpected nature of the assault. Authorities pieced together a chunk of the story based on their investigation.

After a lone 25-year-old attacker barged into the home with a knife, he confronted Paul and forced him to open a secure safe. Paul pulled a gun from inside the safe and immediately started firing at the attacker. The man lunged for the weapon, and while the two men wrestled for the firearm, shots rang out. Paul's wife, Mary, used the chaotic opportunity to escape to a neighbor's house to call for help.

Though Mary had been shot twice, she still managed to contact the authorities. When police arrived shortly after, they tactically entered the home and found Paul and the attacker, both shot.

Sadly, Paul died on the scene. The attacker succumbed to his own injuries a short while later.

Mary, however, seized an opportunity to escape and, by extension, survive.[36]

DECIDING WHETHER TO STAY OR ESCAPE

I remember speaking with an older female home invasion survivor. She watched a pair of attackers rummaging through her things from inside a deep bedroom closet with a slatted door. They took several pieces of her fine jewelry and smashed open her safe, which she kept under the bed. Thinking that everything of value was retrieved from that room, they left the bedroom and headed to the dining room to continue their thieving.

The woman had a difficult choice: She could stay in place, knowing that she was in a room that was already stripped of valuables, or she could try to make it out the first-floor window just steps away to get to safety. While she weighed her options, one of thieves suddenly stormed back in, taking her by surprise. He poked around the safe contents again before leaving for a second time. The fact that the man returned made her decision easy. She needed to get out.

The woman wasn't terribly agile, but she believed she could manage to escape. After quietly phoning the police, she made a break for it. The window quietly slid upward as she dropped down into the side yard.

The woman landed outside a few moments before two police cruisers pulled up to her front yard. Within minutes, the men were arrested and the homeowner's things were returned.

In that story, the woman made the right choice to escape. It would have probably been easier and more comfortable to stay in place, but after she saw one of the intruders storm back into the supposedly clear bedroom, she knew that it was highly probable that they might discover her hiding place. Getting out was the more physical option, but ultimately, it was the better choice.

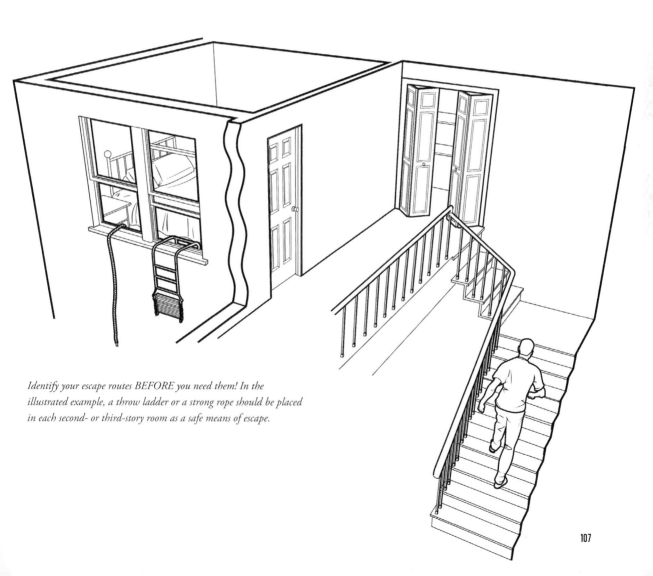

Identify your escape routes BEFORE you need them! In the illustrated example, a throw ladder or a strong rope should be placed in each second- or third-story room as a safe means of escape.

There are never any set reasons why you must stay or escape a home invasion. Your primary goal is survival, and depending on what's occurring around you, you need to be ready to do whatever it takes to help you achieve that primary mission. If that involves staying put until the attackers subside, then so be it. From my experiences, it tends to be more beneficial to get out as expediently as possible. Weigh both selections before committing to one plan, and if you need to change your mind mid-execution, do so responsibly. Fear is no reason to back down from a daring escape, especially if the odds lean favorably toward finishing out an escape plan.

For many targeted by home invaders, finding an escape route is an afterthought. They wait until they are under attack to figure out the best ways to get outside. This is just terrible, and you cannot ever allow it to happen to you or your loved ones. It's no different than going on a cruise ship, then waiting until it starts sinking to ask where the life jackets are located. Rather than building escape routes into their family action plan, the vast majority of victims try to wing it, the results are predictably horrific. When you put off finding an escape route and then scramble to a hiding place, you're most likely just picking the spot where you will soon depart this Earth. Sometimes, I imagine these are the same people who are completely shocked when monsters or gruesome killers find victims hiding in a closet during horror movies!

ESCAPE: SCENARIO EXAMPLES

Escaping is almost always the preferable choice in a home invasion. These vicious attacks do not unfold like you see in the action movies, where mousy heroes rise to the occasion to take down armed attackers. Every option is fraught with significant danger, but going rogue is quite possibly the worst. The surest way to not get burned is to stay away from fire, and the closest thing to guaranteeing survival during a home invasion is getting out right away.

This section lists a few times when escaping is, hands down, your best option. It's not all-inclusive, and as with all home invasion survival tips, remember to judge your situation before implementing any strategy. What works

99 percent of the time may not apply during the attack targeting your family. Think logically, execute tactically and survive successfully!

Escaping is extremely important when your life is in imminent danger. There are times when you know that survival chances are slim. Maybe your attacker never wore a mask and has a creepy, devil-may-care attitude. This generally points toward his intent to murder you at the end of his spree. Your intruder may also be legitimately insane, exhibiting psychopathic tendencies that result in risky decisions, a complete disregard for others' lives and a willingness to do things that make little or no sense. In any of these situations, the only option is escape. Staying behind is too risky a gamble.

Imagine that you're in your living room, between two attackers, and a third is rummaging upstairs. Suddenly, you hear a crash and an excited exclamation.

"Get up here, guys! NOW!"

The other two attackers exchange glances and run upstairs, perhaps even telling you to stay put before they go. You look upstairs, then shift your gaze toward the front door. It's the moment of opportunity you've been waiting for ever since the trio barged into your home. You need to quickly weigh the consequences and outcomes. After all, if the noise was caused by a spouse or child who needs help, you're essentially abandoning them. However, if you know they are not upstairs, and if there is a chance for one or more family members to escape, you should seize the opportunity. Who knows what piqued their curiosity upstairs, and more importantly, who cares. You need to take that moment for what it is and get out of the dire, dangerous situation.

This drive to escape does raise tricky questions, such as whether or not to leave children or spouses behind in their hiding places. Weigh your decisions and the consequences quickly using the scenarios you've planned out in advance. You need to be ready to do whatever it takes for you and your family to survive, even if it means temporarily leaving them in their hiding places while you run out to call for help. This isn't an easy choice, but you need to quickly make it based on your situation and the specific challenges you face. Focus on long-term survival, not the temporary discomfort and fear that your family faces during the home invasion.

Previously, we talked about possibly staying put if your hiding place was not discovered after crooks finish their initial casing of the residence. It's an option, but I'd prefer that you instead wait for the coast to clear and then slip outside unnoticed. This technique enables you to safely call for help while extracting yourself from harm's way. If the attackers were to return and discover you, you would suddenly lose your advantage. In fact, you'd probably be severely injured or killed. Get out quietly and safely.

Engaging and taking down a dangerous attacker will be covered in the next sections. If you are successful in overtaking an intruder, a new path opens for you: escaping before his comrades can return and exact revenge on you. As with the other surreptitious extraction methods, sneak out as quietly and subtly as you can, staying close to cover while you creep away from the property. If you hear a sudden commotion, which could indicate that your successful take down has been discovered, sprint to a safe place immediately.

In quite a few debriefs, I've heard about victims taking an instant of opportunity and making a mad dash to safety. This moment could be an attacker stooping to tie a shoelace, a distraction forcing a momentary departure from the room or even an unexpected knock at the side door. Weigh the pros and cons before running to freedom, preparing yourself to work through any pain that an attacker may inflict. Once you get outside, you can make enough noise to get a neighbor's attention and hopefully be rescued. Even if you are dragged back into the home invasion, you will have most likely alerted the authorities. The goal then shifts to buying time until help arrives.

PRIORITIZING COMMON ESCAPE ROUTES

Just about every American home has multiple entry points that double as escape routes. Some are traditional ones, such as front, side, garage and rear doors. Others are less traditional, like windows and crawlspaces.

Standalone houses usually have more exit points, while apartments and condominiums tend to have fewer. Connecting points within the home with viable, safe escape routes is a challenge unique to each and every residence. I'll share a few of the most common here.

The best escape route is the shortest, plain and simple. The faster you're able to get out of a besieged home, the less likely you are to be caught in an attacker's crosshairs. To this aim, seek out hiding places that are within ten feet of a household entry point. This will make it much simpler to run toward the door as soon as the opportunity presents itself.

Upstairs escapes are difficult due to the significant drop distance between windows and the ground. If you injure yourself in the fall, your cries of pain can result in capture. You could even find yourself paralyzed or knocked unconscious. That's why I recommend either avoiding second-story escapes or storing a foldable fire ladder next to bedroom windows. These tools are great for both home invasion scenarios and fire and carbon monoxide emergencies that require a quick exit. It's a worthwhile investment that serves multiple purposes.

When scoping escape routes, look for ones that will not leave you trapped in an inescapable corner. Examples include dark basements, bathrooms with small vent windows only and attics that do not provide roof access. In the event of an emergency, you can hide in one of these places if absolutely necessary, but avoid placing them on your escape route list.

Some escape routes lead to the outside but are not optimal choices. These include crawlspaces and tight-squeeze doorways, such as those obscured by stored belongings in a packed basement. In both of these situations, you can be slowed down or, worse yet, stuck—making you a prime target for any attacker with a weapon. Keep these places in mind as alternatives, but don't rely on them as primary routes out of a house.

One of my family members had the perfect escape route in their basement. Disguised behind a wall of sliding mirrors, there was a short, three-foot tall playroom for their kids. Just beyond that, there was a little door that led to a storage space. They kept it organized and free of clutter, and it was very easy to maneuver in. I could squat by bending my knees and waddle without hitting my head. The wide, maneuverable storage space wrapped around the entire basement of the house and came out on the other side of the foundation, in the laundry room situated next to a rear door. In the event of a home invasion, they could have slipped behind the silent hidden mirror doors then crawled to safety while the home invader searched for them in vain. At the very least, the crawlspace gave them two escape routes, not to mention ample boxes to hide behind.

PRIMARY, SECONDARY AND ALTERNATIVE ESCAPE OPTIONS

As you conduct your preliminary assessment and monthly walkthroughs, nail down your primary escape route. You should be able to navigate it without thinking, and though it sounds a little drastic, it wouldn't hurt to try running through it blindfolded. This can be a limitation that occurs during a home invasion, so it's best to prepare for it in advance!

Primary escape routes need to be quick, direct and impossible to mess up. If you find yourself asking questions about whether a maneuver is feasible, or if you'll have the strength to quietly crawl a long distance, then it's probably not the first means of escape you should consider. Look for the best way to get out of each room in your home, make your way to an exit and sneak outside in the fastest amount of time without encountering any barriers. The more fuss between you and freedom, the less likely you will be to survive.

That said, you shouldn't rely on primary exit strategies alone. Always have at least one backup plan ready in case your primary way out is blocked. I recommend standing in each room of your house, picking out a primary escape route and then forcing yourself to think up two more ways to get out. The vast majority of homes have more than one exterior door, so think about paths that lead to each. In the event that you only have one exterior door, consider routes that can take you around criminals so that you have a better chance of escape. Crawling around

an L-shaped sectional couch isn't ideal for a primary strategy, but if it's the only way to evade an armed attacker standing between you and the door, then do what you must.

I've listed a couple of primary, secondary and alternative escape options for several house types here. These have been grossly generalized, so be sure to fit them to your living situation before including them in your family action plan.

- **ONE-STORY DETACHED RANCH:** Primary escape routes include front, side, garage and rear doors, with the nearest door to each room prioritized. Secondary escape routes include windows, as falls from first-story homes are highly survivable. If you feel comfortable using a window as your primary escape route, you may do so.

- **TWO-STORY OR TALLER DETACHED HOUSE:** Same primary escape routes as ranches. Secondary routes may include climbing up through basement casement windows, or out from upper-story windows. If a room is located next to a garage or porch roof, climb out and crawl up to hide behind a chimney until help arrives. Alternatively, lower yourself to the ground, into a tree or onto the roof of a shed, making as little noise as possible.

- **TOWNHOUSE, CONDOMINIUM OR APARTMENT:** Front entrances are preferable for primary escape routes, as they will put you in full view of multiple neighbors. Secondary options include rear exits, windows and roof dropdowns. Shared doorways with neighbors are also possible exits, if available.

- **MOBILE HOME:** Primary escape route is the main entry to the mobile home, plus secondary doors (if any). Other secondary routes include windows as well as roof vents or skylights. Many mobile homes also include hatch access through the floor, which can provide a good method for dropping down to safety. Know the limitations associated with this option such as clearance to the ground, hatch mechanics and proximity to utility lines.

With 17 percent of Americans residing in apartments and condominiums, I'd also like to review escape routes from higher levels.[37] It's rarely possible to open a window and drop to the ground from these perches. That's why assessments to determine realistic avenues of escape are so important, in case your front door is blocked. Because most units only contain a single entry and usually a window-based fire escape, it's very important to figure out a backup strategy.

Look to see if you can safely drop down to another balcony just below your unit. Don't underestimate the sway that wind, rain, ice and other exterior variables can have on your drop. In spite of the inherent danger, this is probably your best bet for a secondary escape route. Just be sure to make friends with the occupants below you so that they don't mistake you for a home invader! If dropping down is not a viable option, try emergency ladder systems or foldable ladders that hook inside the window ledge and let you climb down a few stories.

If you live on the second or third story, look out to the nearest building. If you can see the top of the first floor and if it's within ten feet, you can try jumping or swinging to that side. Ropes are the ideal option for climbing down, but you can also make do with bed sheets tied together with strong double or triple knots. Use the knotted sheets to slowly lower yourself down to a lower balcony or flat surface.

Perhaps your unit is located high up with no other buildings nearby. In this case, it makes more sense to escape upward rather than racing toward the distant ground. The roof is a good place to consider, but keep in mind the many limitations that it poses. First, ensure that you can freely access this space. A lot of rooftops are locked or barred. Others are open but tied to alarms, a benefit for those escaping a home invader. Also research to make sure that you will not be stranded on a flat, coverless roof if you do need to escape here. Cornering yourself in a vertical trap is a terrible idea. Look for multiple environmental barriers, areas of cover and even pipes or ledges that you can drop onto in case you need a quick hiding place.

In the event that you cannot escape from an upper-floor apartment, try creating the illusion that you have gotten out. Break the window and leave a hanging shirt or fabric strip on one of the shards so that it dangles out the window. Not only will the sound draw the attackers away from whatever they're doing, but they may believe you escaped. This serves two purposes. First, it forces them to speed up their timeline because they now believe the police will arrive within minutes, expediting their required exit from the home. Second, it removes you from their hostage manifest, giving you the very real opportunity to escape once they've abandoned pursuit. After breaking the window, take up a defensive position in the space closest to the door. That way, when the attacker enters the room, you can defend or escape while he concentrates on the broken glass and mysterious shirt hanging out the window. This technique enables you to manage the attack's timeline and also places the power to take an advantage into your hands.

One final note particular to escaping from apartment units: Use restrictions and alarms to your advantage whenever feasible. A lot of buildings have permanent smoke alarms that can be set off with a match, cigarette or candle. These detectors will automatically call the fire department and route them straight to your unit. Window alarms can be used for similar purposes.

STAY: SCENARIO EXAMPLES

As I mentioned earlier, deciding to stay in hiding during a home invasion is generally inadvisable. It puts you at risk of being discovered, inadvertently injured by gunfire or debris or trapped in a dangerous hostage scenario. However, as you've learned throughout this book, there is no set template for this type of vicious attack. Every home invasion unfolds differently. You need to be ready for anything, and occasionally, that means making decisions that are counterintuitive to the prescribed norm. Here are some of the reasons that you might stay in the residence during a home invasion.

The most common reason you would not try to escape during an attack is because your family is still trapped inside, particularly someone who is incapable of caring for him or herself, such as a toddler. Even if you were able to successfully avoid detection, the fact that this helpless individual might need you or might draw unwanted negative attention is a reason to stay behind. I cannot speak for every situation, but I do want you to realize that this is a gamble. By staying in hiding instead of escaping or defending, you cannot call for help. This leaves you trapped until the attackers decide to leave of their own volition. But if you have a compelling reason for staying behind and waiting longer, you can do so if your head and heart agree.

Another common reason that someone would stay in a hiding place rather than escape is because they are physically unable to make it outside. Perhaps you're an elderly person and you're hiding upstairs. Rather than risking a deadly fall, it may make more sense to remain hidden than attempt to sneak downstairs. You also may be struggling with a leg injury or permanent disability that makes it difficult to maneuver while remaining undetected. In a situation like this, watch for any windows of opportunity that open during the attack. If you sense that you may be able to escape at one particular point, and if you judge that you can do so without alerting any of the attackers, try your very best to quietly do so.

I know that the taste of freedom is alluring, but if your escape routes are all blocked by patrolling assailants, you need to stay put until they clear up. Don't rush into a room where one or more attackers wait; they will be able to easily take you down. Outrunning is not usually an option, either. Instead, bide your time and look for a good opportunity to dash toward a door or window. In the meantime, listen in on your assailants' conversations and try to pick out details about their crime spree, upcoming targets and any identifiable information like names, stash locations or accents. At the same time, scan for weapons of opportunity.

Less frequently, you may find it impossible to escape because exterior entrances are being watched by an additional lookout stationed at the curb. This person may double as the gang's getaway driver. These sentries can be difficult to spot from inside, but if you happen to notice them watching your doors and windows, stay put until you figure out a plan to use a side of the house they cannot see. It may not be perfect, but it will give you a better shot at sneaking outside to call for help.

Another instance where remaining in concealment makes sense is when the police have been called and should be arriving momentarily. In this case, the risk of alerting your attackers to your position is significant, while the risk of awaiting rescue is much lower. As long as you feel safe, ride out the authorities' response time by listening and observing your attackers. That way, you can help the police shut down their network as soon as you are rescued.

It also makes sense to stay put when your position has been cased but the perpetrators missed your hiding spot. If the room is unlikely to be visited again—say, a laundry room or bathroom where valuables are definitely not stored—you may opt to remain hidden instead of risking detection. Crooks may change their mind at any point and barge right back in, so this is not a tried-and-true guarantee for survival.

COVER VERSUS CONCEALMENT

If I asked you to differentiate between cover and concealment, could you do so at this very instant? I've found that a lot of people do not understand the difference between these key terms related to hiding. It isn't entirely your fault, though. Most of the time, civilians do not need to know much about either hiding philosophy. It's not a concept that the majority of average Americans grapple with on a daily, weekly or even annual basis.

However, for those with military or police experience, the difference between concealment and cover is drilled into their brains from the moment they start training. Concealment is hiding out of plain sight, while cover is ducking behind a substantial protective barrier should the enemy fire or attack. Cover does not need to fully conceal. For instance, a refrigerator will defend you from gunfire, though it's hard to be fully hidden from sight in most kitchen configurations. Similarly, a solid oak chair reinforced with metal hardware may deflect blows from a blunt instrument, even if the attacker can see you hiding behind it.

I don't want you to think that cover has to be a piece of furniture or an appliance. Think back to the environmental barriers we looked at earlier. A lot of those illustrate good examples of cover that may be found in just about any household.

Positions of cover can save your life; concealment keeps you from sight! An example of cover is shown on the left—the woman protects herself behind a door while the intruder struggles to thrash at her. An example of concealment is shown on the right—the home invader does not see the woman effectively hiding inside.

Cover can be an architectural element of the house, such as a deep stone fireplace, a thick support column or even a stone countertop. Generally speaking, the best types of cover consist of solid materials that are not easily shattered or punctured. They should be able to stop, slow or deflect a bullet just as easily as they protect against blows from a baseball bat, hammer, chain or machete. Stone accent pieces, hardwood furniture and thick, heavy metal items such as insulated appliances yield the most effective forms of cover.

On the flip side, in very specific conditions, concealment may be more important to short-term survival strategies than cover. Bear in mind that this is exceedingly rare in home invasions. Think back to the reasons I listed for hiding versus escaping. When you're concealed, you're merely prolonging whatever comes next. Anyone can barge in and discover you. You're not truly safe until you escape or the home invasion ends.

Infrequently, concealment can offer benefits when the home invader is not yet aware of your presence. Say you wake to a home invader entering your bedroom in the middle of the night. You're able to drop down and hide behind the bed frame and mattress before he sees you, but he drags your spouse from bed and out into the hall. Because of the particulars of this situation, you may have a chance to remain undetected for the short term by tucking and rolling under the bed frame. If he returns and opens fire into the mattress and box spring, though, the bullets will go straight through these loose, soft materials and rip into your flesh. This option offers no protective cover.

When in doubt, opt for a location that offers cover over concealment. The primary reason may disturb you. Your house probably features one or more photographs of your family. Though nice to have, these portraits provide a face-for-face manifest of the home's occupants. Additionally, scoping generally reveals the names and ages of occupants, making it easier for criminals to compare who they've located with the list of anticipated residents. If you are missing once everyone else is rounded up, savvy criminals will up their search efforts to locate you. They may even resort to indiscriminately shooting into walls, mattresses, furniture and doors to neutralize the threat that you pose. If you select a place to cover, you will be better protected from this type of backlash. Plus, you will then have the option to either escape quietly or surrender in order to save your life. Concealment offers neither benefit.

I'd like to quickly share a few pointers about how to spot cover and concealment, too. Whether you're getting ready to initiate first contact or you're sweeping a room after you've taken down two out of three attackers, you'll want to pick out threats quickly. Think of blind spots that conceal an attacker like a grown-up version of hide-and-seek. The only time you can see the person who's hiding is when they move. To pick out concealment, look at a fixed point. Then, scan left and right, holding the area of focus in the center of your vision. Wait and repeat for a few seconds. If you notice any movement, you've discovered someone's hiding place.

SELECTING HIDING PLACES

Though escape is the primary goal, it's important to identify a handful of good hiding places to use while you wait to make a break for it. Walk through your home to identify hiding places that work well based on your house's layout, furniture and flow. Some places are going to offer excellent concealment or cover for adults, while others are optimized for children. For example, a 300-pound person hiding behind a chair that could just barely obscure a nine-year-old demonstrates the misuse of a hiding place.

If you cannot find a single good hiding place in your home, you only have one option: escape. I don't recommend painting yourself into a one-solution corner. Make it a point to buy or create hiding places, if only to increase your own family's safety.

There are no set rules about what constitutes the best hiding place or the worst hiding place. Having processed home invasions for years, I've seen hundreds of hiding places that fall into each category. Each option has a set of pros and cons. However, good hiding places will always satisfy three key criteria:

- **THEY ALLOW YOU TO SEE DANGER COMING.** Squeezing into a tight space like the underside of a low bed or a low basement crawlspace will often force your head into a position that prevents you from seeing danger coming. If you can only see what's directly ahead of you, you are in a bad hiding place. You need to be able to silently turn your head and neck to get a 360-degree view that remains as unobstructed as possible. If you choose to hide behind a large object, make sure you can still see around it as needed.

- **THEY ENABLE YOU TO DEFEND YOURSELF.** The interior of a tall clothing wardrobe might seem like an ideal hiding place, but in reality, it hampers your ability to defend yourself. The close proximity of the sides and door make it very difficult to move your arms and legs in any sort of defensive manner should you be discovered. Avoid places that are restrictive relative to your body size, as well as places that pose a significant tripping, falling or snaring hazard (such as a cluttered hallway closet). The gap between a bookshelf and a wall is a good option because it does not restrict your limbs yet it still gives you the option to watch, defend and escape.

- **THEY PROVIDE THE OPTION TO ESCAPE.** This is the most important criterion you should consider when selecting a hiding place. All hiding places are temporary, and you need to be able to dash out the moment that staying becomes unsafe. Poor hiding places that inhibit escape include deep holes or wells, loft spaces and ledges outside second-story or higher windows. In all of these places, victims hand themselves over to the mercy of the attacker who found them. Conversely, the end of a hallway is a great option because it connects to multiple rooms as well as the main section of the house, giving you multiple alternatives for escape. If you have a piece of furniture there that you can hide behind, you'll be in good shape.

If you cannot escape, see your threat or defend yourself, you have only selected where you will die! Each of these illustrations shows an effective hiding place that provides an escape route, concealment and weapons of opportunity present.

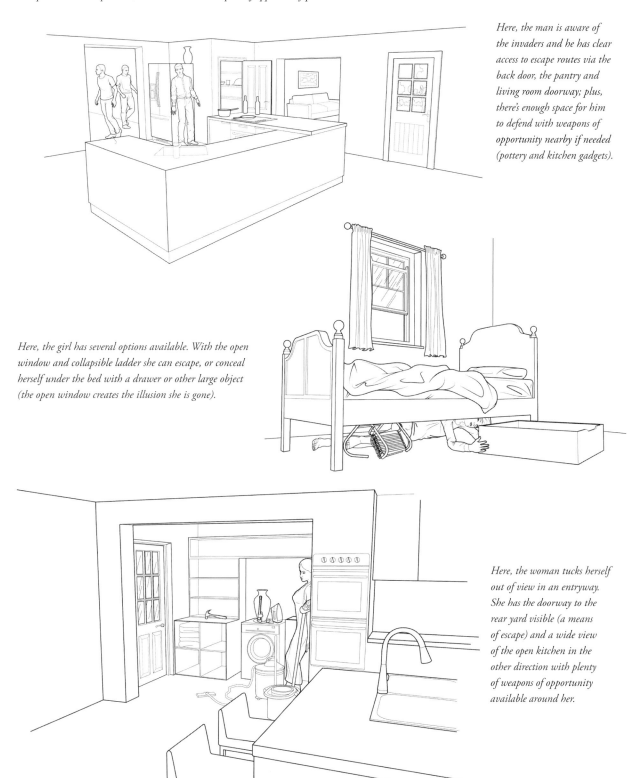

Here, the man is aware of the invaders and he has clear access to escape routes via the back door, the pantry and living room doorway; plus, there's enough space for him to defend with weapons of opportunity nearby if needed (pottery and kitchen gadgets).

Here, the girl has several options available. With the open window and collapsible ladder she can escape, or conceal herself under the bed with a drawer or other large object (the open window creates the illusion she is gone).

Here, the woman tucks herself out of view in an entryway. She has the doorway to the rear yard visible (a means of escape) and a wide view of the open kitchen in the other direction with plenty of weapons of opportunity available around her.

Knowing these concealment criteria, conduct a safety walk through your home to get ahead of the action curve. The longer your list of hiding spots, the better equipped you'll be for any type of confrontation in your home. It can be a little tricky to pinpoint good hiding spots, but with enough searching, you'll be able to find spaces that will do nicely. Add them to your family action plan.

Because they often make the difference between life and death, I'd also like to share some really bad hiding places that you may be tempted to try. Nearly everyone has these places in their home, and you wouldn't believe how often I hear about people using them. A lot of these may surprise you, since they do give the illusion of safety. However, don't let yourself be fooled!

- **CLOSETS:** Though they seem like a natural hiding spot, don't pin yourself inside a closet unless it's your absolute last resort. They have one escape route, and it's the same way that an intruder will enter. There's usually no room to defend either. If someone turns the knob and starts barging in, you are discovered and captured. Making matters worse, closets are the first place that an attacker looks when scoping any room. If you have no other choice but to hide in a closet, tuck yourself behind any hanging clothes or coats first. If there are no shoes in the closet, point your shoes parallel to the door so that the toes do not stick out. If there are shoes, line up your shoes in the same direction they're facing. Pile one or two pieces of clothing over your head to blend in a bit more. If you're in an empty closet and you hear the intruder turning the knob, you can rush the door to slam it in their face and stun them as a last resort. Refer back to the doorway defense techniques in Chapter 4 for more ideas on how to leverage the door in this situation.

- **BATHTUBS:** It's tempting to jump in a bathtub and pull the shower curtain closed, but avoid this at all costs! First and foremost, you're stuck in a place that offers no cover. Additionally, tubs are slippery, so escaping from one upon discovery is very difficult. Even if you can defend from within one, you have few weapons of opportunity and no escape routes. If you're in a bathroom when an attack happens, a better option is to hide behind the primary door. This way, you can

at least brace the door with your legs by pressing the small of your back against the vanity or opposite wall and pushing with the muscles in your upper legs. However, be aware this does not protect you from possible gunfire shot into the door. Alternatively, you can hide next to the doorway instead of bracing the door. That way, you have the options to surprise him with a counter attack or to sneak out while the attacker peers in the shower, the first place he'll check.

- **ATTIC EVES:** Though some homeowners may be able to use attic eves to their advantage, I generally classify attics as terrible hiding places. This isn't always the case—even in the chapter openers throughout this book, I mentioned a few success stories where people survived by hiding and defending in these spaces—but for the most part, treat them like bad news. You're cramped inside a tight place with few escape routes. Additionally, most attics creak, groan or thud whenever someone moves around, providing an audible alert to your location every time you move. When the door is closed, you cannot see danger approaching, making you blind to an attacker's movements. The only exception comes in the form of eves. If these passages connect multiple upstairs rooms, they give you hidden corridors to use as escapes. Not every house has attic eves, so plan accordingly.

- **KITCHEN OR PANTRY CABINETRY:** Just like the wardrobe and closet examples, these tight spaces restrict your movement. They also make it impossible to see an attacker coming due to the closed doors. An added detriment to these locations is the potential to knock down clanging utensils or pantry supplies, betraying your location through sound. Better options are the nook behind a refrigerator or other large appliance, the space beneath a breakfast bar or kitchen table or even the opposite side behind a countertop island. If your pantry is open and not cabinet-style, that can be a good concealment alternative, too. Just be aware of your surroundings so that you can remain silent and safe.

- **FIREPLACE HEARTH:** If you're in a living room and you hear a home invasion starting, the fireplace looks like a great option, right? After all, you can slip inside and wedge yourself inside the lowest portion of the chimney. No one thinks to look there . . . right?

Possibly. But remember that first and foremost, it's really hard to hold yourself up for extended periods of time. If your limbs lose strength or if you slip, you'll fall into plain view while making a considerable amount of noise. Plus, there's no escape route upward. It's a lot like a closet in that regard. Additionally, the soot and ash from the chimney will smear everywhere you go in the house, so even if you do manage to successfully escape, you'll be leaving a trail for your attackers to follow. There's the added possibility that they could turn on the fireplace, especially if it's a modern gas model, to burn you out.

When I'm vetting potential hiding places, I run through a quick exercise I call the ten-five-two test. The numbers refer to the number of feet away from your hiding place you can conduct risk and threat assessments. Ideally, you should be able to see everything within a ten-foot radius. This is a characteristic common to all ideal hiding places. When you can only see everything within a five-foot radius, your time to react is cut in half. Hiding places that only afford two feet of visibility or less are usually bad options, as an attacker can be upon you before you see them.

PANIC ROOMS

I also wanted to devote a short section to panic rooms. A panic room is a dedicated, fortified protective space that some individuals build directly into their home. Many celebrities use panic rooms to hide in their mansions when a stalker breaks in, and world leaders often have several hidden throughout their compounds. If you have a spare bedroom, large closet or basement area, you can consider retrofitting it into a unique panic room.

Professionally constructed panic rooms are encased in steel-reinforced concrete with heavy locked doors and dedicated communication equipment. While you can consider having one built into your home, realize that they're a bit more expensive than most homeowners can afford. For the most part, you'd be just as secure in a lower end, self-made version. By building a lower cost alternative, you will help keep your family safe during a home invasion.

First, find a space near your family's bedrooms that will serve as the panic room. Ensure that there is enough space inside for all of your family members

to comfortably sit. A large walk-in closet is a good candidate, as is an unused guest bedroom. Next, replace the hollow-core door with a steel-reinforced wood exterior door. Install a high-end deadbolt and pin locks with long screws. For added protection, line the walls with sheets of metal or fiberglass, and increase insulation in the walls. These measures will help to slow down and even stop bullets. Install a cabinet in the room stocked with a gallon or more of fresh water (restocked quarterly), a prepaid cell phone, a heavy-duty flashlight, a firearm with extra rounds, a chemical deterrent (such as mace or pepper spray) and at least one bludgeoning weapon. If you can afford them, purchase ventilation masks for your family members to minimize irritation from chemical weapons and smoke. The goal of a panic room is to provide a place to hide while authorities come to your aid. If built successfully, a homemade one should be able to keep most attackers out for at least several minutes.

DRILLING FOR SUCCESS

Now that you've gotten this far into the book, you've probably noticed a trend. There are three "P's" associated with every aspect of home invasion survival strategies: planning, preparing and practicing.

After you've analyzed your home and picked out hiding places as part of your family action plan, you should tidy them up and get them prepared for use. Stock hiding places with weapons of opportunity as well as concealment objects. Once the prep work is done, it's time to practice using them.

Drilling escapes from hiding places is immensely important. I cannot stress this enough. In the chaos of a home invasion, your plans have to be flawless if you want them to succeed. Think back to that example I shared earlier, the one about the man who couldn't remember how to deploy his flotation device when he started drowning during a swim exercise. He had everything he needed to save himself, and in his mind, he knew what needed to happen. But without the muscle memory of actually having pulled the flotation device's cord, he couldn't connect the dots. Work proactively to keep that from impacting your own ability to make it out alive.

As part of my law enforcement career, where I was involved in ending and investigating home invasions, I had the opportunity to interact with the perpetrators. Let me tell you that these guys are not nice. It doesn't matter what pushed them to a life of crime, or their circumstances. They were out for loot and blood, and their greed forced them to bring innocent families into their terrifying plans.

Anyway, there is a very real concept that a lot of home invaders talk about fear of capture. If they're in the middle of a crime and see the authorities closing in, they frequently think about committing suicide by police force rather than facing the criminal justice system. The most traditional way is to walk outside with guns blazing, aiming haphazardly to inflict as much collateral damage as possible before they fall. If your hiding place is near an entry point, it could be subjected to a hail of gunfire.

Alternatively, a lot of criminals also set homes on fire when they see no other way out. Sometimes, this is a suicide measure. Other times, it's combined with suicide by police force to add dramatic effect and notoriety. I've also seen it used as a diversion to allow them to escape out back while the authorities tackle the flames at the front of the home. Regardless of their motive, setting the house on fire becomes a major problem for you if you're hiding in an inescapable spot. You can burn to death, or smoke inhalation may overcome you. Even if you just wait a little too long, your escape routes might be blocked by flames.

Drill often and drill hard to avoid this potential danger. Time your escape routes, and look for ways to shave seconds off your break. Also consider route variations that can prevent you from bumping into attackers. Work the drill schedule into your family action plan alongside safety walks and other periodic exercises. It might sound like overkill, but be sure to drill during different times of the year to experience how shifts in weather, holiday décor and other seasonal changes impact your escape from hiding places.

As I mentioned, I'm a military guy. Before I was stationed overseas, I wanted to make sure my family had the right training to follow through on their hiding and escape plans if something happened while I was away. I taught my children a game I called "Go Hide and I Find."

Go Hide and I Find could start on a moment's notice, which aligned with the potential for an instant home invasion. Whether we were watching television, eating breakfast or even having a family cookout at home, the game started the moment I displayed the OK sign with my right hand by pinching my index finger and thumb into a circle, then raising my other three fingers.

As soon as the kids saw that signal, all six children and my wife would stop what they were doing and either hide or escape to a designated location outside the house. Those who made it to the escape location were deemed "safe." If their route to the designated location was blocked and they had to hide, they had a few seconds to find a spot before I went through the home to find them. I would check every room and either say "Clear!" or call out their hiding places. The objective was to make it to the safe spot or find a successful hiding place. Every time we practiced, the kids got better at the game. Finding them became harder and harder, which meant they were safer. Go Hide and I Find served its purpose, and while I was deployed, I knew they were that much safer.

Another important item to work into your drills is the art of good illusions. These are little tricks that you incorporate into your hiding places to make them more effective. Here's an example of an illusion that can easily be instituted. During your drills, hide sneakers poking out of cracked doors or from behind large furniture. They can even be placed upside down under beds. The goal is to make it look like you're hiding in any of these places. The sight of peeking shoes makes it seem like you didn't fully conceal yourself, and it lures attackers to that spot. Every time the trick fools a home invader, they'll stop and investigate—buying you time. They may also become impatient or frustrated by the little tricks, emotions that speed up their casing efforts. This can force them to miss obvious hiding spots that you and your family might actually be using.

Another fantastic drill practice for children is hiding in the laundry room. Though the washer and dryer are too small for most adults to fit inside, many young children can easily slip into one of these appliances. Have your children practice opening the door, getting inside and covering themselves with laundry, then closing the door as quietly as possible. The more frequently children drill this routine, the faster and quieter they'll be if they actually need to execute it. Bear in mind, of course, that I only recommend children hiding in laundry appliances. For adults, abide by the three criteria for a good hiding spot instead so that you can observe and defend if necessary.

PRACTICE EXERCISE 7: YOUR GREAT ESCAPE

Escaping is often the only choice for safely ending a home invasion. When you make the commitment to escape, you take your survival into your own hands and leave the attackers behind. This route gives you the leg up to call for help and bring your assailants to justice.

For this exercise, buy several pieces of poster board from your local craft store. You'll need one sheet for every level of your house. On the boards, sketch out drawings of your home's layout. Make them as close to scale as you possibly can. Then, draw or print pictures of the furniture, décor, stairways, doorways and windows throughout the house. The more accurate each is, the more impactful the planning will be. Make sure the assets are produced on heavy stock paper. On the back of each, affix a piece of double-sided tape or movable adhesive putty. Finally, place the furniture and assets where they belong on the schematic.

Sit down with your family and introduce the tools. Plot out strategic escapes and hiding places on paper, showing the best techniques as well as pitfalls to avoid. Make sure everyone has a chance to contribute to the discussion. You can even have family members trace their escape routes and hiding place locations on the poster board with their fingers or a laser pointer. This should be a fun exercise, so treat it like a huddle and keep the conversation open and productive.

Next, practice making your escapes from at least four rooms in your house. Position yourself and your family members in various rooms for each repetition of the exercise, reviewing the planned escape route with all parties each time you reset. Then, ask your significant other or a trusted friend to enter through the front doorway, shout out the word "START!" and begin casing each room, starting from the entry and working their way inwards before moving up or downstairs. The casing path should be identical each time, as the situation would be fresh to an intruder.

The goal is for each participant to follow their preplanned escape routes out of the house without being detected. When someone is detected by the intruder, they must sit on the floor against the nearest wall and wait for the exercise to finish. After each round concludes, discuss the exercise as a group, paying particular attention to the successful escape tactics as well as the less successful ones. Use the posters as illustrations of what went wrong, along with remedial paths.

You can tweak this exercise to enhance its realism. For instance, have the attacker enter from a different entry point than you'd usually expect, or enlist two or more attackers. Vary the practice exercises frequently, and conduct them as often as your schedules allow. You can even build in hiding place drills to practice getting into designated locations. (You really can't over practice!)

Store your game plan posters, house assets and any notes from the exercises in your family action plan dossier so that you can periodically review them. You can even consider hanging the posters in a secure but visible place so that family members can practice whenever they have a few spare minutes.

8

ENGAGE:
PUTTING LIFE OVER DEATH

Three months after moving into an East Orange, New Jersey, apartment, James Dittrich took his dog out for an evening walk. Afterward, he headed back inside the building to wind down for the night. As he arrived at the front door of his third-story home, two men rushed him from behind and pulled a gun.

James quickly surrendered his wallet and hoped it would satisfy the attackers. It didn't.

The men forced their way into the apartment where his fiancé, Meredith Duffy, was asleep in the bedroom. Though James tried to make noise to alert her or the neighbors, the assailants found her in the bedroom and sexually assaulted her.

After dragging Meredith into the living room, the men forced her to empty her purse. Her cell phone tumbled out along with the other contents. James spotted the cell phone, glanced at Meredith with a knowing look and made the split-second decision to act.

He grabbed the gun pointed at his back with both hands and held it, giving Meredith enough of a distraction to grab the phone and call for help.

The two men didn't notice Meredith making the call. The assailants beat on James, breaking his nose, cheekbones and eye socket. But as soon as they subdued him, they fled. Thanks to James' decision and Meredith's fast response, both victims managed to survive the brutal encounter.

They suffered severe physical and emotional scars, but they both kept their lives.[38]

STAND DOWN, OR STAND GROUND?

Home invasions happen fast. On the spot, you need to be able to quickly and definitively answer a tough question: Do you live—a choice that requires you to fight back—or do you sit tight, do nothing and potentially die as a result of your inaction?

To those with prior combat experience, the answer comes easily. However, for many people with no related background or training to pull from, making this choice may actually be very difficult. Terror ups the stakes when you are confronted with life-threatening chaos in your own living room. Frightened for your family's safety and unsure if you will get out of a dangerous situation alive, how do you decide what to do?

Making the right choice comes down to intuition. I often tell my clients that in do-or-die situations, only they know in their hearts what action to take. Selecting between fighting or dying is a decision that you must make confidently and immediately. After all, you need to live with your choice.

In this chapter, I break down a handful of key decision points and share guidance about rooting out your best options. I will help you understand what these decisions are, the types of consequences you might face and how to appropriately take the right action. Then, you can use these points to craft a plan that suits your home, your family and your drive to survive.

When you are unable to safely leave your home during an attack, your family's lives are at extreme risk. The decisions you make during a home invasion directly impact the lives of those you care about most. Unlike the majority of choices you face on a daily basis, survival decisions can have life-ending consequences.

Sometimes, doing absolutely nothing is the best short-term course of action. Other times, cooperation is a necessity. Most often, you need to engage the assailants to bring the situation to an end. This is a major decision you need to be able to make confidently. It's do or die, plain and simple.

Fortunately, there will always be moments of opportunity you can seize. Happenstance situations will unfold that can give you an edge, if you leverage them the right way. If you've done your due diligence and preselected a few engagement locations throughout your home, you've taken the first steps toward yanking control away from the people who want to wield it against you. I want you to become an expert in your own engagement strategies so that you have the best opportunity to hide intelligently, defend successfully, escape efficiently and take control over the situation.

REASON UNDER FIRE: LOGICAL VERSUS TACTICAL REASONING

Many people struggle to pinpoint the difference between logical reasoning and tactical reasoning. Though the two types of thought usually share a common goal, they often lead you there along very different paths.

Take the following scenario, for example. Imagine standing in the center of a square ten-foot by ten-foot living room. In one corner, you notice a ten-gallon vase filled with fresh flowers and water. The next corner holds a five-gallon terra cotta pot with a leafy plant in potting soil. The third corner features a small three-foot by five-foot decorative rug on the floor.

Finally, in the fourth corner, you notice a fire smoldering away. It has already engulfed a pile of papers and is quickly creeping toward two long window curtains.

The instant you see the flames, you are faced with a choice. What do you do to immediately put the fire out?

LOGICAL REASONING: A simple, one-dimensional, "knee jerk" reaction to a single issue.

TACTICAL REASONING: A rapidly calculated, multidimensional strategy spanning a scenario.

Using logical reasoning, your gut pushes you to reach for the vase full of water. After all, water puts out fires, right?

But tactical reasoning breaks the situation down into smaller parts. Instead of grabbing the vase, you would quickly assess the situation and prioritize all available options, mentally rating them in order of effectiveness. Tactical reasoning helps you consider all the alternatives that you might need if the first option turns out to be ineffective.

In the case of the fire, you'd first survey your three options. Skipping the vase, you would snatch the pot full of soil and dump its contents onto the flames to keep the fire from spreading. Next, you could use the vase full of water to put out any lingering sparks or embers, if the soil hadn't already extinguished them. If both alternatives failed to do the trick, you'd have the rug available to smother the remnants of the fire.

Does that seem like a lot to process instinctively? It is. Tactical reasoning may not come naturally to you. But when you must answer the core question at the center of home invasion survival—fight or die?—you need honed tactical skills to make the right choice. Start building this type of thinking into your family action plan now so you're ready when an incident happens.

CONSIDER WHAT HAPPENS NEXT, RIGHT NOW

I can tell you that the action required to pull the trigger of a firearm is very easy. You simply need to grab the weapon, slip your index finger over its trigger and squeeze. The entire process usually lasts just under one second.

But what happens the instant after that bullet leaves the gun's barrel? The decision to defend yourself with a lethal firearm can have life-ending results that create emotional, mental and physical consequences for you

Quick tactical thinking will safe your life! In this illustrated example, logic would have you first throw water from the vase at the fire. However, that likely won't be enough to stop the fire. Tactical reasoning is much more effective, and would lead you to first use the potted plant's soil to keep the fire from spreading, then the water in the vase to put out the minimized flames and finally the rug to smother the embers or lingering flames.

and your loved ones. Sure, firing a deadly round may protect you from an intruder. But can you live with the fallout, second-guessing and what-ifs of a split-second decision for the rest of your life?

The mere thought of risking someone's life—even an attacker who unfairly puts your life in jeopardy—can present emotional issues that override the necessity of protecting yourself. When you think about hurting, maiming or killing another human being, in many ways, you end up feeling sorry for them. Remember, this is not the right mindset to adopt when defending your life.

In reality, you have to be focused on how to best use the weapons of opportunity available to you, how to leverage key target areas, successfully control your weapon and execute the take-down strategy. Tactical reasoning makes you consider a number of possible scenarios, such as: What if my weapon breaks while I'm using it? What if my weapon proves less effective than I hoped it would be? This mindset also requires you to think about what you will do next and who in your family can help you.

There isn't any room for error or second-guessing.

Comparing yourself to an attacker causes a lot of people to freeze, including highly trained professionals. Hesitation derails protective measures, leaving those in harm's way open to dying. In my opinion, this option is neither rational nor acceptable.

Mentally, those under attack often struggle with why they are being targeted rather than honing in on what needs to be done. Think back to the mental and emotional limitations we analyzed earlier. A tense situation like a home invasion creates doubt, heightens anxiety, increases fear and, if emotions are not managed correctly, can induce a blind panic. This chaotic turn of events compromises their safety while handing an advantage to the intruders. This isn't just undeserved, it's downright dangerous.

It's too common that I see defenders wrestle with the results and consequences of their actions rather than simply initiating physical measures. Quick actions, like pulling a trigger, swinging a bat, slashing with a knife or choking with a cord, weigh heavily on the defender's

mind. But you need to act quickly, and decisions cannot be approached from the vantage point of what someone else might do in the same situation. You're there in the moment, others are not. No one can tell you when it's time to fight or leave. If someone tries, they are not on your side.

Prepare for consequences in advance. Frame your perspective around your family's wellness, not the intruder's comfort. For every uncomfortable or unsettling consequence associated with a particular action, make a mental checklist of the opportunities it maintains for your loved ones. No good person wants to hurt someone else for any reason. But home invasions and violent crimes force you to think differently. Good people question the results of their own actions, but smart people survive. And here's something to chew on: You can be both good and smart so long as you make the right preparations.

TRANSLATING YOUR PLAN

Before you can put a survival plan in motion, you must make a life-bonding commitment to see the strategy through to the end. Say to yourself: I can do this, and I will do this. Then, when the time comes, follow through and do what you must with all your heart, energy and focus, no matter what happens.

"No matter what" is not an exaggeration. It means that you will go through with your defense plan wholly and entirely, even if you are hurt and need to push through discomfort, pain or even rivulets of your own blood. Remember that you can still defend yourself with a broken finger, or if you cannot see, or if your breathing becomes forcibly restricted.

After committing, congratulations! You've just cleared the first obstacle barring your way to successfully engaging and beating an attacker. You can make this commitment at any time, and I recommend you do so right now while the idea is fresh in your mind. The rest of your family action plan (except regular practice) kicks in once you find yourself ensnared in an attack.

Now, we're going to leap forward to that moment. Someone raised an alert, and a moment later, they sent out the alarm. Your family scrambled to their hiding places and double-checked their weapons of opportunity. Someone tried defending at the door, but the attackers still made it inside. One by one, they've discovered members of your family in their hiding places and tied them up in the living room. You're still free, but you sense that danger is rising. Your daughter raised her arms to shield a slap from an attacker, and your son has fallen down after feigning a seizure.

Now it's up to you to start the engagement. From your hiding place, you can see or hear almost everything going on in the house. Begin by choosing which attacker to take down first. That's right, you, who just a few seconds ago was marked as a helpless victim or prey, now becomes the hunter. To win in attack situations, you do not hide from a hunter. Instead, you hunt back, developing a plan and taking action.

There are a few things to consider as you make your choice. Use a rating scale like the one shown here to judge the targets.

> I can't mess with this person.

= I stand a 50-50 change of success.

< I can take this one!

Start by looking at heights and weights, as well as overall fitness levels. Use your own stats to make realistic comparisons about what you can and cannot achieve.

Do your assailants stand with their feet close together, or are they planted shoulder-width apart and balanced? Additionally, how does each target walk? Do they use long or short strides? Are any of the attackers limping or showing signs of injury? Or are there any physical disabilities present, such as wearing prescription glasses, hearing aids or diabetic insulin pump devices? Overall, is their movement natural and fluid, or does it appear erratic and nervous?

Steal a glance at your attackers' faces. Are their breathing patterns normal, or are there irregularities? When speaking, are their words clear and concise? What tone of voice do they use? Attackers may sound confident, assertive, timid or weak. Do they have a specific accent or recognizable speech pattern? For each, determine if the attacker gives or takes orders. You're trying to figure out who's leading the charge and who's following commands.

Take a moment to listen to what is said between the assailants. How do they speak among themselves? What are their demeanors? If they are casual when speaking, they are very likely familiar with one another. On the flip side, if one attacker gives specific orders to another and that individual repeats back what is said, the situation indicates a lack of trust. Seeds of doubt have already been sowed between them. You can use that to your advantage!

Try to get a feel for your attackers' emotions. This requires a slightly different engagement scenario. Now, let's say you're tied up and they're moving you from one room to another. Slip and fall on purpose. See who comes to help you; that attacker has the most compassion and may not want to be there in the first place. If no one comes to your aid, and they start kicking and dragging you instead, it tells you that you won't find any care from the group. Attempts to appeal to their emotions will go unanswered.

Home invaders are humans, too, and they have their addictions and bad habits. Listen for breathing difficulties and other medical conditions. If you notice that someone leaves every ten minutes and comes back inside reeking of smoke, you know they're suffering from a nicotine addiction. Similarly, if one smells of alcohol and sips from a mysterious bottle or flask, you can bet that they're an alcoholic. Use these vices to your advantage. Tell the smoker about the pack you have in your bedroom drawer, and show the alcoholic the liquor cabinet. Get them impaired, relaxed, loose. They'll let their guards down, and you'll gain valuable weapons of opportunity like breakable wine or liquor bottles in the process.

Watch who paces and who stares out the window. Is one of the attackers glancing down at his watch? What about the one who's texting on his phone? It's a tense situation for all involved, and by lighting the powder keg, you might just be able to turn them on one another.

"Who's your buddy texting?" could be a great question to start unraveling the camaraderie between them. If your assailants think that they might have a traitor in their midst, their focus will shift very quickly. Trust me on that.

Though these types of points may seem minor, they are actually very important. If you choose your first target wisely, you can gain an advantageous position and increase your chances of emerging safely. But pick the wrong attacker and you might just lose right away, sealing your own fate before you even put your plan into motion.

FROM IDEA TO ACTION

Once you've selected your first target and picked out a weapon of opportunity, it's time to put your plan into action. If you're dealing with multiple threats, instigate a separation. The goal is not to separate yourself from the attackers, but to break up the pack of assailants so that you can take them down one at a time. One way to accomplish this is by telling the attackers you need to take a medication for a medical condition, or even by faking a serious acute medical issue. Examples include high blood pressure, tightness in the chest, displaying stroke symptoms or signaling the need to use the restroom. Be as convincing as possible. Embarrassing though it may be, forcing an accident or episode lends credence to your request.

ASTHMA: Difficulty breathing.

LOW BLOOD SUGAR: Nausea and dizziness.

HEART ATTACK: Short breath and tight chest.

STROKE: Disorientation.

PANIC ATTACK: Hyperventilation.

Examples of some common medical ruses are listed at left. Become familiar with at least one ruse that suits your abilities and personal attributes.

Reflect back to the scenario described in the previous section. Your family is tied up, and your son has pretended to have a seizure. You remain in hiding, and it's time to bring the plan to life. One attacker heads upstairs, while the other two remain downstairs. One is very quiet and mousy, clutching his gun nervously, while the other seems slightly bored with being left on guard patrol. He's sitting and complaining, his gun left in the waistband of his jeans.

Putting on your tactical reasoning hat, remember to always think ahead to what happens next after the primary threat is incapacitated. A common secondary plan is escaping the premises. This decision must be made in accordance with your own physical abilities and skills, though. Alternatively, you may need to take down another attacker before you can escape. Though the media makes these scenarios seem exciting, it's often unreasonable to eliminate an entire group of attackers.

Part of putting ideas into action is communicating with your family. If your mouth is gagged, try silently communicating your readiness with your eyes. Look at them with concern, then open your eyes and close them tight twice in a row. If they are all right, they will repeat the concerned look, then open and close their eyes three times. This confirmation goes a long way in building up the emotional strength that may have drained over the course of the attack. That strength is very important when it comes to enacting your strategy.

Back in the scenario, the jumpy attacker states that he has to go to the bathroom. He hurries from the room toward the hall bathroom, and suddenly, you get the perfect window of opportunity to take down the bored one. You make eye contact with your son, who conveys that he understands the plan and is ready to help. Your son immediately begins to feign a second seizure, making enough noise for you to emerge from your hiding place to take down the first enemy with your weapon of opportunity, a heavy tabletop lamp base.

STANDING GROUND

As soon as you're out in the open, the second man grabs you. He finished his bathroom break sooner than you anticipated, and you've been caught. As he pulls you from hiding, you think about using his distance from the man upstairs and the one in the living room to incapacitate him. It may be the only time you have alone with him, so you know you need to use every moment, weapon of opportunity and defensive strategy wisely.

From the living room, the bored man approaches with his weapon drawn. The original plan is instantly out the window.

Your heart pounds in your chest. Suddenly, your attacker shoves you.

"Get in the closet, now," he growls. "Move."

You've run through your family action plan twice while observing the three men ransacking your house. You've decided on your weapons of opportunity, and you know your family has prepared the ruses or strategies that come next. You know in your heart that it's time to end this vicious assault. You are ready to stand your ground and begin to fight back.

The instant you decide to stand ground is the moment you stop giving your attacker what he wants. You're no longer a docile sheep, you're another wolf, his equal, and you're ready to take back what's yours by any means necessary. Plans have been made, and the pieces are in place. It's now a matter of executing on what you've been preparing for months.

I tell people to look at standing their ground as though it's a tactical sequence. Extract the fear, anxiety and panic; those emotions will only hurt you and hold you back. You have to be 100 percent ready to mount your assault. Focus on the actions, not the consequences. As long as you prepared yourself in advance, you will be able to grapple with those later.

In a way, a hostage situation isn't entirely dissimilar from a game of cards. You have to carefully play the hand you're dealt, and you can't let your emotions betray your strategy. You need to root out your strong suits: which attackers can be riled, which ones communicate more, who will do what they're told. You've also got to be on the lookout for jokers and aces, those wildcard moments that throw your plans into flux.

Choosing to stand your ground is a difficult moment for many victims of home invasions. You need to be ready to follow through on your plan, regardless of the consequences if you should fail. You've also got to be prepared to defend yourself, protect your family and potentially end another human being's life.

The concept of standing ground has its roots in battlefield tactics. Two opposing forces clash, with one weakened by the fight while another takes a dominant, aggressive position. Rather than retreating or fleeing entirely, troops dig their heels in to prevent the enemy from advancing into their territory. Standing ground occurs when the lesser force decides to actively put a stop to its submission or weakness by choosing to fight back.

You need to consider a lot of variables when standing your ground in a home invasion. Is your attacker significantly stronger than you? Are they equipped with weapons that will dwarf the power of your own weapons of opportunity? Will they be able to overpower you and exact revenge for your rebellious behavior? If so, you can expect to suffer dire consequences, including death.

Fortunately, family action plans prepare your responses to these situations, taking a substantial amount of the guesswork out of the equation. Nothing can guarantee your success, but planning can tilt the odds closer to your favor.

Many jurisdictions have stand your ground laws, which are occasionally referred to as "line in the sand" laws. These enable defendants to use force without retreating to defend or protect against threats. They protect people who are in a place where they are allowed to be, such as a private residence. The laws cover your use of deadly force to push intruders and attackers out of that particular space. While you're at it, look into related Castle Doctrines that govern self-defense measures in your town and county. It's important to know both your state and local jurisdiction's laws, but during a home invasion, you're generally within your rights to defend your family with any force necessary.

Don't ever be afraid to turn the tides of a home invasion. Your primary goal is getting a bad person out of your home, and sometimes, you need to stand up to them and engage them in order to enact that outcome. Sitting back and cowering is not often the best option.

When should you stand your ground? The easy answer is the moment that you're ready to engage the home invader. This means that you've conducted your threat assessment, you know what you're up against and you're ready to face off, regardless of the consequences. Weapons of opportunity are at the ready, and you have a realistic plan for how to use them to incapacitate or drive out the intruders.

Houses have a lot of different rooms suited to engaging. I wouldn't necessarily recommend one particular part of the home as the place where you decide to begin the engagement, though I will say that small rooms and spaces (like hallways) tend to be more beneficial to defending victims. The optimal location depends on a lot of factors, including the number of enemies who are pressing you. That's why it's important to conduct a thorough analysis of every interior space in advance. You don't want to be burdened with this decision when your life is on the line.

ENGAGEMENT CONSIDERATIONS AND OPTIONS

There's no such thing as *an* engagement strategy. Rather, there are dozens of engagement scenarios, each with intricate complexities that cannot be predicted in advance. You don't know if you're going to be dealing with one attacker or four, and you don't know if they'll split up once inside your house. You could get stuck with the weakest assailant, or you could be guarded by a tough veteran of crime who isn't afraid of your pushback. What if they're wearing masks, or what if they show their faces and up your stakes?

My advice is to build out engagement arcs for every room, hallway and space within your house. By arcs, I mean that you should draft multiple what-if scenarios

that could happen, understanding that individual factors will change. Arcs plot out general directions and guidelines without getting muddy with specifics, which are liable to shift wildly out of your control. Plan for varying numbers of attackers, as well as contingencies for breaking the group up. Think about distractions that can enact those break-ups to separate the pack and manage your own safety. Similarly, think about what happens when the full family is home, when certain individuals are out and when you're all alone.

The first step is to separate attackers. Never try to overpower several together. Sifting the chaff from the wheat enables you to manage their offensive maneuvers while reducing threats to those defending alongside you.

Once your initial target is separated, follow the disruptive protection pattern we discussed earlier: obstruct breathing, impair vision, induce pain. Get the focus off of you and onto their own plights. Whether that distraction is labored breathing, a temporary or permanent loss of vision or the triggering of a crippling pain overload is up to you and the situation you find yourself in.

Accept that you may be injured in the process. You could suffer a broken bone, or you could be stabbed in the shoulder, or you could have a bite ripped from your cheek, or you could have a finger jammed in your eye, or you could be shot at close range. As hard as it may be to understand, you need to hone in on tactics and block these consequences out. Push through them. You can't focus on your physical needs yet. People finish obstacle courses with broken legs, or wrestle weapons with gunshot wounds through their palms. Pain is very temporary in the scope of life. But death? That's final.

The second you see a break, run for it. Teach your family to do the same. You could be engaging like a pro, doling out one heck of a retaliation strike, but if your golden moment appears, don't hesitate to fly the coop. Your escape and survival are far more important than your pride. By getting out, you enable yourself to fight the perpetrator in court where you have the law on your side. He'll be looking at years of lockup, not icing the bruises from a one-night scuffle.

It's easier said than done when you're trapped with family members. The instant you leave, they become hostages. It does not play out like you see in the movies. For example, let's say you have an eight-year-old daughter. You know that if you cannot escape, you'll both die. In that case, you need to set it up so that you're fighting the criminals while she escapes. She might not want to leave, but she has to. It's a difficult conversation to have, but it's one you must share before a home invasion happens.

I had that conversation with my family a few years ago. In the event that a home invasion occurs, I will be the one to sacrifice myself so that my wife, sons and daughter get out alive. If I fall, my wife assumes the leadership role. She will fight back until she falls. The chain continues down my list of children from oldest to youngest. No one wants that to happen, but if it's the only way, it's a reality we are all prepared to endure.

With the right engagement considerations plotted out in advance, you'll increase your own survivability. Listen, I'm not going to blow smoke and tell you everything will definitely be all right. If it works out, that's what we in the police community call a rare happy ending. But if you don't get a happy ending, you have to be willing to go down fighting with the hope that the others in your family will use your actions to facilitate their own escapes.

That's why I've written this section about engaging the enemy. I want you to have the best shot possible. Over the next dozen or so pages, I cover engagement techniques in many common spaces in every home, as well as some unique places that only select readers will have in their houses. Learn them, and use them if the time comes.

DEFEND IN CLOSED OR CONFINED SPACES

Small and confined spaces in your home will give you the best advantages for engaging multiple threats. These areas include hallways and doorways, which are spelled out below, as well as bathrooms, pantries and mud rooms. There are ways that you can improve your odds while defending in a small space, and I'll share them here.

First, even though these utilitarian spaces are not generally known for their aesthetics, consider relocating some useful decorations to each small space in your home. Tuck conventional weapons or weapons of opportunity around each small room for easy access during a home invasion. Good items include picture frames and mirrors that can be shattered for edged weapons, electrical cords that may be used for strangulation or swinging weapons and heavy pans and flower pots with which to bludgeon an enemy.

In our laundry room, for example, we keep the usual things you'd find in such a space like detergent, bleach and dryer sheets. However, my wife also keeps a bottle of stain remover in the cabinet over the washer. This squirt bottle is kept in the spray setting whenever it's not in use, providing a readily accessible vision impairment. We also have several camping pots, pans and rotisserie skewers stored there. They hang from hooks in the pegboard wall. With a quick snatch, anyone can be armed and ready to engage.

I've also seen defenders make smart use of foyers and mud rooms. These spaces usually connect to an entry, making them great places to engage. Generally, you'll be defending the door or fighting your way out of the house here. Keep that in mind as you store weapons of opportunity and other tools. Potting tools, including vessels to hold plants, make for excellent blunt objects. Spades, trellises and digging tools are outstanding instruments to jab enemies while keeping significant distance. You can even use soil, powdered plant food and mineral garden supplements as visual impairments by grasping a handful of material and thrusting it into the attacker's face. A lot of foyers and mud rooms include a small bench to sit and remove dirty shoes. This can be used as cover if it's large enough to protect your body, or as a shield if small enough to be held. If you don't have one already, I strongly recommend investing in a short, stocky solid wood piece to use for defensive purposes.

Small spaces also offer an attractive benefit to people with diminutive statures. Larger, muscular individuals may have trouble maneuvering in these places, which can constrict their movements. This gives tiny people

If you cannot escape where you are, you need to barricade and/or defend yourself! Here, the woman shown has a safe position away from the door in case of gunfire. If an attacker enters, she has the advantage of surprise to jump up and injure him with her weapon of opportunity—the scissors.

(including youth) the position of advantage. Use your nimbleness to your credit, evading with quick dodges and jumps in order to get your opponent cornered. Then, use a weapon suited for a small space, such as a stabbing instrument or strangulation cord, to take him down. Avoid long weapons or bulky furniture that will be difficult to wield.

Reach down and squeeze your calves and thighs. What you're feeling between your pinched fingers is raw power. Even in individuals who do not regularly exercise, these muscles tend to be quite strong. We walk everywhere, and as such, these leg muscles are constantly being flexed.

Use them to your advantage in a small space! With your back against the wall and your arms bracing furniture, a sturdy door or another perpendicular wall, raise both your legs and thrust a forceful double kick into your attacker's legs (to disable their movement) or groin (to trigger a pain overload). Push back into the wall as you kick while tightening your arms, bracing yourself against the structure to gain even more power.

DEFEND IN COMMON AREAS OF THE HOME

In this section, I'll provide some pointers for defending and engaging in rooms and areas that are common to most modern American homes. Bear in mind that your home's layout and furniture configurations may require you to adjust some of the strategies I outline here. If this is the case, adapt the techniques so that they better fit your living spaces. You can also review the strategies for uncommon areas in the next section to see if any of these apply to your home's unconventional features.

Perhaps the best place to defend in any home is its heart and hearth: the kitchen. Not only is this space very often centrally located—making it accessible from most other rooms and hallways throughout the structure—but it's packed with hiding places, escape routes, weapons of opportunity and positions of advantage. In fact, I think the only downside to defending in a kitchen is the fact that its rich arsenal is available to both the homeowner and attacker. However, you can even control that with a few inexpensive upgrades.

Purchase child protection locks for your cabinetry and drawers. These small plastic devices screw into the interior of cabinets and prevent them from being easily opened. In a dark kitchen, they can trip up an intruder searching for a knife, meat mallet or other weapon. As long as you practice, they will not offer any resistance to you or your family. Keep countertops clear of flour and cookie jars, knife blocks, small appliances and other debris that an intruder could scoop up and wield against you. Instead, store these items in your cabinetry for easy, controlled access.

If your kitchen has an island, use it to create distance between you and the attacker. Duck to evade blows, and move around it to remain as far from them as possible. This also gives you an opportunity to line up with an exit to escape. If your island has a sink, turn it on and grasp the spray nozzle attachment to soak the floor and distract your attacker before making a break for it. The tactic will at least give him pause, and at best, slow him down enough for you to make it outside. In the confusion, knock over a bottle of soap or dishwashing cleaner to make the floor extremely slick. If your island is on wheels, subtly unlock each with a tap of your toe while circling it.

Then, prior to making your escape, jam the whole piece directly into the attacker. Press him up against a wall, cabinet or counter, if possible. If you can, lock at least one or two wheels before running off to keep him pinned for a few more seconds.

Flick on your range as soon as you become aware of a home invader's presence. Lay a metal utensil with a stay-cool silicon handle on the hot burner to create a brand. In my kitchen, I have a pot rack behind the stove that also includes some hanging barbecue tongs. The points are extremely sharp and, when heated, they'd cause a lot of pain if poked or scraped against exposed skin! You can also attempt to slam your assailant's hands or face into the hot burner, though be on your guard to avoid having this weapon turned against you.

Beyond the plethora of edged and blunt weapons available, kitchens also hold a number of abrasive cleaning products. Use these liberally in your home invasion defensive strategy! Oven cleaners are extremely caustic and can be sprayed into an attacker's face to blind them. The same goes for degreasing solutions, ammonia-based window cleaners and cleaning detergents. You can also create something I like to call a "chem cloud" with items from under the sink. Powdered dish soap, carpet agents and other granulated chemicals can be flung across the room, creating a cloud of noxious chemicals that stuns and disables anyone who breathes it in. Take a deep breath before flinging the materials and make sure you can instantly duck out of the space to minimize contamination. You can also cover your mouth with a dampened shirt or rag to prevent breathing any of the chemicals yourself. By surprising the attacker, you can maximize his chances of him gasping or quickly inhaling, then sucking in a large quantity of particulate. If any of the aerosol cleaners are flammable, pair them with a barbecue lighter to create an effective flamethrower.

As you defend in the kitchen, stay one step ahead of the fight. With your free hand, open and close drawers that do not contain sharp objects. Pull out the garbage can and tip it over. Fling stools or chairs erratically. Basically, clutter up the space with objects that make poor weapons of opportunity. This chaos makes it hard for an intruder to follow you without climbing over debris or banging into obstructions. It also makes them less aware of things happening outside their immediate area—giving your family members in other rooms an opportunity to escape.

Moving on, let's look at the living room from an engagement perspective. Though I generally discourage against fighting in the living room due to its open nature, it tends to be the room that home invaders use for their center of operations. You need to be ready to defend here if necessity calls for it.

Looking at your living room, first identify architectural and layout details that you can use to your advantage. Examples include columns, nooks, fireplace hearths and bay windows. Some living rooms also adjoin the foyer and hall closet. Plan for ways to use each space to your benefit. For instance, you may be able to press yourself into a nook to shield blows or avoid gunfire. Fireplace hearths can provide trip hazards, and most are also flanked by sharp, heavy tools used to stoke a roaring fire.

Examine the furniture you have in the space. If you have a tall buffet or sofa table with sharp, pointed edges, you can use this to injure eyes and dislodge teeth by shoving an attacker's face into it. Flatten yourself against the side of the piece, then pop out and thrust their head into the corner before they know what's happening. Coffee tables and ottomans are good objects for maintaining distance. If your table has a glass top, try to knock the intruder onto it. The glass will shatter and cut them, and they'll also be stuck in the frame, which will take some time to escape. If you're having trouble getting them near the table, pop out the glass top and thrust it at him. The shards can yield significant lacerations, and the distraction can create enough time for you to quickly crouch behind a sofa or overstuffed armchair.

Because they are difficult to defend in, use as many ruses as you can when engaging from the living room. A friend told me this fantastic idea, and it'd be perfect for fooling home invaders from this space. Purchase an inexpensive wireless doorbell from your local home improvement store. Plug the receiver in, but keep the ringer hidden inside a living room drawer or key bowl. As soon as your family action plan alarm sounds, grab the button and slip it in your pocket, bra or underwear. Then, when you are ready to engage and need a distraction, press the button. It will sound like your doorbell ringing, startling an intruder and prompting him to walk toward the entry. Use that moment to engage him with one of the closest weapons of opportunity. Just remember that the doorbell noise may bring all intruders down to the entry, so be prepared to separate the group and take them down from an advantageous spot like a doorway.

Defending in a recreation or family room has similar advantages and disadvantages to defending in a living room. Use any additional furniture, toys or games that are stored in this area to boost your arsenal. Because recreation rooms tend to be a bit darker than other common areas of the home, they have a lot of lights. Consider investing in a sound-activated switch for all the lights in this room. That way, if you and your family are being held in this space, you can clap, stomp or cough loudly, then become shrouded in darkness. Though your attacker may figure out the ruse quickly, there will be an opportunity for one or more individuals to slip away into a hiding place as he fumbles to clear his hands.

Bedrooms are relatively easy to defend from, as long as you stock them appropriately in advance. Make sure you have objects that double as weapons of opportunity in every corner, mounting some on the wall for good measure. Prepare multiple escape routes from each bedroom, including one or more using windows and foldable emergency ladders.

Some defensive techniques require constant vigilance even when an attack is not underway. For instance, when sleeping, keep bedroom doors shut and locked. This prevents attackers from sneaking in unnoticed while you're unconscious. Additionally, consider sleeping with a conventional weapon nearby. I've seen mattresses with pockets for firearms and knives, as well as headboards that double as miniature gun lockers. When you go to sleep, keep your cell phone charging nearby. This allows you to call for help while also providing a useful strangulation weapon via the charger.

When defending from a bedroom, avoid falling onto the bed mid-struggle. This position makes it harder to fight back, and it opens victims up to the additional threat of sexual assaults. Brace against the wall or a piece of firm furniture, such as a dresser. Keep as much space as possible between you and the attacker. If you can, get between him and the bedroom door to prevent additional home invaders from bursting in. Concentrate on taking him down before shifting focus to the others elsewhere in the home.

One of the most significant challenges associated with defending in the bedroom is the lack of adequate cover. Excepting dressers and vanities (if available), there are few places to shield yourself from gunfire. Instead, I recommend relying on concealment while in the bedroom. Open or break a window and create the illusion that you've escaped, then hide under the bed with clothes or other debris hiding you from view. Remain perfectly still and, once the attacker leaves, quietly text a friend to call the police for you.

Home offices are filled with sharp tools and heavy equipment that make them great spots for engaging the intruders. Use desks and credenzas for concealment and, in some cases, cover. Then, seek out weapons that make sense for your situation. Staplers are heavy blunt objects that can inflict significant head trauma, while letter openers, pens, sharp pencils and scissors are effective edged instruments. Computer cords make great devices for restricting air flow or binding enemy hands. If you have a large waste basket, throw it over your attacker's head and rapidly trigger pain points, using the confusion to take him down.

The final common areas we'll look at are semi-outdoor spaces, such as the garage or a screened-in porch. The obvious advantage to using these areas is the close proximity to the home's exterior, and by default, freedom. Unfortunately, it's rare that attackers use these locations for tying or corralling their victims. The limited insulation and enhanced exposure do nothing to muffle sounds, making quiet attacks difficult. If you do find yourself against an invader in a semi-outdoor space, make as much noise as you can. Fight hard to bring attention to your situation.

Make use of flammable liquids such as gasoline and torch fuel to spray or soak attackers. These liquids have an overpowering odor, and the threat of being set ablaze will give smarter criminals pause. Even if it does not faze the assailants, use it to impair vision by splashing it in their faces, scooping your throw upward to get the liquid behind goggles, glasses or visors. If the attacker does catch fire after you've doused him, use his panic to either escape the space or subdue him by striking the back of his head with a blunt object.

DEFEND IN UNCOMMON AREAS OF THE HOME

All homes are somewhat unique, even those that are prefabricated or built to a standard plan. Many feature uncommon rooms, peculiar architectural details and interesting elements that can be leveraged for your defense. Here I've listed a few uncommon areas that I've seen successfully incorporated into home invasion survival strategies. If you have a similar space in your home that doesn't quite fit what you see listed here, adapt the strategy provided below to make it better fit your home's layout.

- **SOLARIUM:** Some homes feature an enclosed greenhouse, sunroom or solarium. These rooms provide excellent sun exposure for growing plants, but unfortunately they are also lucrative to criminals due to the fact that they are constructed with large amounts of breakable glass. Solariums are frequently located off of kitchens and formal dining rooms. Though defending in such a space is not generally advisable, you could use the garden tools and pots as weapons of opportunity. Additionally, you can use the glass to your advantage for a quick getaway by shattering a pane and running to safety. If you have a solarium attached to your house, I strongly recommend that you install a security camera inside the structure and place several sensors on the glass panes to detect break-ins. Also, install thick glass doors to the exterior, and use a protected, reinforced exterior door for the entry from the solarium into the house. It may not be as aesthetically pleasing, but it will make the solarium into more of an external structure than an inviting entryway to your family's abode. If possible, use thorny landscaping around the exterior of the greenhouse and install a gravel walk-up to force a noisy approach.

- **SAUNA:** Though not as common in the United States as in European and Asian countries, private saunas are not completely unheard of. In fact, some home improvement stores now sell do-it-yourself sauna kits that can transform any spare room into a wet or dry sauna! To make it more defendable, hide weapons of opportunity inside one or two rolled towels in the sauna area. Inform your family and guests that they are there, and keep them in the same location at all times. That particular towel should never be used. You could even use a slightly different color to mark it. Additionally, consider hanging a decorative coal rake, heavy wooden ladle or other sauna-related tool in the area, even if your device is electric. This aesthetic touch will double as a weapon if needed.

- **INDOOR POOL:** For those fortunate enough to have an indoor pool, you have a great place to defend yourself and your family! Slippery floors are an accident waiting to happen—use that to your advantage. Lure a criminal into the pool area, then startle him and wait for him to slip. If necessary, you can even push him or knock him into the pool to buy some time. He will struggle to stay afloat wearing heavy boots, weaponry and thick clothing. Powdery pool chemicals are also great for impairing both vision and breathing, and long skimmers and brushes make for excellent bludgeoning instruments. If your pool connects to the exterior of your property, you can even use it as an escape route.

- **BUTLER'S PANTRY:** I've seen quite a few butler's pantries in older, historic homes. Some newer houses also build them into the floor plans. They generally store serving utensils and silverware. Use them as you would other confined spaces, and make sure that weapons of opportunity are available to you but not to criminals. Keep drawers locked when not in use, but store a few edged instruments in places where you might reach them, like under a cookbook, beneath the sink cabinet or even in an apron pocket hanging on a door hook. Keep a heavy object such as a cast iron door holder or soup tureen in a corner of the floor as well.

- **LIBRARY:** Libraries may be separate rooms in a house or simply a wall that contains a large bookshelf. They contain a number of useful weapons of opportunity. Heavy books may be used to strike intruders, and bookends are equally suited as bludgeoning tools. Larger libraries have movable ladders that can also be used to maintain distance. If bookshelves are movable, you can topple them on intruders or create a hiding place by gently tugging them away from the wall. Remember that hollow books are great ways to camouflage traditional weapons like firearms.

- **WINE CELLAR:** Like libraries, wine cellars can range from custom underground caves designed to preserve rare vintages to simply an extensive collection of bottles on movable wine racks. Use bottles of wine as both blunt instruments (when intact) or as sharp, edged weapons (when shattered). Some bottles of sparkling wine can be shaken up to shoot the cork, though I recommend using this as a distraction instead of a weapon. Spill a dry light-colored wine on stone or tile floors to make a slippery surface. If the cellar includes multiple racks, you can dodge behind them to temporarily hide.

- **HOME THEATER:** Home theaters are one of the newest trends in mid-level and luxury homes. A large room with a projection screen (or large television set), mounted speakers and one or more chairs, they are not terribly well-suited to defending. However, you can leverage the large chairs for space between you and an attacker. Be sure to store valuable weapons of opportunity in the theater in the case of a home invasion. Examples include countertop popcorn machines, decorative statues and High Definition Multimedia Interface cords, which can be used for strangulation. You can also tie a cord around a heavy remote control to create a swinging device. Additionally, if you have a home theater, consider turning the speakers on as loud as you can the moment a home invasion begins to add chaos. Hide the controller, then leave the room. This may successfully lure home invaders into the space, giving you an opportunity to escape.

- **LOFT:** Lofts are popular in vacation homes, but they are terrible for defending. The low ceilings make it very hard to maneuver, and they often have a single ladder for escaping. However, if you find yourself trapped in a loft during a home invasion, there are still creative ways to defend from that location. First, use gravity to your advantage by dropping a heavy object onto an intruder's skull. These items could include wooden slats from beneath the bed, a lamp or a book. Second, you can also use the ceiling to brace yourself for a strong kick to an intruder's neck or clavicle as they emerge over the top of the ladder. Timed right, this has the potential to seriously injure an attacker through blunt-force trauma coupled with the ensuing fall. Finally, use loft bed sheets to cover an intruder's head and impair their vision, or twist them into a rope for a strangulation instrument.

- **SPIRAL STAIRCASE:** Though spiral staircases are widely seen as archaic and inconsistent with modern zoning codes, some older structures still use them to traverse levels of a house. Use them like other small spaces to brace yourself and time strong kicks. If the staircase is open on the sides, you can also use it to drop down and escape while an attacker attempts to climb up.

DEFEND IN A HALLWAY

Let's say you're up against three attackers. If you try to engage them in your wide-open living room, the large, unsheltered environment will let all three spring toward you at once. They will surround you, grab you and hold you down while the others attack relentlessly. Your wrong decision about where to engage gives them additional time to think through their actions rather than reacting haphazardly. You're going to be lucky to emerge in one piece.

In this situation, it'd be far better to engage the three attackers from a hallway. The tight space limits the number of attackers who can readily get a piece of you. This translates to a positive: you're essentially fighting off one attacker at a time. It's a heck of a lot easier for one to fight three individually than all at once!

What's key to note with hallways is the proximity of the walls and the location of the doorways. You can use both of these details to engage home invaders.

Beginning with walls, push your back against one wall and extend your legs to the other side. You can use this to break down a door. Better yet, if an attacker is opening a doorknob, slam your legs into it to blow them back with a stunning forehead slam. For doors that open into the hall, brace them shut with your legs instead. After a few attempts, many attackers will charge at the door to get out of a room; stand aside and let them crash into the hallway's drywall before you knock them out cold.

If you're being pursued, use the tight space in a corridor to your advantage by taking out the first attacker with a sharp blow to the neck, groin or face. While he struggles with his injuries, other attackers will either trip over his slumped form or gingerly step over him. Use this hesitation to take the bad guys down one goon at a time.

If you live in an apartment, take note. Hallways leading to apartment doorways are considered to be semi-public spaces. While you can defend yourself from an ongoing attack, the use of deadly force may not be protected, especially if the attacker is backing away or fleeing. Evaluate your options for a non-lethal protective countermeasure, such as pepper spray, and use it carefully to avoid disarming yourself. Consider the attack to be over as soon as the perpetrator leaves your private domain, but don't treat the danger as anything less than imminent. Call the authorities and warn as many neighbors as you can. If your building employs security or a doorman, notify them immediately with a phone call to prevent the attacker from escaping.

DOORWAY TACTICS AND APPROACHES

In Chapter 4, we talked about defending the doorway connecting your home to the world beyond. Taking the fight inside to an interior door, your tactics need to shift slightly.

Interior doors are far weaker than exterior ones. Many are hollow-core, and they'll give way with a single strong kick or punch. The hardware keeping them in place is similarly flaky, with most screws less than on and a half inches in length. Trust me that a single good shoulder ram will take down almost every hollow-core door. And deadbolts? They're practically non-existent indoors.

But don't let those facts dissuade you. You don't need interior doors to be as strong as primary entries, so long as you use them the right way.

The first thing you need to adjust is your expectations. You won't be keeping anyone out with an interior door, and you'll be lucky to buy much time using one as a static barrier. However, couple an interior door with the strength and mass of an adult human, and suddenly it becomes an impressively versatile shield on hinges. Use the doorway to trap an attacker, slamming the door on his body as he begins to step into a room. Continue to press on it with all your weight, leaning into it with all the force of your legs, hips and core. While he's struggling to get free, punch his throat as hard as you can with your free fist to disrupt his airway. If that fails, go for his eyes with your thumbs. If neither area is accessible, knee him in the groin as hard as you can. If other attackers are present, they'll have to fight one another to get to you, since the doorway limits exposure. This presents a unique insight into aggression levels of each attacker.

When my kids were young, I taught them to be on the lookout for me fighting off one or two guys at a doorway if we ever experienced a home invasion. If that situation ever happened, I said, they were to run outside and start yelling, "He's in here!" as though speaking to the police—even if the authorities weren't there yet. That illusion would have been enough to scare them considerably, possibly buying the advantage I would have needed to knock one or both out.

Look at the hardware on interior doors, including latches, locks and hinges. Ripped from the door or simply forced in the locked position, they can be used to impale, slice or bludgeon an enemy. A lot of homeowners place decorative furniture like tables with picture frames, candlesticks and trophies next to interior doors. By slowly and gently reaching inside a frame, you can grab for something without your attacker seeing. Be sure to place these types of objects all around doors and hallways so that there aren't open spaces lacking weapons of opportunity.

Another key benefit to interior doors is their capability to open up new spaces. For example, say that an attacker drags you out of bed in the middle of the night. Rather than facing him in your bedroom, you take three steps toward the door and suddenly, you have multiple places to engage. If he comes at you, you can also retreat into the hallway to move the fight elsewhere. You're not constrained.

If you're in a room and you hear an attacker approaching, hide along the wall where the door swings open. You can also stand at a corner opposite the door to avoid the intruder seeing you first. That's why I recommend not standing right next to the door handle, since you'd be totally visible the second he cracked the door open. Do not stand where the door can hit you either. This position could force you to lose the position of advantage before you engage, and there's a very real possibility you'd wind up getting seriously injured if the door handle cracked into your own face, gut or groin. Crouch down just outside of where the door swings, extend your arms and get ready to grab him the moment he steps through.

As he walks into the room, grab his arm with your dominant hand and pull down, disabling his weapons with a surprising jerking motion. At the same instant, swing your free elbow up into his face, aiming square for the nose. As he reels, slam his head into the door frame, the door itself or an adjacent wall. The door frame is the best option since it features the most solid construction. Grab the weapon, shove him to the floor and take aim at him. At this point, you can disable him with a non-lethal shot or strike to the extremities, a stab to the arm or a swift blow to the temple. Once he's down, back off and close the door, preparing for the next attacker. It's critical to back away, just in case he comes to and lunges in your direction.

Any weapon you choose can have multiple uses, so always have a plan B. The images below show multiple ways you can use a door to engage an attacker.

1 A locked door can be used to put distance between you and an attacker while you escape or hide.

2 It can be swung as a blunt weapon—with special emphasis on the knob.

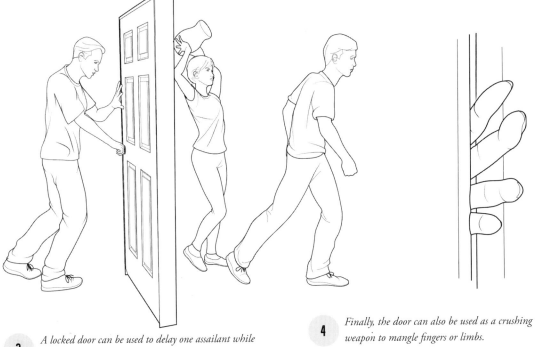

3 A locked door can be used to delay one assailant while you take down another with a weapon of opportunity.

4 Finally, the door can also be used as a crushing weapon to mangle fingers or limbs.

MANAGE DISTANCE AND MAINTAIN THE CONTROLLING POSITION

We've discussed the importance of managing distance when keeping attackers out of your home, as well as the critical need to put as much space as possible between you and the assailants while defending from the inside. Now that you are actively engaging them, the philosophy sticks—even though you must implement it a bit differently.

When engaging an attacker, you're going on the offense by initiating a fight that you believe you can win in order to protect your family. That goes right back to the difference between defending and protecting. When you switch to an offending engagement position, this forces the attacker into defensive mode. Many of the same instincts and techniques I discussed earlier in this book are going to apply to them when they attempt to defend against you. That's right: The tables turn, and you now need to be ready to dodge their blocks and avoid their return strikes.

Managing distance is key to staying on top during any engagement scenario. If your attacker gets too close, generally within arm's distance, he can injure you and destroy your capacity to fight. In other words, you lose. Hand-to-hand combat is off the table. By keeping yourself outside of the distance at which he could grab or kick you, you avoid limiting your options or stepping into a trap. You also afford yourself the space to duck into another room, make a break for it or grasp a different weapon of opportunity. These surprises can be enough to maintain the controlling position. They force your opponent to react, and reactions are seldom intelligent. They are primal and prone to failure.

Top-notch illusions are another way to maintain the controlling position. Even if you cannot physically defend yourself, make it seem like you're ready and able to do so. Create the image that suits your plan, whether it requires you to come across confident or cowardly. Watch for signs of weakness, such as referring to victims with honorifics like "sir" and "ma'am." These show an immature grasp of the situation. Prey on the attackers using these terms, getting them to calm down and let

down their guard. Paint a passionate picture that you're not a threat to them until the second you are ready to engage. Then, easily usurp the controlling position and keep it until help arrives.

Whenever you see a window of opportunity to maintain or grow your controlling position, take it. Home invasions aren't neat and tidy. Sometimes, you've got to break the window of opportunity to make it out alive. Sometimes, it isn't that big of a window to begin with. But do whatever you must to get out alive. When your home is under assault, the window of opportunity you need could be little more than a single crack that lets in a single ray of sunlight. Take it and run with it.

When you select a weapon to defend yourself, make sure you know how to use it and have the space to properly wield it. A baseball bat, as shown here, can be an effective weapon to manage distance between you and attackers.

REVIEW BACKUP OPTIONS

First of all, if you're reading this book, you have no excuse for being so underprepared that you run out of primary and secondary options. Backup options are unstable, unpredictable and unwise. They come into play when your alternatives dwindle down to two choices: doing nothing and accepting death or doing something that might succeed but will probably still lead to death. Never let yourself become trapped in this situation.

I don't even like going here. To me, it's like training a bad habit. But for the sake of illustrating some last-ditch efforts in the hope that they might save someone's skin, I'll share a few examples. Promise me that you'll do everything in your power to plan for a home invasion, and you'll only use these backup options if everything else fails.

Pretend that you're underprepared, unarmed and helpless, and two or more attackers are closing in on you. You know there is no way for you to successfully engage them. Where do you go from here?

Some people think that acting ballistic and mentally insane in an attempt to scare the attackers away is a good idea. I disagree wholeheartedly. It's foolish and will probably result in you getting a bullet straight through your skull. The attackers don't want someone who is unable to follow directions risking their cover and bounty. In fact, the only reason I could ever see someone using this strategy is if they wanted to distract their attackers so that their spouse and children had a sliver of hope to escape alive. It's self-sacrifice, nothing more.

Instead of acting insane, a better option would be to fake a medical emergency. Start shaking as though suffering an epileptic episode, or clutch your chest to indicate that it's getting extremely tight. Change your breathing to mirror an asthma attack or general respiratory distress. Pretend to have an airway obstruction by gagging, drooling and convulsing to get your mouth gag removed. The difference between a medical ruse and acting berserk is that one condition is manageable, while the other is not. If they sense it's a medical issue, the attackers may even try to help.

Of course, this goes back to understanding as much as you can about your attackers. I've also heard stories about victims suffering anxiety attacks only for their assailants to wrap plastic bags over their heads, suffocating them. These are far rarer than home invaders rushing to help, however.

The moment the ruse takes root, you have something to work with. You can separate an enemy from the group, and a family member can lure them away to the medicine cabinet to get the "required" pills. You can stash some generic ibuprofen in an old prescription bottle if you'd like, though it's not necessary. Even if you do not have generic pills at the ready, your bathroom will be stocked with many other weapons of opportunity that the family member can use to engage the lone attacker. As soon as they're out of the room, you can take on the other attacker from your location to take full advantage of the opportune separation. You're no longer in a worst-case scenario. You've got seeds of hope once again!

Again, these last-ditch efforts are not recommended, except in moments of extreme danger. Plan as much in advance to avoid having to use any of them.

At some point during a home invasion, you may have to physically remove a family member from peril. If you see a family member about to be murdered, rush them and push them through a window. Even with the threat of glass shards and the fall, they're more likely to survive than if they were shot at point-blank range in the forehead.

You can also set the room you're in on fire to distract the attackers, even though you may burn to death because of it. It could also go out, leaving you holding a match while intruders bear down on the soon-to-be-dead man or woman who tried to smoke them out.

Not all last-ditch self-sacrifices are fatal. You might have to break or dislocate your own shoulder to get out of rope ties that hold you in place. Or, you may need to plant your hands on a table, slam down a weight and snap your own knuckles to wriggle free from a pair of tight handcuffs. There have been situations where people gave up their own arms, hands and other body parts in order to live. Once, I even heard about a man who head-butted his attacker with an open mouth to bite his attacker's jugular, a brazen move that cost him several teeth, broke his jaw and nearly got him killed.

When it comes to engaging the enemy, never begin an effort without the end in mind. Don't rely on last-ditch efforts as part of your plan. Keep them as an ace up your sleeve.

PRACTICE EXERCISE 8: ENGAGE, THE GAME

I won't sugarcoat it: Weighing whether or not to engage your enemy does not rely on a single preprogrammed response. It's a complex decision that requires you to balance a number of smaller responses, factors, benefits and consequences. The vast majority of these microdecisions are not things that you can perfectly plan to address.

A better strategy is to ramp up your decision making skills in advance so that you are ready for anything that comes your way. I came up with a game to do just that, which I like to call "engage." It's a strong way to practice your engagement skills, and it can be played by preteen children, teenagers and adults to up family-wide readiness.

Go to your local office supply store and purchase index cards in four different colors. The first color will be for "Situations," which describe the home invasion at a high level. The second color will be used for "Locations" around the home. The third color will be used for "Weapons of Opportunity." The fourth color will be "Stakes," which detail specific threats that are on the line.

Come up with a list of at least fifteen to twenty topics for each card type. You'll write these on one side of the card, leaving the reverse blank. Examples for each follow:

Situations
- Three masked men burst into the home during dinner.
- After a family member answers a knock at the door, a single criminal pushes his way into the home.
- Your neighbor's new landscaper approaches your house with a weapon in hand.
- In the middle of the night, you go downstairs for a glass of water and encounter an intruder.

Locations
- Kitchen
- Living room
- Hallway
- Child's bedroom
- Backyard

Weapons of Opportunity
- Vase
- Umbrella
- Candy dish
- Telephone cord
- Wooden spoon

Stakes
- The rest of the family is tied up with rope.
- A gun is held to Mom's head.
- An attacker moves to assault a child.
- The intruder is about to open the door where someone is hiding.

Once compiled, sit your family down to play this unique learning game. Shuffle the cards within their separate colored piles. The current player pulls one card from each pile and then puts the cards down on the table for all to see. He or she then has sixty seconds to decide whether or not to engage their attacker, listing the factors that weigh in on their decision.

After each turn, discuss what the player did well and areas where they should consider other alternatives. Remember that each factor needs to be examined from the individual's perspective. For instance, a preteen child may not have the strength to use a baseball bat effectively, but a teenager might gauge their abilities differently and use it to engage the enemy.

The goal of Engage isn't winning or losing, it's all about responding more quickly and effectively to a random threat that puts your family's lives at risk. In competitive families, you can assign an Olympic-style scoring scheme where every family member rates the responses on a scale of one to ten. The "winner" at the end of the game is the person who accumulates the most points.

If playing with teenagers and older children, be sure to acknowledge their successes with praise or a small treat. Gently coach them on mistakes to help them want to understand how to perform better in the future. This positive approach will groom them to make positive decisions in real-life home invasion scenarios. While Engage is not suitable for very young children who lack the emotional maturity to understand engagement considerations, you can still let them sit in on the game while explaining what's going on in terms they comprehend.

Wrap a rubber band around your cards, and store them in your family action plan dossier. Break out the game every month or two to keep everyone's skills sharpened. This is also a good, portable exercise that's perfect for long car rides and weeknight dinner table conversation.

9

ARM INTELLIGENTLY

On July 19, 2016, an attempted home invasion took place in Surrey, British Columbia in Canada. The criminal attempted to gain entry into a residence, but he was met with significant force.

The residents fought back against the intruder, disabling him with their fists and a belt. They were even able to bind him with the belt, restraining him on the front lawn until the police arrived.

Additionally, neighbors who heard the commotion came running to help. By the time the authorities arrived on the scene, the quick-thinking residents had the situation under control. The perpetrator was brought to the hospital with non-life-threatening injuries, while two residents were also examined for minor injuries.

None of the residents faced charges stemming from the incident, and all those involved recovered.[39]

WEAPONS OF OPPORTUNITY

The word "weapon" calls up many different images. For some, it's a protective measure that helps them sleep soundly. For others, it's a terrifying reminder that sometimes we need to fight in order to survive.

In reality, a weapon is nothing more than an object you use to defend yourself or others. Weapons do not need to be crafted for killing. In fact, they can be as innocuous as a spoon, pencil or kitchen pot. It takes training to think about everyday objects as aids for personal safety. I'm hopeful that this chapter will give you a taste of this critical survival mindset. My goal is for you to walk away with a few key tips for using the items around your house to save lives under pressure.

So far, this book has focused on protective strategies that avoid requiring the use of firearms. In this section, I will continue to favor unconventional weapons over traditional weapons, though there are several areas where I provide tips for using both kinds of tools. Remember that firearms are not required to protect your family, despite being beneficial in many survival situations.

Slip back into the engagement situations we looked at in Chapter 8. Once you have decided to engage and have selected your target, shift your focus to looking for factors that can tip the balance of power in your favor. I call these "positions of advantage" and "weapons of opportunity."

What do I mean by "weapons of opportunity"? These are everyday objects that you transform into protective mechanisms out of necessity. You must know how to properly use the weapon in order for it to be effective. For example, if I asked someone to pick up a pen and use it for protection, most folks would grab it like a steak knife. However, what they don't realize is that when the pen makes contact with the target, the worst it will do is scrape the skin or snap because of the way you're holding it. It won't penetrate into the flesh. However, if you grip the pen along your index finger with the base nestled in your palm, you can jam it into an attacker's ears, eyes or throat without risking it snapping. The different position and targeting adds significant strength, and coupled with a hard jab to soft tissue, this lowly writing instrument can do some real physical damage.

Before diving deeper on weapons, I also want you to better understand positions of advantage. These are the locations where you can find specific weapons of opportunity. They connect to a few important survival factors.

First, selecting the location is critical. The place where you engage winds up becoming a big part of your plan, and depending on your needs, it can provide you with an escape route, weapons of opportunity or the simple advantage of knowing the environment. Remember that when an intruder breaks into your house, they're on your turf. You have the home team advantage, so use it!

Allow yourself to think ahead and predict how the defensive scenario might play out. For instance, what would the success rate be if you took action in your current location versus waiting to take action in a different part of the house? Are the intruders staying put in one location, or could they be strategically separated? Does conflict exist between the perpetrators?

Consider the room itself. Is it big or small, cleared or cluttered? What is the weight of nearby furniture, and are there any small objects that could be repurposed as an impact weapon? What types of sharp objects are accessible to you, and which ones are accessible to the attackers?

Every room in your home provides you with certain advantages and access to different types of weapons. Conversely, they also come with specific disadvantages on the arms front. I'll walk you through a few key rooms now and provide some examples.

Bathrooms are small, confined spaces. But don't let that deter you from using them to your advantage! Even though they are not ideal because they lack multiple escape routes, as far as closed and confined spaces go, bathrooms are full of hard tiled walls, firm countertops, glass mirrors and hard porcelain fixtures such as toilets and tubs. Small sharp objects (such as tweezers or nail clippers), aerosol room and hair sprays, lotions, creams, power cords from blow dryers and even toothbrush chargers sit within arm's reach. Leveraged correctly, each of these items provides a means for protection that anyone can use.

Take powders and creams, for example. You can use them to impair an attacker's vision by slinging them into an intruder's face, or you can alter grips and change the balance requirements on hard surfaces. A slip is the perfect opportunity for you to take advantage of an intruder and turn the table! Similarly, cords can be used to restrict movement, choke an attacker or be swung forcefully as an impact weapon. Once you get someone down for the count, tie them up with the same cord if you can.

Bathrooms afford you an opportunity to access small, sharp instruments like scissors or clippers. Use them to sever rope, tape or other soft binds that restrict your motion. Thanks to the small, solid layout, you can also leverage the walls by driving an attacker into hard, unforgiving tiled surfaces.

Kitchens tend to be slightly larger with an open area for cooking. Many feature cabinets filled with glass cups, dishware, eating utensils and pots and pans. You can use larger objects for striking, blocking or defending yourself. Woks, for example, make for exceptional shields that have built-in handholds. Additionally, kitchens are full of useful objects like knives, spice racks, countertop items, fruit bowls, appliances and toxic, flammable cleaners. When defending inside your kitchen, know where these weapons of opportunity reside. But keep in mind that the smaller the weapon, the closer you need to get to the target to be able to use it effectively.

Creativity is a must when it comes to weapons of opportunity. Think about what action you want to elicit, and then consider what tools you'll need to make that happen. A great example of creative thinking is a quick do-it-yourself torch. Combine a candle lighter with a spray-friendly flammable liquid such as cooking spray or disinfectant. Or, simply throw certain liquids into an attacker's eyes to create blindness and facial burning. I'll give you a tip that never fails: If your cleaner has a health hazard warning on it, use that knowledge to target your attacker. If the label cautions against getting the spray in the eyes, aim for the pupils. If it recommends wearing a breathing mask when in use, try to spritz it all around the assailant's face to make them sputter and cough.

Many common household items can become effective weapons once you shift your thinking. Aerosols can be sprayed to impair an attacker's vision and breathing, keys can be used to stab at the face and eyes, picture frames can be smashed for a sharp edge. But remember: Practice using these items ahead of time, and never pick a weapon you haven't practiced with beforehand, or you have just given another weapon to your attacker.

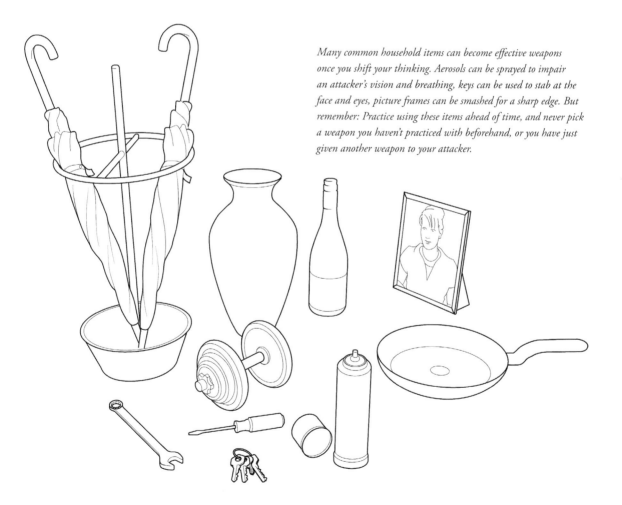

Use kitchen knives for slashing, stabbing and stopping threats. Target their throat, rib cage or the location of major arteries. When all else fails, stab whichever body part they give you. What I mean by that is if they punch you, slash at their hands. If they kick you, stab their feet, ankles or legs. Nothing is off-limits when your life is on the line. Take every moment and transform it into an opportunity to survive.

Hallways create narrow passages, a quality that makes them excellent for limiting the number of attackers who can confront you at a single time. Most halls feature large framed pictures of family or friends, often fitted with protective glass. Smash the covers to create quick edged weapons of defense. Use the shards to target major blood vessels such as the jugular vein (on the side of the neck), the femoral artery (on the inner thigh) or, if the shard is long enough, the lungs (via the soft under-arm area along the ribs). If you can, use a potholder, glove or piece of thick fabric such as denim torn from your jeans to hold the shard so that you don't cut yourself. Drive attackers' heads into walls, and use handheld objects to strike hands or faces. Also, remember that hallways lead to other rooms—quite literally opening doors to additional weapon locations.

CONVENTIONAL VERSUS UNCONVENTIONAL WEAPONS

There are two primary classes of weaponry: conventional weapons and unconventional weapons. Let's take a quick look at the definitions of each to better understand our options for defending during a home invasion.

Conventional weapons are items that are designed to be used for protective purposes. They include firearms such as pistols, rifles, shotguns and Tasers, as well as blades, clubs, maces, brass knuckles, pepper spray and localized explosives. Conventional weapons do not cause wide, large-scale destruction. They are usually small enough that they can easily be used by a single attacker for multiple strikes.

On the other hand, unconventional weapons are items that are not primarily designed to serve as offensive or fighting tools. However, under the right circumstances and wielded correctly, they can transform into useful tools for cutting, striking, bludgeoning and strangling.

Whenever I teach homeowners the best techniques to protect their property, I remind them that they are surrounded by unconventional weapons. A lot of times, people initially scoff at me, thinking that I'm a little bit off-kilter. But as soon as I start listing the kinds of unconventional weapons that everyone has in their living room, and kitchen, and bathroom, and bedroom, jaws hit the floor. No one thinks of the urn containing Grandma's ashes as a bludgeoning tool, but in a home invasion, that revered object could just save your life.

It takes a sneaky mind to see all the unconventional weapons that surround you. That's one of the reasons I constantly encourage people to think like a criminal when building their family action plan! But truly, weapons of opportunity are numerous, and they are located almost everywhere.

Go ahead and think like a bad guy as you survey the room you're sitting in right now. Take a good, long look at that wine bottle, and just imagine smashing it and brandishing the jagged edge at an intruder. Or maybe you're looking at your phone charger and thinking about how you could totally choke an attacker with it, if push came to shove. The more you think about it, the greater your arsenal becomes. Quite frankly, after reading this book, you'll have trouble looking at a home goods store the same way ever again.

That's the type of thinking you need in order to see unconventional weapons in everyday objects. Don't be afraid of thinking creatively and let your inhibitions fall away. Survivors thrive on creating good self-preservation strategies that work within their environments. Use that mentality to conduct a weapons assessment around your home.

From this point on, your mindset should be permanently changed in regards to how you look at everyday objects and the word "weapon." You should always have a minimum of three unconventional weapons available in every room or corridor of your home. More importantly, you need to know how to use each in order to protect yourself and those in your family.

One word of caution, though. Just like conventional weapons, unconventional weapons can be stolen by an attacker and used against you. I'll share some tips on how to hide your weapons all around the house later in this chapter. Prepare yourself with multiple options. As you think about ways to use weapons of opportunity as defensive and offensive tools, you should also be thinking about how you could block that same item should it get away from you.

WEAPON DYNAMICS

Every weapon you select must take three important considerations into account. If you don't think about these in advance, you'll pick the wrong tool from a bountiful arsenal. Please don't let that happen to you; it's like tripping at the finish line when all your competitors are half a lap behind.

First, you need to ask yourself what you're trying to accomplish. This is called determining physical solicitation. If you're just trying to hit and hurt the assailant, you might pick one weapon over another. But if you're trying to kill them and stop them dead in their tracks, then you need to choose more wisely.

Second, you need to determine how much distance needs to be maintained between you and your attacker. Every weapon will give you a certain specific distance from your threat. However, these vary wildly. For instance, a shard of glass requires you to be no further than one arm's length away from an attacker. A broom handle gives you up to four or five feet of distance, while a projectile can give you the length of an entire room. Blunt instruments tend to provide greater distance than edged weapons, though there are exceptions to this guideline. On the flip side, blunt instruments require greater physical strength, abilities and endurance.

Finally, you need to ensure you have the abilities required to successfully use whichever weapon you choose. Ensure that you have the emotional strength and mental conditioning to follow through with your physical actions. If you're elderly or frail, you'll probably want to lean toward a weapon that cuts or stabs instead of a bludgeoning tool. But for younger defenders, blunt objects are better because they increase the distance between you and the attacker. Weapons of opportunity are not one-size-fits-all tools.

You'll also want to verify that you have the right target in mind before using any weapon. Targeting a weak, lesser individual in the attacking team may not have as big an impact as taking down the leader. That said, it may still be beneficial to knock out the weaklings first so that you thin the pack. You have to make this decision based on the group you're facing. Similarly, think about the impact your actions will have on an individual. If you're going up against a tremendous figure with thick, tough muscles, you're going to need a lot more strength to do the same damage you'd easily cause to a thin, wiry assailant. You must scope out areas of soft tissue that you can hit with the amount of force needed to enact the desired reaction.

Weapons generally fit into a few main categories. These correlate with the damage or injury caused by the weapon. Note that many weapons fall into more than one category, depending on how they are used.

- **EDGED:** Weapons with a sharpened edge that are designed to lacerate or amputate flesh. Examples include knives, peelers, razors and thin sheet metal.

- **IMPALING:** Weapons that puncture or stab. These may be pointed objects designed for making holes or blunt items that are forcibly inserted into an enemy. Examples include pens, pencils, screwdrivers, forks, sticks and pointed furniture edges.

- **BLUDGEONING:** Weapons that cause massive trauma when slammed into an enemy. These impact weapons usually target the skull, neck or chest, but they can be used to break limbs or trigger pain points as well. Examples include heavy potted plants, statues, bookends, sturdy metal tea kettles, cast iron pans, Dutch oven pots and weights.

- **STRIKING:** Weapons that enable a defender to strike the enemy from a significant distance. Though less powerful than bludgeoning tools, these weapons have the advantage of creating greater distance between the defender and attacker. Examples include rakes, flags, ironing boards, curtain rods, canes and oars.

- **CONSTRICTION:** Weapons made from cords, twine, wire or rope that are used to restrict breathing or blood flow. Constriction weapons may induce strangulation, or they can be used to bind, pull or restrain assailants. Sharp wire can also be used to lacerate skin and muscle, while rough ropes and twine may be rapidly rubbed into the skin to create a stinging burn. Examples include cell phone chargers, audio-visual cables, garden twine, fishing line and dental floss.

- **SPRAY:** Weapons that emit a noxious or irritating mist when sprayed, splashed or dumped on an attacker. Examples including caustic cleaning solutions, battery acid, lemon juice (particularly when aimed at sensitive tissue such as the eyes or skin lacerations), toilet bowl cleaner and crushed or powdered glass.

- **PROJECTILE:** Weapons that initiate damage from a distance. Firearms fall into this category. Other examples include thrown rocks, glass pieces and sharp instruments like darts. Note that items can be combined to create a projectile weapon, such as rubber bands, Y-shaped sticks and rocks to make a slingshot, or PVC pipe with a rubber band and sharpened dowel to make a crude harpoon.

- **FLAME:** Weapons that burn an attacker's body and clothing. Examples include matches, lighters with aerosol cleaners and Molotov cocktails. Most flame effects are amplified with the use of a flammable agent such as gasoline, high-proof alcohol or aerosol solution.

- **ELECTRICAL:** Weapons that cause electric shock, disabling muscular responses. Examples include Tasers, exposed arc wires and broken lamps or appliances that complete a circuit when forced into contact with human skin.

Train with as many weapon categories as possible. Be ready to use any or all of them at a moment's notice. If you cannot use these valuable tools to protect yourself, then an intruder will use them to harm you and your family.

COMMON HOUSEHOLD WEAPONS

If I had a quarter for every time someone told me they didn't have any weapons in their house but then ate their words after I pointed out ten items in their living room alone, I'd be a rich man. The fact is, our homes are surrounded by weapons everywhere we look. Perhaps these aren't the types of weapons you see in action movies, like guns and shivs, but they are protective tools all the same.

Throughout this chapter, I'll list specific examples of room-by-room weapons that you can add to your defensive arsenal. Here, I'd like to share a few common classes of weapons that everyone has in their home. The goal is to get you thinking about the objects you have and the various ways they can be used to protect your life.

- **TOOLS:** Even if you're not the handiest person, everyone has a screwdriver or two lying around somewhere! Tools that make excellent weapons of opportunity include hammers, awls, drills, punches and wrenches. Tools can be hidden in nearly any drawer, nestled into the soil of a potted plant or even taped beneath furniture for easy access, no matter where you're defending. The use of each tool is governed by its attributes and purpose. For example, a screwdriver would be used to impale an attacker, while a wrench would be used for bludgeoning.

- **UTENSILS:** Utensils are items used for dining and food preparation purposes. Just about every American home uses forks, knives and spoons. Most of us also use specialized steak and bread knives, can openers, spatulas, ladles, tongs and peelers, to name just a few. I generally separate utensils into two categories: items that can double as edged weapons, and items that can double as impaling instruments. Nearly all utensils fit one or both of these categories. A few, such as meat mallets or old-fashioned ice cream scoops, can be used to bludgeon.

- **DECORATIONS:** Home décor is wide-ranging. Look at the types of decorations you have, and think about how to use each piece as a defensive weapon. For instance, hanging photos and paintings beneath glass covers create excellent edged weapons when smashed. Wooden frame pieces can also be transformed into edged or impaling instruments. Statues, vases, pots, bowls and lamps make for excellent bludgeoning tools. Cords from electronic décor (such as lamps, neon signs or candle warmers) may be used to strangle or bind enemies, while hot light bulbs can be smashed into an enemy's face while a device is still plugged in to burn, lacerate and possibly even electrocute him. Some decorations even hide secrets, such as bookends that lift to reveal spiked edges or hanging shields and replica weaponry that can be wielded in a pinch.

- **FURNITURE:** Use small pieces of furniture as bludgeoning tools as well as shields. They can be forced between a victim and assailant to set and maintain distance. Furniture that you assembled can be snapped into tools for stabbing or striking. Finally, you can also hurl certain pieces of furniture at enemies to induce chaos and potential injury. Avoid throwing anything that might be repurposed into a deadly weapon against you, however, and always be prepared to duck into a place that provides ample cover after tossing the piece.

- **EXPENDABLE SUPPLIES:** This class includes cleaning solutions, craft adhesives, construction supplies and beauty or hygiene products such as hair spray, powders and fragrances. It can also include aerosol food items such as cooking spray, acidic juices and spicy cooking liquids.

Just because you own a firearm does not necessarily mean that you will be able to use it during a home invasion. It could be locked in a different room, or it could simply be inaccessible due to an attacker standing in the way. Sometimes, it just isn't the best weapon to get the job done—and that's coming from someone who has used a gun to save his own life on quite a few occasions. That's why common household items are important even for armed homeowners.

I think about it like this: If I was on a range with three of the best shooters in the country, they could all fire faster and with better accuracy than me. But tactical strategy is where I might have an edge to beat them. It's not always about how fast you are, or about outshooting your adversary. It's about knowing the dynamics of a weapon and how to use it to safeguard, protect and engage. That's what will get you out of a home invasion faster. Yes, sometimes a gun or another conventional weapon is the best option. But in a lot of situations, an unconventional weapon is even more compatible with survival.

DISTANCE VERSUS MAXIMUM EFFECTIVENESS
Throughout the book, I reiterate the importance of distance between you and your attackers. Nowhere is this concept more important than when using a weapon.

Weapons are dangerous to all in the immediate vicinity. Pro-gun activists champion the point that "guns don't kill people, people kill people." This sentiment is entirely true, regardless of your stance on the Second Amendment. A weapon does not think, discriminate or act. In the hands of a human being, it performs a single lethal function regardless of who stands in the crosshairs.

Whenever any kind of weapon is used, the greatest danger exists for those who are targeted. Another person is putting their focused efforts into causing them harm, and it will result in some form of injury. But weapons can also backfire and strike the person using them. You can slip, or a freak incident can throw you off balance (such as an explosion, earthquake or even a honking car outside) and cause you to miss your opportunity. If you're not injured, someone else in the room with you might be hurt instead.

When brandishing a weapon, position yourself at least one arm's length away from your attacker. If they can lunge and grab your neck, you've lost the position of advantage. The easiest way to avoid that is staying out of their grasp. If a weapon requires you to get closer, such as an edged blade or an impaling instrument, stay back until you're ready to strike. Then, lunge quick and unexpectedly at your target, inflicting maximum damage in one or two hits. Immediately jump back as soon as you've completed your strike.

Even if your attacker appears incapacitated, don't trust that you're safe yet. I've seen Academy–Award winning performances from criminals who don't want to give up. They'll hold their breath, stop all bodily movements and wait until you let your guard down to spring up and take the weapon from you. Keep a few steps away with your weapon drawn until the police arrive. Let the trained professionals handle him from that point forward. If you see him moving or getting up, use a projectile weapon to knock him back down. Throw a book at his head if you have to. Don't lean in for any reason, as he could reach up and grab your hair, a necklace, your clothes or even the skin on your throat to pull you down in a heartbeat.

Physical distance is by far the most important factor when using a weapon. But you also need to establish an emotional distance between you and the people who want to take everything from your family. This reflects back to what we discussed earlier about overcoming limitations. If you're brandishing a weapon that could kill someone who wants to kill you, you absolutely must go through with what you're doing. Your feelings do not matter in that instant; your survival does. Separate your actions from your compassion, and focus solely on consequences.

If you do not act, you will die. If they take the weapon from you because you hesitated, you will die. If you try to act but cannot go through with it, you will die.

Think back to what I told you about following through with your plan no matter what. That's exactly where you're at in this instant. Put up that emotional distance and follow through. Get the deed done, and move on with your life intact. You will have time to process your actions and responses once you're safe.

Don't fall for pleas, displays of terror or bargaining. Just like you're trying to buy time throughout the defensive process, the now-defensive attacker is doing the same because the roles have flipped. He may be waiting for backup, or he might be trying to play off of your indecisive nature. He might simply be waiting for the police to show up so he can be arrested instead of dying.

But you can't get inside his head, and you need to assume the worst. Leverage the emotional distance to stay the course you set out when you built your family action plan. If you need a quick shot of fortitude, think of the most horrifying scenario: your spouse, children or loved ones laying in a morgue, their bodies cold and gray after being shot. Do what you need to do to keep that from happening, if nothing else.

You also need to consider the maximum effectiveness of weapons. Anything can hurt you; even a tiny notepad can give you one hell of a paper cut! In a home invasion, the key is wielding the selected weapon correctly so as to maximize its effectiveness while reducing its danger to you.

When swinging a long striking tool, such as a baseball bat, clutch your knuckles close and swing from your dominant side. I'm right-handed, so I would raise the tip of the instrument toward my right shoulder, twisting as far back as I can to maximize my power. Unlike a baseball game, however, I want to restrict the movement of the bat so that it doesn't strike a wall or other object by accident. Swing overhand if you must to make your target.

For a slashing instrument, grasp the handle or widest part as firmly as possible in the palm of your hand. Position your thumb at the end of the instrument to brace it in place. With the pointed end facing down, away from your face, dig into your enemy with downward strokes. Use your other hand to block when going in for a slash. After puncturing your attacker, quickly pull out as jaggedly and erratically as you can without dropping the weapon or letting it slip due to blood spatter. This will cause the most crippling damage, while a clean in-and-out motion loses out on some effectiveness.

Bludgeoning uses gravity for assistance. Lift the object with both hands and quickly bring it down on your target. I recommend going for the temples or back of the skull to render the person unconscious. You can also aim for the nose to trigger a pain overload. If necessary, strike the collarbone or chest as a backup option, though keep in mind that these areas are protected by strong bones and will be harder to injure.

To this aim, I recommend that stronger individuals trend toward bludgeoning and striking weapons, while weaker and frail individuals opt for edged weapons. This enables various demographics to select a weapon suited to their strengths and compatible with their shortcomings. We've all got them, and there's nothing to be embarrassed about. Know where you're weak, then prevent anyone from using those failings against you. That's all there is to it.

MAXIMIZING TARGET AREAS

Just like you need to maximize the effectiveness of your weapon, you also have to aim for the right target areas to make them work for you. This requires a basic understanding of human anatomy, specifically the circulatory system.

The center of the system is the heart, located left-of-center beneath the ribcage. This organ pumps blood throughout the body. When the heart stops and is not restarted via electrical or massage intervention within a short period of time, the individual will die. This vital organ connects with arteries and veins throughout the body and its extremities.

Those arteries in particular are major targets whenever you're using an edged or impaling weapon. They lead away from the heart, and as such, any wound will cause the injured to bleed out. In the neck, the carotid artery runs along the sides of the neck. It throbs when a person is under stress or physical duress. The carotid connects to the subclavian artery, which runs along the collarbone.

The arm contains the axillary arteries, which are lesser targets than the others due to their secondary nature. Wounds to these areas can be addressed with pressure via a tourniquet or by simply raising the arms to use gravity to slow some blood flow. Instead, consider targeting the femoral artery, located in the upper leg. It's much harder to stop blood loss at this location.

If you're not using a puncture weapon, look for opportunities to interrupt consciousness. Even if you are not able to knock someone out, you can make them dizzy, disoriented or confused with a strong blow to either temple, the side of the forehead next to the eyes. The weakest point of the human skull, a strong blow here can cause the brain to bounce and the lights to go out, so to speak. Alternatives include the top of the head as well as the solar plexus, located just below the ribcage.

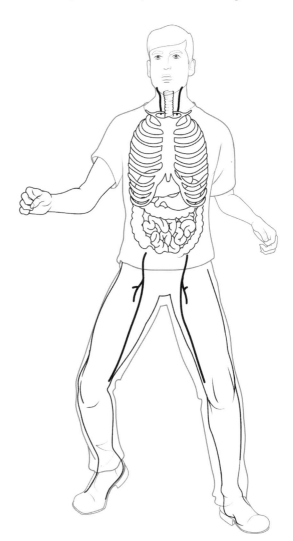

Remember to use HARD weapons on SOFT areas of the target, especially where important organs and veins are located such as the throat, eyes, gut, groin and inner thighs.

Generally speaking, the face is a good target. It contains a lot of nerves and crushable cartilage, making it an excellent space to land strikes, bludgeoning attacks and even lacerations. Sometimes, extreme bleeding from a broken nose, split lip or cut to the cheek can make an intruder panic, buying you time to plan your next strike. Additionally, the pain resulting from facial injuries tends to be quite extreme. Solid strikes to the jaw can also knock someone out, if landed correctly.

Think about what an attacker values during a home invasion. They need their wits about them, for sure, but they also cherish their ability to move freely. Targeting their legs with a well-placed defensive strike is a great option. Knees are particularly easy to knock out of alignment with a strong kick, punch or hit from a weapon. If you are hiding and an attacker walks near you, you can also try to slice behind their knees with your weapon to bring them down immediately. They will no longer be able to walk with this area out of commission, transforming them into an angry trapped rat.

Some self-defense experts rave about pressure points, but I find them to be really difficult to master. Instead of gambling with your life by trying a complex technique, go for the targets that will reap immediate returns. Make it simple, clean and effective with the fewest number of blows.

PLACING AND POSITIONING WEAPONS

The key to placing and positioning weapons is making sure that you always have something at hand to protect yourself in a home invasion. Everywhere you sit or stand in your home, you should be able to reach at least one life-saving tool. This includes the floor, since you may have fallen, crawled or been tied up. Maybe it's an object hidden in the soil of the potted plants near your front windows, or a knife buried among the ashes of your fireplace. It could be a wrench at the bottom of a garbage can, or a loose wire hung behind a family portrait on the wall. Put weapons in places where they won't be spotted when glanced at, but where you'll know they reside. If it doesn't draw attention, then it's a very successful placement.

My wife is an outstanding interior decorator, and she meticulously sets the dining room table every day. But she has a secret; the casual place settings don't include flatware flanking the plates and glasses. Why? Rolled up inside the napkins, she keeps a pair of sharp, metal chopsticks for each diner to use. No one knows about these unless they look in the napkins—making them perfect weapons of opportunity if a home invader was to break in.

A lot of homeowners ask me what to do if the criminal gets to their weapon before they do. It's a very real possibility. My biggest piece of advice on placing weapons is that you need to keep conventional weapons out of sight, but you can store unconventional weapons anywhere. If they can't see it, there's a good chance they won't fumble around trying to find it.

Prior to considering the next suggestion, please remember that state gun laws vary. Some states require you to keep weapons locked in a secure safe or locker at all times. I strongly recommend following your local laws at all times. Remember that you can easily adapt your strategy to accommodate legal requirements and provisions. That said, when possible, consider storing guns and knives in hollowed-out books. You can make these devices yourself, or you can buy them premade online. Store them around your house in a few different locations to provide access to multiple conventional weapons. Knives may also be tucked away inside plant pots for quick access from the floor, or even under couch cushions. I've even hidden them in opaque vases and decorative vessels.

Fire makes for a great unconventional weapon, though realize that it can have devastating consequences. Your home could be severely damaged or destroyed if your technique gets out of hand. However, if it can make the difference between surviving a home invasion or perishing at an intruder's hands, weigh your options accordingly knowing that you can always repair or rebuild a lost home. Matches and lighters are common household objects that don't seem out of place in most rooms. A spray can of aerosol room freshener next to a long-stemmed barbecue lighter doesn't draw a single glance when placed in a kitchen, bathroom or living room, but it makes a mean blazing torch. I've even seen people keep a decorative vase

Be smart and prepared: Place weapons throughout your home where you will need them. Shown here, the lamps, figurine and plant pot are good bludgeoning tools, the phone cord can be used for strangling and the letter opener is an excellent edge weapon. Can you think of other ways you could protect yourself in this room?

filled with marbles and—get this—lighter fluid instead of water. In a home invasion, they throw the vase at the attacker, soaking them in fluid before flinging a match or lit candle in their direction.

If you have a fireplace in your home, use it to your advantage. In my house, I keep two bookends that look like tribal masks on the mantle. But when you pull the mask off the mantle, its base is a sharp stake that can be used to jab or stab. Additionally, use the ashes and charcoal of a fireplace to hide weapons like knives. You can also repurpose the fire poker or ash rake as bludgeoning tools.

Have you seen those removable hooks that stick to any solid surface thanks to a strong adhesive? They are perfect for hiding weapons! Stick one or more on the inside of cabinet doors, drawers or just behind tall pieces of furniture such as entertainment stands. Hang a weapon on each. They're invisible to those who aren't looking closely in the shadows, and if you ever need to paint or move furniture, you can always remove the hook without damaging your items. No mess, no worries, just strong preparedness. You can even use them to create holsters underneath tables, countertops and furniture. Place non-edged weapons in these places for easy access when you're on the floor. The reason I don't recommend putting edged weapons here is because they can be jostled accidentally, cutting an innocent person.

Another great place to hide small weapons is the bathroom medicine cabinet. If you're faking a ruse based off an illness, a family member can beg to go get the medication, but emerge with a pocketed knife, screwdriver or other tool to fight back. The same goes for weapons tucked in the refrigerator.

Your pantry is a good place for convincing weapon storage. Buy a big can of tomatoes, ravioli or any other food that your family likes. Open the can from the bottom to enjoy your food. Then, wash the can thoroughly and file down any sharp edges on the bottom. Put it back in your pantry, but tuck a weapon inside. It'll be undetectable to anyone snooping around. Another great hiding spot is the inside of a toilet tank lid, as long as you carefully wrap the weapon in plastic bags first to prevent it from rusting or decaying.

Dedicated media rooms can be hard to defend. Take ownership of them by creating innovative weapon stores. Hollow out a portion of the wall and make a small cubby to hide a weapon or two. Place an outlet cover over it, but don't screw it in. Instead, attach it with some easily removable adhesive or tape. This gives you an opportunity to grab and pocket a blade without anyone seeing you take it, especially if you're tied up. In fact, there are even some kits available to turn a false outlet into a drawer that opens and closes! A similar hiding spot is the bottom or side of a speaker cabinet.

No matter where you place your weapons, make sure you can reach them from anywhere you need to defend. The more weapons you have stored in strategic locations, the better off you'll be if a home invasion happens to you.

UNCONVENTIONAL WEAPONS: CORDS, STRINGS AND ROPES

If you have a landline phone, you have one of the world's best corded weapons in your home already. I know it sounds weird, but thin, metal-based cords are far better than bulky ropes, twines and other string-like instruments in the house. They are strong, flexible and easy to maneuver, not to mention numerous. Look around your room right now—I'll bet you can find at least two of these within arm's reach. Charging devices, corded phone wires, Ethernet cables, power cords, appliance plugs; they're everywhere! Even dental floss functions as an exceptional corded weapon. Wind out an arm's length of floss, then fold it in half, wrapping each end around your hands. This is a perfect, strong choking instrument.

If you are using a bulkier rope, there are a few techniques that you can employ to improve your odds of disabling the attacker. Use a slipknot to drape the rope over his neck, then pull tightly. You can use this as a choking mechanism by continuing to pull, or you can utilize the distraction it provides to escape. Another technique involves standing behind the attacker, wrapping the rope around both hands, laying it across the attacker's throat and crossing your arms before pulling, adding significant strength. Tie a few half-hitch knots in the rope to add pressure on the larynx, helping it to crush the soft cartilage of the throat or Adam's apple. This will restrict both blood and airflow, incapacitating the assailant.

If the strength to strangle someone eludes you, do not despair—there are other ways to make rope-based weapons work. Transform a cord into a lacerating device, almost like a swinging medieval mace. Securely tie something sharp on one end of the cord, then swing it in a figure eight toward the attacker. This will cut at their skin and keep distance between you and them. Avoid using heavy objects like paperweights or staplers, as these require significant arm strength to use effectively. The heavier the swinging weight, the more effort will be required on your part.

The U.S. Department of Defense has published guidelines for soldiers using rope and cords to defend themselves. The following tips come from Field Manual FM 21-150 Combatives, published in 1992. The manual has since removed this section, but the techniques are relevant to citizens looking to protect themselves with unconventional weapons.[40]

These approaches require three feet of rope or string. You can use a belt, shoelaces, a necktie or a winter scarf twisted to make a rope-like structure. Hold the cord at both ends, pulling it taut to make a stick-like weapon that you can strike with. Alternatively, keep the center slack, raise it to meet your opponent's body and repeatedly snap it tight to strike soft tissue like the throat or key joints such as the elbow. Hit until he stumbles or falls. You can use these same techniques to disarm or redirect a lunging attacker, then strangle him with a second movement to the neck.

Ropes aren't just for strangling, bludgeoning or striking. You can also use them to trip attackers. This is a great technique for children who may not have the emotional fortitude to directly injure someone with a weapon. In your family action plan, have two children kneel on either side of a doorway. Each should hold one end of a jump rope, shoelace or cable. Teach them to wrap the rope around their hands or mid-sections, leaving enough slack for the center of the cord to lie across the floor. Keep it loose on the floor until the approaching attacker is one step away from the door frame. Then, quietly pull it tight and let him stumble or fall. While he's down, another family member should use a bludgeoning tool to render him unconscious.

Lastly, you can use ropes and cords to set traps around your house as soon as you're aware of an attack. Tie doorknobs together to trap assailants in rooms. You can also tie some floss or fine thread to an object on top of your refrigerator. Then, loop the floss onto the refrigerator handle. If a hungry attacker opens the door, it'll pull the object down onto his head. At the least, it will startle him and buy you a moment to act. It could even knock him out.

UNCONVENTIONAL WEAPONS: EDGED OBJECTS

Edged objects, by their very nature, make for fantastic unconventional weapons. There's a reason your mother always yelled at you to stay away from broken glass and sharp knives: They can do major damage! Lacerations expose many nerves housed in the skin, causing searing pain. In addition to inflicting a lot of discomfort, they also draw blood and cause chaos. From a home invasion survival standpoint, edged weapons are a really good option for most defenders, though bear in mind that their short distance is not always ideal.

Anything with a thin point or razor-like edge can be wielded as an edged weapon. From a wire coat hanger to a bathroom mirror shard to a lamp base with a thin metal rim, there are potential edged weapons everywhere in your home. Right next to my front doorway, I've placed a large portrait of my family on the wall. My wife and kids are my pride and joy, and it's a blessing to see their faces every time I come home. But the picture serves a dual purpose.

You see, the frame is of really good quality, and the thick glass it holds would shatter into large, sharp shards with a quick strike to the center of the picture. Those shards are excellent edged weapons that I could produce by myself in a matter of seconds, all while defending at the door. Just remember that when using anything sharp, be it a glass shard, knife or other weapon of opportunity, you will be at risk of getting cut and injured yourself. If using shards, I recommend holding the center of the piece between your index finger and thumb, resting the flat, dull surface against your palm if possible.

This isn't the only weapon of opportunity I store in that area. Inside a large, five-gallon decorative bucket, I keep a collection of walking sticks. We'll use all of these when we go out for family hikes. That is, all except one, which has a distinct blue handle. That's because this particular walking stick is actually a long blade in disguise. By ripping off the protective cover, I suddenly have a long, sword-like instrument available to me—and the best part is, attackers have no idea about its hidden purpose. In the same bucket, I keep a pronged trident for picking up litter on my front lawn. The tips are protected with rubber caps. However, if I push hard enough, the sharp metal points rip through the rubber and become a formidable weapon. At a glance, it looks like just another walking stick.

I frequently recommend using wine glasses in home invasion situations. Simply hold the glass by its slender stem, then strike the top portion of the vessel against a table, countertop or wall. The goal is to maintain the stem for added distance while creating a sharp tube of glass that you can thrust into an attacker's face. Good china and crystal are excellent options for when you need to defend within the dining room.

In living rooms, studies and family rooms, look to fragile ornaments hung on walls or displayed on shelves. These objects create sharp pieces when cracked. Position these types of objects throughout your house—entranceways, exits, large rooms, bathrooms, bedrooms, hallways—to ensure you always have something sharp at your disposal.

Home offices have letter openers, scissors and even computer equipment. Basement gyms have removable bars and pins that hold equipment together. Kitchen drawers are filled with knives, peelers and preparation gadgets that are inherently sharp, as well as smashable casserole dishes, glass pitchers and serving plates.

Everyday tools and utensils aren't the only sharp items that can function as bladed weapons. Do you have baseboard hot water heating in your home? Recently, I went to clean my hot water pipes before the cool weather caused the furnace to turn on. As I went to lift the cap, I sliced open my finger and caused a bloody mess. Those pieces are incredibly sharp, and with a swift kick, they detach from the wall. Better yet, they also offer significant distance between you and the attacker.

When conducting assessments, I often tell those with children to put their parental caps on. Think about all the different items you disposed of, hid or placed out of reach so your children wouldn't get hurt when they were young. A lot of these qualify as edged weapons that could prove extremely useful in an attack. For parents who double as weekend warriors, I tell them to think about something around the house that inadvertently sliced them open at some point or another. Those memories stick!

UNCONVENTIONAL WEAPONS: BLUNT INSTRUMENTS

Of the unconventional household weapons discussed in this book, blunt instruments are quite possibly the most common and versatile. That's a great thing for you as a protective homeowner!

The kitchen is a treasure trove of these types of tools. One of my personal favorites is the paper towel holder, which few people see as threatening. However, freestanding holders have heavy bases that keep them from tipping over, as well as long handle-like rods to maintain distance.

Another great blunt instrument from the kitchen is the coffee maker. A lot of models have one or more sharp edges that can be jammed into soft tissue for added power. If you have hot coffee already brewing, swing the carafe into your attacker's face, then finish your move by dumping hot liquid on him. This two-for-one defensive maneuver will send just about anyone reeling backward.

Family and living rooms are chock full of blunt instruments. Coffee table books are usually heavy, hardcover volumes that can be quickly accessed and swung into an unsuspecting nose or throat. Video game systems are also excellent bludgeoning weapons, and their controllers can be swung around for distance-conscious attacks. Any similarly sized objects will work, especially crystal picture frames, metal lamp bases, magazine holders and candy dishes.

Bedrooms are a bit weaker when it comes to blunt objects, but they're not entirely absent from the scene. Besides wall décor, look at removable under-bed drawers that can be picked up and swung around. Jewelry boxes and bulky vacation mementos are good options. If your bed knobs twist off the frame, they can be used as heavy bludgeoning tools, too.

Laptops and tablet computers are great blunt weapons of opportunity as well. A lot of people keep them in their bedrooms at night. Due to their sensitive electronic equipment, they tend to maintain some heft. However, modern equipment is designed with ergonomics and portability in mind, which yields a near-perfect blunt weapon that balances usability and maximum effectiveness in one convenient object.

In your bathroom, use any personal supplies or equipment to double as a blunt weapon. A great option is the heavy top of a porcelain toilet, the piece that you remove to toggle the plumbing components. Swinging this into an assailant's upper abdomen is a surefire way to knock the wind out of him. You can also slam it down onto his neck, across his knee or into his groin.

Some blunt instruments have other helpful features built in. In a pinch, a hot hair curling iron or straightener can cause significant burns. Let the device heat for a few minutes before unplugging it and aiming for your attacker's hands. This will make it harder for them to use weapons, bind you or strike you, and it will slow down all of their efforts. You can also jam the hot iron into his neck, face or groin to elicit an extreme pain response.

Garages and storage areas are rich in blunt instruments that may be leveraged as weapons of opportunity. Old, half-full paint cans can be swung at arm's length or tied to cable or rope to make a heavy swinging weapon. Rechargeable tool batteries are also good to use for this purpose. Pipe fragments, old light fixtures and other half-completed projects are easily transformed into weapons of opportunity when necessary.

CREATE AN EFFICIENT, LIFE-SAVING WEAPON OF OPPORTUNITY

Necessity is the mother of invention, they say, and this quote applies to home invasion survival techniques. In this section, I'll provide tips on a few weapons of opportunity that you can make during a home invasion. My intent here isn't to say that you'll create each of these tools, it's to provide inspiration. Look around you and see what materials you have. For instance, a socket wrench and a piece of twine are useless as weapons on their own. But if you tied the twine to the wrench and swung it around, they'd make a formidable weapon that could be swung into an attacker's face. This focus on an item's potential, or its potential when combined with other items, can have a big impact on your survival. Don't be afraid to think creatively when it comes to home invasions!

These are some ultraeffective weapons of opportunity that you can quickly throw together in a home invasion situation to save your life and protect those around you. Remember that you can substitute materials based on what room you find yourself in.

The first technique is a homemade cowl that restricts breathing and irritates the face and eyes. Grab a pillowcase or garbage bag. Fill it with any sort of fine inedible powder you have on hand. Great examples include cosmetic powder, baby powder or talcum. Dump copious amounts into the bag or pillowcase, then sneak up on your attacker and thrust it over his head, cinching the open end tightly so that he is forced to breathe in the powdery material. These options will all dry out the moisture in his nose, mouth and throat, leading to choking and vomiting.

Take this a step further by using smashed, pulverized glass. Place your bag or pillowcase on the floor and fill it with delicate glass objects, such as light bulbs, trinkets or Christmas ornaments. Avoid heavier objects like drinking glasses and vases that make a loud noise when shattered. Once your glass objects are inside, gently crush them with a shoe until they form a shard-laden powder. Yank the pillowcase over the attackers head, or simply fling the glass dust into his face and eyes. This abrasive material will impact vision, irritate the respiratory system and can also cut the face. It also sticks to fingers and clothes, creating a lasting irritant.

Do you have indoor plants that use thin wooden stakes for support? A lot of people do, myself included. Rather than using blunt dowels to hold up the stems, take these wooden supports and sharpen them to a fine point in a pencil sharpener first. Then, place the sharp point into the soil. No one will know that these tools double as weapons, and you'll have a great spear-like object at the ready whenever you need it.

Homemade pepper spray is a great item to keep prepared, and you can put it in any pump spray container. Store one in every bedside table! Just mix a container of hot pepper flakes, rubbing alcohol and baby oil in a blender. Then, pour the liquid through a fine cloth to strain out the flakes. Shake the solution every few days to keep it from separating in the mister bottle. An added benefit is that it won't create as large a noxious cloud as professionally made sprays.

If you've seen a lot of adventure movies, chances are that you're familiar with bullwhips. These leathery rope-like instruments issue a loud crack when swung through the air, and they can strike enemies, incapacitate them and bind them. Though it won't be as dramatic, a homemade whip can be crafted from a few electric cords. Knot them together, and then braid them until the whip is approximately eight feet long. Then, knot them again. Swing your whip to maintain distance and inflict stinging pain upon attackers.

Combine the sharpness of an edged weapon with the distance and blunt force of a bludgeoning tool by assembling a crude axe. Take any pole you have handy—shower rods and curtain rods work perfectly—and a glass shard from a broken mirror or picture frame. Using tape, shoelaces or even chewing gum, fasten the shard perpendicular to the pole with the sharpest section facing out. This doesn't have to be the strongest axe. In fact, one swing that embeds the glass in an attacker's throat or chest makes your crude crafting efforts worthwhile. Plus, the materials can be readily found in just about any room of your home.

PRACTICE EXERCISE 9: ARM AND L.E.G.

Weaponry is pretty easy to talk about, but it can be harder to actuate in your home environment. When you look at a beautiful engraved plaque on your mantle, you might think about the occasion it commemorates—not the heavy item's potential as a life-saving bludgeoning instrument. Break past those preconceived notions and life-obstructing mental barriers with this simple training exercise.

Have a family member sit with their eyes closed. Take an object from somewhere in your house and place it in front of them. Instruct them to open their eyes and analyze the item using the List, Exhibit and Gauge (L.E.G.) arming technique.

First, the family member should *list* the key weaponry attributes: the type of weapon, its potential, its consequences and its distance tradeoff. Next, the participants should *exhibit* how to use the weapon in a manner that keeps them safe and in control. Critique their technique as required. Finally, have the participant *gauge* which family members could easily use the weapon and which would struggle with it. This may include physical, mental or emotional limitations.

Switch roles to get multiple points of view. Review at least a dozen objects that are currently out around your home. Explore a variety of different items for the exercise, and open your mind to creative uses that another family member might suggest. The more information you have available to make a sound tactical decision, the better off you'll be when fighting off a home invader.

Create a journal entry after each L.E.G. session to remember the objects you looked at, your findings and any recommendations for better stocking the home with weapons of opportunity. As with your other entries and notes, keep a copy in your dossier.

10

END THE INVASION

Melissa Burke is a county marshal administrator. When a group of home invaders attacked her Fairburn, Georgia, home on January 4, 2013, she knew what to do.

Melissa immediately called 911 and relayed her situation to the authorities. She then took to the nearest hiding place, a closet, to await rescue.

The attackers made it to her first, shooting her fourteen times. But Melissa survived, and thanks to the quick response of the authorities, the attackers fled before they could kill her.

Melissa later recounted the terrifying incident to the police. With input from her and her neighbors, the authorities were able to pursue and track down the car they had stolen to get away from the scene. Though the attackers remain at large, Melissa survived the ordeal and has since regained the ability to walk following a lengthy recovery.[41, 42]

ENDING ON YOUR TERMS

In my professional coaching and training travels, I've come across a lot of emergency response plans that can be summed up in three words: Call for help. I constantly tell people that if their plan for surviving is calling someone else for help, they've already lost!

It sounds harsh, but that's the truth when it comes to home invasions. Emergency responders play a critical role in your survival and escape, yes, but they cannot be your only line of defense. If your only plan is to call for help, that means you were not prepared! They need to be the relief hitters that step in after you've given the situation everything you've got.

Think about it. In mere seconds, attackers gain access to your home by inviting themselves in or by forcing an entry. Without regard for your safety, they snatch accountability for everyone in the house. Either they roam through every room and drag occupants to a central location, or they make threats until the unprepared surrender. They work diligently to separate adults from children. They may ask questions to try to figure out your strategy, working to sink your family action plan before it gets thrown into motion. If you're trying to survive, your responses to all these tasks have to be realistic in order to buy time and opportunities. You've got to have all the right answers ready to go.

Ending an invasion is not wildly different. In fact, in a lot of ways, it echoes the start. The key difference is positioning. You'll no longer be in a defensive, reactive posture; you'll be protecting and holding the controlling position. The attackers made a conscious decision to target you. But after taking control over the attack, you make the decision about ending the engagement.

I've mentioned that real life defensive situations are not like what you've seen in the movies. This can be said about ending attacks as well. In the media, you may see a victorious defender maim, kill or exact just revenge on someone who has terrorized his or her family. They may use phrases such as "getting a taste of their own medicine" or "seeing how they like it." But in real life, this isn't just unsafe, it's possible grounds for a lawsuit against you. It sounds crazy, but once the clear and immediate danger subsides, any harm you induce can come back and haunt you in court.

Do you remember how I coached you on looking for opportunities to take the controlling position? Well, guess what the subdued attackers are doing at the same instant that you're plotting revenge? That's right: They're formulating a plan to overtake you again. Don't waste your efforts on a last-minute failure. Use every second to end the engagement safely and completely.

Just like your gut tells you when it's time to engage, you'll know inside when it's time for you to end the home invasion. Maybe you've taken down two out of three attackers and you've just landed a sucker punch to the gut on the third. Or, perhaps you and your family have regrouped in a neighbor's house and the danger to your life is over. Ending on your terms can even occur when you're in hiding and snag a few seconds to call the police.

It all comes down to a fine balance between tactical execution of your family action plan and a fleeting moment of opportunity. When the scales balance, don't waste time thinking about petty vengeance or regrets; end things firmly and immediately.

FINDING SAFETY

Staying calm during chaos is critical. Sometimes, you don't get that perfect opportune moment to end an engagement on your terms, and instead, you need to force your way to safety to draw the encounter to a close. I don't think this is a poor choice; in most situations, I actually think it's quite smart! Getting out is your number one priority.

In the context of a home invasion, safety is any place that the attackers cannot or reasonably will not be able to harm you. It's not the same as concealment or cover, which serve as temporary cloaking techniques. Simply getting outside of the assaulted home is the first moment of safety that most home invasion victims find. Remember that your odds of surviving increase the further away you go, so don't stop on your stoop or porch because it's on the other side of your front door. Keep going. You're out of the house, but you're not yet out of danger.

Some individuals are able to get their family into the car and drive off, though be aware that the noise from slamming doors and a starting engine is not always helpful. There's also a period when you become easy motionless targets while waiting for the car to start and then backing out of the driveway. If you can minimize this time, you will be better off.

The best nearby safe place is a neighbor's house. While creating a family action plan, think ahead to a safe location where you can go request assistance. Avoid selecting someone directly next door to your property as the intruders could follow you. Make standing arrangements with several of the neighbors on your street, and be sure to introduce your children to them as well. You want to be able to trust these individuals to shelter you after you've escaped a home invasion. Swap escape route plans and offer your home as their rendezvous point if they pledge the same in return.

While building your family action plan, designate three or four rendezvous locations. Decide why you might use each during a home invasion. For instance, if there is a location that is more suitable for home invasions

When planning escape routes, make sure you don't just know how to get out, but also where to go! And further, when escaping, always put barriers between you and the attackers' line of sight and the weapons they use.

that happen in the middle of the night, discuss this with your family. Set one location as the default location where family members should plan to go unless the circumstances prevent it. This fallback should be the best, most convenient location of the group, and it should be the place where the family would regroup in 90 percent of escape situations.

Additionally, create a code to quickly alert your family to the precise rendezvous location while you're running away. The easiest is to assign nicknames to every neighborhood house on the street. These shouldn't include the homeowners' names or address numbers,

as home invaders may overhear the plan and act upon it. Colors are a great option, as are adjectives associated with the people who live in each house. For example, if you have a neighbor with a very friendly demeanor, their code word might be "happy." In the event that the family leader whispers or yells out "happy!" during the escape, everyone knows to meet at that person's house. You will need to make the decision of which safe location to use on the fly, looking for cars in the driveway, lights on throughout the house and the blue glow of electronic devices leaking out from behind curtains. Send at least one family member to a rear or side door to knock, just in case knocking at the front door is not heard.

Escaping to safety sometimes doesn't go as planned. If you're fleeing with the attackers in hot pursuit, break a neighbor's house or car window to set off their security alarm—this will trigger a police response even before you can call for help. As you run, select a curvy path that takes you through shrubbery, around dark corners and even over fences to lose the assailants bearing down on you. Fling garbage cans to cover the path behind you with debris. Scream and shout while you run to draw attention to your survival plight, using short key phrases such as "Help, call the police," and "Don't hurt me." These cries for assistance will not be ignored by anyone who hears them.

If you live in a city or a bustling downtown area, safety can even be found in the middle of a crowd. Most attackers are not ready to take on dozens of opponents. Watching their victims run into a huge sea of people is a major deterrent. Crowds will also give you the ability to blend in while you call the authorities. Just be sure to plan for escapes that occur during the busiest times of day as well as moments when the surroundings are not as busy. The last thing you want to do is rush outside hoping for a crowd only to find a ghost town.

OPTIMAL TELEPHONE BEHAVIORS

Getting to safety is your first priority. Your second priority must be getting professional support from your local emergency services department. Even though you will want to comfort and calm your family, this has to take a backseat to initiating a police response. There will be time to debrief and process the day's events soon.

Calling for help is most commonly achieved via a telephone call placed directly to the authorities. Remember that landlines can be cut, and cell phones can be jammed. To combat interruptions of service, use phones as quickly as you can. Immediately call 911 once you are secure. Keep your answers short, brief and to the point, as I recommended earlier. Remain calm, even if the threat persists back in your home. Listen closely to the operator's questions and only answer the questions they ask to speed up dispatch procedures.

The most common mistake when calling authorities is not knowing what to say. Traumatic situations cause people to act irrationally despite their best efforts to remain calm and collected. Rambling is a common side effect. Practice your conversations in advance. Work on keeping answers as concise as feasible. Do not give information unless it's requested, and be sure that your name and address are disclosed immediately so that dispatch can get units to your location. All other information is optional. If you cannot remember secondary details, or if you are not able to speak cohesively, you can hang up on the operator and wait for the police to arrive. They are trained to work with victims and survivors, and they will not take offense.

Sometimes, people pick up the phone after getting out of a home invasion situation only to launch right into their story. They'll even forget to tell the operator their name and location! This does not help you, and it only continues to delay the response time. Force yourself to take a deep breath and rehearse what you need to say. Position the phone's microphone several inches away from your mouth to avoid muffling sound.

What about children? Coach them to be experts at calling for help. This is a fantastic task that they can master without stretching their emotional maturity levels. While practicing, stand outside the room so you cannot see any head nods or shakes, as these nonverbal communication is useless when dialing for emergency assistance, and children need to learn this crucial fact. Additionally, if your area uses 911 for its emergency number, refer to it as "nine-one-one." Calling it "nine-eleven" can confuse children who will look for an eleven key on the phone when trying to dial. That could derail the entire call for help. If they're having difficulty getting the full script into their heads, teach them to say three basic things: their name, their address and the phrase "I need help." Most operators are trained to send immediate police support upon hearing a child say that phrase.

If using a phone does not work, there are other ways for people to get the attention of the authorities, such as tripping their own security system and giving the wrong code word when the operator calls. A lot of elderly people wear wireless medical pendants to get medical help to their locations as quickly as possible. If your smoke detectors are connected to your security system, light a match, candle or cigarette next to the detector and let it call for you. Requesting assistance could also mean flicking on a certain light to alert the neighbors or sending up another distress signal, as long as you rehearsed this during your family action plan development.

After the police have been called, contact one local family member or friend and tell them the situation. They may want to come to be with you, or they may request that you spend the night with them. In either case, tell them you will take them up on any offers after the police clear the scene. It may help soothe your mind to know that a short-term solution is ready to go once the investigation wraps up for the day or evening.

EMERGENCY RESPONDER DIALOGUE POINTERS

Let's dive a little deeper into the actual dialogue you should employ while talking to an emergency responder. I've listed the primary questions that you're likely to hear, along with good responses in bulleted lists beneath each. Build these answers into your rehearsed preprogrammed response to ensure they're never far from the tip of your tongue.

"911 operator. Is this an emergency?"

State your problem and your need for help in one or two short sentences. Keep it brief. By default, the operator will send police response units and Emergency Medical Services. Listen closely to their questions and be as direct as possible when answering them.

After confirming that the situation is an emergency, the operator will say,

"Tell me what is happening."

Example responses to this question include:

- One or more armed people broke into our home. Please send help.

- We have people inside our home and we need help.
- I just escaped from a home invasion, but my wife and son are still inside.
- My family just escaped from a home invasion. I've been shot in the leg.

"Where are you located?"

A simple address works perfectly. If your house has another identifier, such as being located on the corner with a cross street, you can use this to speed up reaction times. Even in the 2010s, with GPS technology and smartphone maps available just about everywhere, I've heard stories about emergency responders having difficulty finding private roads, hard-to-find streets and little-used byways. If you live on a street like this, relay simple instructions on how to find the location.

Example responses include:

- 555 Sycamore Lane.
- 555 Sycamore Lane, right at the corner with Oak Street.
- 555 Sycamore Lane, the blue house with two silver cars in the driveway.
- 555 Sycamore Lane. We're a private driveway right off of Oak Street, near the intersection with Maple Boulevard. Turn at the yellow hydrant on Oak.

"What is your name?"

This question is simple. Provide your first and last name. Two words, no more and no less.

"Help is on the way. Are you and your family all right? Were you hurt?"

At this point in the conversation, you can hang up at any time. Remember that staying on the phone is only a good thing when you are no longer in danger. Only answer these questions if you are in a safe place and feeling up to it. Traumatic events can cause partial memory lapses or difficulty speaking, and operators are trained to understand this. If you cannot speak, excuse yourself and reiterate the need to send help right away.

If the operator asks for additional details, provide responses such as the following:

- We are safe at the neighbor's house, with everyone accounted for. No one was injured.
- I'm still inside, but I saw my wife and kids get out and run down the block. I don't think anyone's been hurt. Please send help.
- My son has a cut across his face, and my daughter is limping. I think she has a broken leg. Send an ambulance, please.
- I'm having a lot of trouble speaking, but send help quickly. It's urgent.

They may also ask: *"Are the attackers armed?"*

This question helps provide vital safety information to the responding officers. Tell the operator if the attackers were armed and with what kind of weaponry. Even if it wasn't used against you but you saw it on their person, quickly relay this to the operator. Do not be afraid to say what the weapon looks like if you are unsure about its exact identity. You can state that it looks like a knife, or a handgun, or a rifle.

"Are the attackers still in the home?"

You have three options when answering this question. Keep your answers brief, as the police will assess the situation when they arrive.

- Yes.
- No.
- I'm not sure.

"Can you describe what your attackers looked like?"

- I am six feet two inches tall and they appear smaller than me.
- One is walking with a limp in his right leg.

This is where you should use your observation skills to begin describing your attacker. Remember that emergency calls are recorded, and this description may be used to corroborate the story that you share during the police interview. It's a good way to increase testimony against your attackers as well.

List the number of attackers and any key defining characteristics. For an emergency services call, keep this brief. The operator may ask a number of prompts to get information. Use your own build and body as a comparison. Some examples of prompts and responses follow:

"How many attackers are there?"

- I believe there are two or three men.
- I only heard one.
- I'm really not sure. It sounds like more than one, though.

"Can you tell me anything else?"

- One called another by the name Mike.
- They looked like they know what they are doing. They are organized.
- I heard an accent. It doesn't sound like they are from the United States.
- I heard one speaking with a stutter.
- I smelled a strong odor of whiskey on one man's breath.
- One has a tattoo of a spider on his neck near his left ear.
- One is missing his middle finger on his right hand.

"How did the attackers get into the home?"

- They entered through the rear window.
- The man pushed his way in through the front door.
- I don't know, but there was a lot of broken glass in the living room.

Give a short overview. Did you defend at the door, or was it a forced entry through another window or entrance? If you discovered them inside and don't know how they entered the property, simply tell the operator that you do not know. However, if you noticed a specific break-in point, every little piece of information is valuable, no matter how minor you feel it may be.

"Is there anything else you can remember at this time?"

• No, that's all I can remember.
• Actually, there was something else…

Avoid rambling. Only tell pertinent information at this juncture. For example, if you heard the assailants talking about not giving up or forcing a suicide by cop, lighting the house on fire, causing an explosion, booby-trapping the doors or performing other malicious acts that could injure the police, repeat these overheard plans to the operator. The police responders may alter their tactics to evade any such traps.

If you don't have anything to add, you can say no and hang up. Otherwise, follow the operator's lead.

To practice, try scripting and rehearsing a mock report. Have each member of your family report the mock home invasion by pretending to call emergency services and repeating their part of the script. All kids should practice telling their first and last names, address and parents' names as well as how to answer basic questions an operator might ask. Teach them to not be afraid or shy. Scripting as much of this as possible will ensure that each family member has something to say based on what they can remember, say or answer. It will keep reporting aligned with their individual abilities. The better the information received, the easier the police responders' jobs will be.

At this point, the police will be on their way to save you.

HELPING THE POLICE TO RESCUE YOU

The authorities will do everything in their power to safely end a home invasion. Their goal is to get to your house in time, stop the attackers peacefully, subdue them and arrest them. They will also strive to attend the family's pressing treatment needs and provide assistance with retrieving stolen belongings.

There are certain steps you can take to assist the police with ending and processing your home invasion. I've split these steps into three categories: before, during and after a home invasion. Just like surviving thanks to a family action plan, helping the police starts long before an attack occurs.

As soon as you finish this book, research neighborhood watch programs in your area. If one doesn't exist, look into starting one for your block, street or neighborhood. Neighborhood watches connect you with those in your community, bringing like-minded neighbors together. You get to learn about the families living near you, as well as the types of vehicles they drive, and perhaps when they're hosting parties or unfamiliar holiday visitors.

In addition to the watch, begin regular walks of your neighborhood. These can be quick, fifteen minute strolls after dinner. Look for anything that seems out of the ordinary, and investigate or report findings as necessary. If others wish to join you, encourage them to do so. Not only is walking a healthy way to maintain stamina and physical readiness, but it's also a great social event that connects you to the happenings in your neighborhood.

Modern police forces rely on community-oriented policing to fulfill their duties. Officers want the neighborhood to know them by name. This allows them to better protect the citizens in their town, and it also encourages improved open communication. If you see a police officer patrolling in a squad car, riding a motorcycle or simply walking his or her beat in your neighborhood, introduce yourself and thank them for keeping you safe. Start a positive, healthy dialogue that will help them better understand your interests in the local community. This friendship can blossom into a productive partnership that keeps home invasions and crime down thanks to improved vigilance and cooperation.

After the home invasion wraps, remember that the police investigation is just beginning. Do not touch anything in the house, and do not search for what was taken. Instead, stay put in one area. Confirm that everyone is safe and unharmed. Wait to shower or clean up the house until after the scene is processed. Call the police to update them on your status at any time.

Upon arrival, police will case the perimeter of the property and structure. They will then enter and confirm your identity before initiating a dialogue. Keep calm and slowly answer any questions asked. After this point, you and your family will be asked to surrender yourselves to assist with the investigation.

Let me be very clear: You are not in trouble! At this stage, you, your family and your home have become crime scenes. Police need to collect as much physical and mental evidence as they can in order to catch the criminals. They will treat you with dignity, but be prepared to answer a lot of questions and possibly undergo examinations for DNA evidence left behind, such as hair samples, blood or saliva. The forensics team will examine each room and collect phone records, surveillance tapes and other evidence. They may also canvas the neighborhood and talk to others to collect scattered puzzle pieces about the perpetrators' motives and identities.

You might work with a police officer who has a bad attitude or a poor outlook. Remember that these hard-working officers are people, too. He or she might be dealing with family issues or other personal troubles. But once they step onto your property to help you, they will treat your case like it's the number one priority in their life, even if their demeanor is a bit rough. As someone who trains police forces around the country, I promise you that my brothers and sisters in blue will take good care of you and your family. Be patient with them, follow their directions and let them assist. They will not take your case lightly. It could have been their home that was targeted, after all. They want justice and resolution as much as you do.

WHAT TO SAY DURING A POLICE INTERVIEW

As soon as the police arrive, it's important to follow their directions. Let the police tell you what to do. Though it may be uncomfortable and unfamiliar, the process is carefully designed to extract the best information possible to nab the suspects and put them away for a long, long time. Just because a former attacker is bleeding on the floor doesn't automatically mean that they're going to be arrested. The police will need to gather enough facts and evidence to prove his guilt.

Before the interview, emergency medical technicians will conduct a quick medical check on all survivors, including injured assailants. If injuries are severe, you may be transported to the hospital. An officer will be assigned to monitor you and ask questions after you've been treated.

Once any minor injuries are patched up, the investigators will begin collecting physical evidence from you and your family members. This includes materials from your person, such as hair and nail samples to source DNA. They may ask you to change your clothes and shoes in order to process the outfit you were wearing. If you endured injuries, these will be fully documented as well to determine if they were inflicted by weapons or the home invader's hands.

THE SEQUENCE OF INVESTIGATIONS

1) Gather as much information as possible.

2) Place the information in a sensible sequence known as the timeline.

3) Return to questions to ensure information matches the timeline.

4) Ask new questions generated by responses to confirm information.

These first ten to fifteen minutes are frustrating to many victims. They crave immediate relief and resolution, but they forget that the police need to stabilize the scene in order to collect as much evidence as possible. This is where you'll experience two competing mindsets clashing: your desire for justice and your desire to get out and take your family to a safe place. Remain patient. You are safe, surrounded by dedicated professionals. Follow through until the end of your plan, which is putting the perpetrators behind bars.

Detectives want to build a timeline of the crime as soon as possible. This begins with the very instant you make contact with the home invaders and continues all the way through to the authorities' arrival. The purpose is to match the criminal's modus operandi, or MO, in your case with other past and pending crimes. Locating crossovers can help pinpoint the identity and whereabouts of perpetrators.

During the interview, it's very important to answer the questions they ask first. Then, add supplemental information afterward. Your mind is going to be scattered, and by letting the police drive the interview, you'll be able to transfer your thoughts in a way that helps build that critical timeline.

When asked about criminals, list as many distinguishing features as possible. These include names used, speech patterns, dialects and the internal group dynamics you observed, such as who acts as a leader and who follows. Maybe an attacker turned sympathetic and signaled ways for you to escape; this person should be called out during the police interview as they may be more willing to betray their colleagues during formal questioning.

The first questions asked during the police interview might not mean a lot to you. But rest assured that the police are trying to paint a picture. These first few items build a frame, and subsequent questions fill in the blanks. Think of it like a model car kit. You need to have the framework in place before you can layer on the detailing and ornamental touches.

Don't get discouraged or upset during the police interview. It's a bad idea to suppress information, even if you're fearful, angry, ashamed, remorseful or filled with regret.

I can assure you that every victim struggles with the same types of negative emotions. You've done everything right, and because of your actions, you survived. You are victorious, and you have nothing to be ashamed about.

As the questions become more detailed, take a few seconds before responding. Close your eyes and picture the situation as it unfolded. Formulate a strong, accurate, concise answer. Don't fill in the blanks with assumptions. Only use the facts. Gaps are better than inaccurate information, since the detective can always add to the timeline from other sources.

The first interview needs to happen immediately after rescue. The reason for the timing is that your mind suppresses unpleasant memories in the days, weeks and months after an incident. The detective is focused on extracting those memories before your mind has a chance to clear them away.

How does questioning work? Here's a scenario. Pretend that a home invasion began at some point this afternoon, but you can't remember the exact time. A police interview might go something like this:

DETECTIVE: What time did you notice the knock on the door?

VICTIM: Gosh, it was sometime in the afternoon, but I . . . I really can't remember. I got scared, and everything was a blur.

DETECTIVE: That's understandable. You've been through a lot today. Can you remember if you were doing any particular activity when you heard the knock? Maybe making dinner, helping your daughter with her homework or watching television?

VICTIM: That's it! Yes, I was watching the six o'clock news.

In this example, the police officer used questions to direct the victim's brain. By doing so, he learned that the crime started sometime after six o'clock but before the news ended at six-thirty.

Or did it? Further questioning sometimes causes us to revisit our previous responses, uncovering additional details. Take a look at a later part of the mock interview:

DETECTIVE: So, remind me. . . . What were you doing right before the attack again?

VICTIM: We were eating dinner.

DETECTIVE: But I thought you were watching television? The six o'clock news, right?

VICTIM: Oh, yes, that's right. We were eating in front of the television. There was a story about the school superintendent announcing the closure of Miller Elementary School next year.

DETECTIVE: That's odd. I remember that story from last night's broadcast. Is it possible you were viewing a copy of last night's program on your DVR?

VICTIM: You know what. . . . You're absolutely right. It was last night's news. I taped it because we were out of the house and I didn't want to miss that story about the school.

The victim was not lying, but it's clear that his memory started to falter just moments after the attack. It's not his fault, as we are hardwired to suppress negative memories. However, this natural urge makes nailing down a timeline very challenging if the police wait even a little bit too long to act. Detectives and investigators are trained in techniques to help victims remember details. Inconsistencies will still pop up from time to time, but as long as the story does not contradict itself, many of these gaps and inconsistencies will resolve naturally.

The interview process may seem roundabout and peculiar, but it almost always works. And when you do start remembering details, don't get defensive or treat it like a bad thing. You are in a supportive atmosphere, and you are not being interrogated. Every fact you recall helps them act on a solution. If you're having trouble concentrating, ask to come back to it in a few minutes. The officer will be happy to oblige. Get comfortable, calm down, accept a glass of water and take breaks. Never force false information to just get through it.

After finishing questioning, most detectives will ask if you want to add anything. At that point, feel free to share any other details that you didn't get to discuss. Be as detailed as you would like. The more you share, the more information the authorities get. Let them backtrack on the new information to confirm and verify the added details. The full process may span several meetings over the course of a few days, but it's the best way to paint a full panorama of the incident's timeline.

For instance, I once investigated a series of break-ins conducted by a group called the Fast Food Felons. Yes, you read that correctly. Each of the attackers had a themed name—Cheeseburger, Nuggets, Large Fries, Milkshake—that they used during attacks. By cross-referencing these unique nicknames that victims recalled during their interviews, we were able to piece together their strategy and bring them a super-sized helping of justice.

AFTER THE INTERVIEW

Based on how rapidly all evidence is processed, the detectives may ask you to stay in another house or a hotel room at least overnight. In that case, they will let you gather up your belongings before securing the house and posting a guard. You will be allowed to return with an escort until the scene is fully processed. At that point, you will be able to return to the property and carry on as usual.

I can't speak for every police department's efficiency, but if no violent crime occurred, evidence collection may be over in as little as one hour. For violence with associated DNA (such as blood or sexual fluids), multiple broken belongings or homicides, the process can take several days or longer. Your access will be severely restricted during this time. Most detectives will recommend putting you up in a hotel for a few days. An investigator will be assigned to the case, and you will be encouraged to contact them with any questions or for daily updates. The detectives will facilitate this initial connection. The investigation will remain open until the perpetrators are apprehended and the case is closed. Bear in mind that this can take months or even years, and sometimes, the case remains open forever.

After your immediate needs are taken care of, the police will conduct a thorough neighborhood canvas. They will drive around, knock on doors, talk to people walking dogs and interact with those in the immediate community. The goal is to find out about every little concern in recent memory. These points may range from suspicious characters spotted around the neighborhood to pranks like egged houses, crank calls and trash disruptions. If the police uncover burglaries or attempted burglaries, they will work closely with the other victims to determine if there is a link between the crimes. All of this information feeds into the timeline, adding pieces to a multidimensional puzzle.

Technology makes this process even more robust. Officers will track down traffic camera footage and surveillance from nearby homes and businesses to examine footage bleed. Footage bleed occurs when a camera captures more visual data than the intended watched area. This can yield incredibly valuable information.

Next, many police organizations will connect with the local news. A public information officer may leak certain details and request the public's help. They may also educate the public by providing a synopsis of the crime. The public information officer's job is to determine how much information can be safely released without posing an addition threat to victims. Most of the time, an interview will appear on local television indicating the neighborhood targeted but not the specific home. A hotline for leads will frequently appear onscreen.

The day after the interview, you'll have a follow-up interview with your investigator. This serves as a wellness follow-up, a briefing on case updates, an opportunity to review newly uncovered details and an opportunity to ask additional questions. As more details trickle in, the timeline will be updated and the investigator will continuously match suspects and motives to other cases.

Depending on your demeanor and the severity of the crime, the investigator may encourage you to seek counseling. They'll give you a list of groups or professionals in the area. I recommend talking about your experiences, even if it's simply connecting with your local religious leader to find a support group. Home invasions and burglaries are traumatic events, and the emotional burden will persist even if your family isn't brutalized. You have to live in a house that was invaded, a place where your happy memories have been replaced with terrors of being tied up and taunted. I've seen a lot of people put their homes on the market days after an invasion because they cannot face living there anymore. This drastic move is perfectly acceptable if it's what you need to do to move on, but please try counseling first.

PREPARING A STATEMENT

Long after the home invasion, you'll still be forced to deal with lingering tasks. Cleanup is high on the list, as is installing protective measures. You'll also need to go to court once the criminals are caught to provide testimony and to get them locked up. Be ready for this postinvasion requirement so that you can enact the appropriate justice on those who wronged you.

One of the tasks you need to accomplish shortly after a home invasion is writing a police statement. This document is prepared routinely during an investigation, but you can get a head start on it by drafting your side of the story.

The statement is essentially a summary of your interview questions and any supporting information that you provide. It's written or captured in your own words.

In the statement, provide the most up-to-date contact information for you and anyone else in your family who will be cosigning the document. Individuals may also elect to file their own police statements. This is encouraged when family members witness different portions of the crime, usually due to their proximity to specific events. For example, if half the family is tied up in the living room, while the other half is kept in an upstairs bedroom, they will have different perspectives on the particulars of the crime based on where they witnessed events unfolding. These varied perspectives are valuable when the detective builds out the timeline.

In addition to your contact details, capture the name, rank and badges for all detectives and investigators present. Though this information will usually be documented by the responders, it's always a good idea to include it in your documentation for cross-referencing. If you cannot collect the information, write down as many details as you can remember and fill in the blanks later.

The most important part of the statement is describing what transpired from start to finish. Use your own words, and do not mix stories from multiple family members who had differing experiences. Use multiple reports to file these types of discrepancies. Note that the police may combine this section with their notes from the interview process. If you remember any elements later, you can inform your investigator. He or she will add the new information as a supplement to the initial report.

First, sit down and gather your thoughts on a piece of paper. Write down everything you remember right off the bat. At first, do not rack your brain trying to remember the right sequence of events. Instead, just write down everything that comes into your mind. You are gathering the pieces of a puzzle that will unfold over time, and you'll have the opportunity to organize everything later. Put it down and walk away! Give it a few hours, or even wait until the following day.

Next, read through what you wrote and make additional notes. Go through your notes, and as the memories and sequencing appears, start to arrange everything in the correct order. This will help you start writing your story line.

Skip a few spaces between your sentences to allow yourself to revisit and add details when memories reveal themselves. This step will add missing pieces to the puzzle, contributing toward a fuller picture. As each day passes, your memories will flash back to moments of the attack. You will want to capture these and add them to your statement. Sounds, smells and even movement will help these missing pieces to reveal themselves. Once the statement is complete, read it carefully line by line. If anything does not match your memory of the home invasion, correct it immediately. Avoid cross-referencing details with other people, as this may pollute your perspective. Once you are certain that the statement is accurate and complete, sign your name to it. If you prepared it yourself, bring it to your investigator and allow him or her enough time to review it with you. If it was completed for you during the interview, you can ask for a copy.

If at any point during the interview or statement preparation you notice that the investigator is not asking questions or prompting you, it's a bad sign. This means that you may have too much information—and you may be on the radar as a possible suspect. Criminals tend to get chatty, and working with a very talkative witness can raise flags that something is awry. If you think this is the case, slow down your discussion and wait to be prompted. This is not a race, and you won't get any points for finishing quickly. Give control back over to the detective so that he can get the information he needs and effectively scratch you off the suspect list.

WITNESS TIPS

In order to best help the police bring justice to the criminals, include in your statement as many details about the attackers as you can recall. During the invasion, you will need to rely on your senses to pick up any distinguishing features of the assailants. Your ears are impossible to plug, so prioritize them as your top sense. Listen for the dialect used by attackers and their tones of voice. Pick out leaders from followers, assigning names if possible. Note whether your attacker is talking to you or about you, as this can make all the difference in pinpointing their motivations.

If you can figure out names or other identifying characteristics, make mental notes with word associations or other memorization devices. These can help the police determine whether the MO matches up with other crime scenes and leads, even those in other states. If you've been victimized by serial home invaders, they may be able to piece together the details to stop other home invasions in the vicinity.

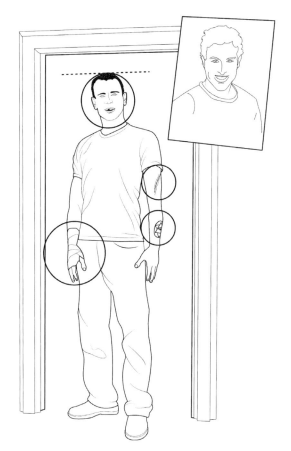

During an invasion, pay attention to key non-removable features of the invader(s), such as tattoos, scars, hair and eye color, which will help you and authorities confirm their identity later.

Even when home invaders leave the room, strain to hear what they're up to. If they're on the phone, determine if it's a landline or their own personal cell phone. Try to figure out who they're talking to. Attackers who check in aren't on their own clock, meaning that there are outside connections to your home invasion. They may also use the Internet to contact others outside the home.

You can also feel for subtle differences in the ways that attackers touch you. If they handle you gently and show concern, it means they either don't like the leader's orders or are sympathetic to your plight. If they help you up and escort you from place to place, they're softer than a criminal that drags you around.

Vision is the first sense to be disrupted during a home invasion, usually via blindfold. If you are lucky enough to have your eyes available, scan the attackers for any and all identifiers. Look for tattoos and piercings, as well as birthmarks, deformities and accidental losses like missing fingers. These things stand out, they're hard to cover up or fix and they can help with your police statement.

If a voice sounds familiar, or if a pair of eyes seem to belong to someone you know, it's a very real possibility that you are already acquainted with your attacker. According to the U.S. Department of Justice, victims knew their attackers in 65 percent of home invasions. Complete strangers only made up 28 percent of these crimes from 2003 through 2007.[43] Be mindful of how the attackers move through your house. Determine if they are looking for something that they know is there, signaling intimate knowledge of your belongings, or if they're looking to see what pops up.

Practice remembering details as frequently as possible to help sharpen your witness skills. Though you won't be able to get the full line of interview questioning down pat, you can work on your answering strategies. To get started, think about something you witnessed earlier today. This could be something completely innocuous, such as a trip to the grocery store. Recall as many details as you can, and test yourself later in the day. Alternatively, snap a cell phone picture of a scene, then wait ten minutes before recounting the specifics. Compare your mental notes with the photograph.

FAMILY DEBRIEFS

After a home invasion, you will feel shaken, scared and violated. Your home will never be quite the same. Once someone has broken in, they've come into your home and taken away your privacy, dignity and sense of self. It changes the whole tone and atmosphere. Fortunately, you've done everything possible to make it hard on them. You've stayed safe, stayed strong and stayed alive. Helping your family to understand this should be your top priority once you've completed your official police statements.

The scars from a home invasion last for a lifetime. Remember that story I relayed in the introduction about the home invasion that I survived down in Hialeah, Florida? To this day, I still think about it every time I hear a knock at the door. It feels like it was yesterday, not four decades ago. You never forget the sound of a door being kicked in, or the sight of a revolver pointed between your eyes. The sounds of your mother and brother crying and screaming as you're kicked mercilessly on the floor echo forever in your ears. Even as I look back on it now, I keep thinking about how lucky we were to survive on hope and prayers alone. It makes me shake.

Formal family debriefs help to ease these bad feelings once the police leave the premises or when you safely arrive at another family's member home or at the hotel. During a family debrief, you confirm the welfare of those around you. Begin by establishing eye contact, then soliciting verbal and nonverbal confirmations that each individual is emotionally well. I recommend sitting in a circle and starting with the oldest family members first. Confirm they know where they are, the first step to establishing presence. Ask for their name, address and wellness status next. If something seems off, or if you sense any hesitation, probe deeper to ensure the person is fully present after such a jarring crisis situation.

Next, have the group stand up and move. Flex arms and legs, and encourage everyone to gently twist their abdominal cores. Make the motions calm and soothing. Shift the head and neck from side to side, then in circles. The goal is to locate any trauma or injury that may have been suppressed by adrenaline and shock. I know you think it sounds far-fetched, but I've even seen people with broken fingers who don't realize that their digits are in poor shape until long after the emergency medical technicians are gone. The same goes for stab wounds, abrasions and even gunshot wounds to the extremities. It's normal, especially since your brain was focused on survival. As normalcy returns, so does the pain we've suppressed.

Once mental and physical wellness checks wrap, start collecting their stories. Yes, each family member was already interviewed by the police and may have prepared an individual statement. However, some children and teenagers might not feel comfortable talking to a stranger about their ordeal. Discussing it in a family-only setting may uncover additional details that are vital to solving a crime. Jot down notes, or capture them with your phone's audio record function.

Build your own timeline to figure out what each person remembers. Make the environment relaxed and comfortable, but keep your notes as formal as possible. Don't forget that your family has already been questioned by the police. Make sure they feel safe and relaxed talking to another family member to see if anything else surfaces, including emotions and lingering feelings. Trace the stories to capture everything the individuals recall. After the fact, you'll supply these notes or recordings to the detective to further flesh out their official timelines. Fish as deep as possible with your questions. Begin with pointed, direct questions that uncover major facts, and then slowly unravel the finer points by exploring in greater depth. Little details can have a big impact, and information is never irrelevant!

After hearing everything, draw your own conclusions. Compare notes to see if stories corroborate or disprove certain details. As patterns emerge, ask the whole family questions, such as:

- Did you speak with anyone out of the ordinary today?
- Did anyone approach you while you were outside?
- Did anyone do anything strange in your presence?
- Were there any out-of-place phone calls today?
- Do you feel like you were being watched by someone?
- What happened while you were out at lunch/school/work/football practice?

If you're not getting answers, focus your questions in with a specific checklist. Why does it matter? The following example hits the point on the nose.

Years ago, there was a mobile home community with about 30 units that experienced a series of break-ins. Most of the burglaries followed the same pattern. Someone forced their way in the back door or a cracked window, then grabbed the pillowcases off the bed. They threw all valuable items inside, climbed back out and then hit a half dozen more units.

Now, this particular community was a favorite among "snowbirds," retired individuals who went north during the summer and came back south during cooler weather. About half the residents were part-timers. Since these were vacation homes, some individuals knew when units were not occupied. Initially, investigators ruled out family members due to multiple specific targets being hit. The police instead looked at employees who were familiar with residents' comings and goings. Nothing stood out, and the case reached a standstill.

That all changed one morning after patrols increased. A police investigator casing the neighborhood spotted an elderly widow walking her dog. She followed the same routine every day at five-thirty in the morning, just before sunrise. The officer introduced himself to the woman and met her dog. The friendly exchange seemed ordinary until the officer asked if the woman had seen anything strange. She said she hadn't and the conversation nearly ended. The police officer thought he'd dig a little deeper before continuing his route.

He pressed. What about people on bikes, or even shady-looking passersby? Perhaps she'd seen a car driving slowly?

The woman's eyes lit up. She commented on a so-called weird car she'd seen driving very slowly a few days prior. It was blue, she added, with a rear taillight out and no headlights on. In the faint light of dawn, she noticed the out-of-state license plate almost matched her anniversary date, a string of numbers that stuck in her mind.

The officer ran the tag number and found that it belonged to a stolen vehicle. Later that day, they found a blue car abandoned under a highway overpass with one taillight out. Officers staked out the position, and two days later, they observed a guy changing the plates and driving off. They stopped him at a light and caught the criminals.

The moral of the story is that the break in the case would not have been discovered if the officer hadn't pried with detailed questions. They made all the difference. Use them in family debriefs for similar revelations.

At this point, you will have to begin your own closure. This means returning to a sense of normalcy in your own life.

First, you will need to accept what has happened to you. It wasn't your fault. You did not want it to happen, and you are not responsible for the outcome. However, you do need to start managing your family's recovery.

There are entire disciplines and techniques dedicated to getting through grief and hardships. They are designed to rebuild your emotional strength. Over the past 30 years, I've built up a number of approaches that work for me. I'd like to share them with you, as I think they would be very helpful in the emotional recovery that follows a home invasion. Below are some of the common stages of emotional response:

DENIAL: The reality that something horrific happened to you is a shock in and of itself. You will be filled with disbelief, and many people build an inner wall to protect themselves from this knowledge. Fortunately, shock does serve a positive internal function: It helps protect your emotional equilibrium. This balance enables you to keep moving forward. However, bear in mind that it may take weeks or months to heal if you do not force yourself to get ahead of it.

GUILT: You will blame yourself. The pain you feel inside during times of loss or hardship is often described as excruciating. Often, this pain leads to dangerous softening mechanisms such as drugs, alcohol and addictions to cope with your feelings. The sooner you can bring yourself to accept that the invasion was not your fault, the better off you will be.

ANGER: Your pain develops, evolving from guilt to rage. You fail to find justification for the anger that you feel. Your attitude causes you to target others, and you spontaneously burst into fits of outrage. Many times, this will ruin your relationships with friends and family, and may even cause you to question your faith. Again, the sooner you can accept that the attack was not your fault, and that you did everything you could to protect your family, the better able you will be to avoid some of these negative consequences.

DESPAIR: You will isolate yourself. Many on the outside view this as you improving and moving on with your life. However, you may actually want to be left alone just to sit in your own dark corner of despair. You may smile on the outside while feeling lonely inside. This is the time when you need to be surrounded by your closest and dearest loved ones.

INSIDE HEALING: You start to open yourself up to new things, beginning to move forward. You understand that you are the only one who can put these events behind you. As you start to adjust, you clean up your home, put new locks on the doors, get a security alarm system and take other precautions. You feel less pain, and you begin retaking control over your life.

MAKING YOURSELF OVER: Next, you will speak with family members and close friends about what has happened. You will start to become more emotionally aware of yourself, working through realistic solutions to some of the feelings you've encountered based on your home invasion experience.

ACCEPTANCE: Finally, you will start to move beyond the invasion's grip on your life. You will accept that it happened, that it was not your fault, and that you are lucky enough to have the rest of your life ahead of you. You can now move forward.

So, what can you do immediately to set this emotional healing into motion? Within the first zero to eight hours, the period that occurs immediately after the attack, sit down and write your notes about what happened. Talk with your family about what transpired and make sure they are processing the incident. Within 24 hours, seek out a counseling group. This may be found through your church, or via an independent support group in your area. Continue to engage your family about their feelings and responses over the course of the next three days.

EVADING FUTURE INVASIONS

People are creatures of habit. After experiencing a home invasion, it's hard to break those habits so that you avoid being victimized again. But you have to. If it happened once, it can happen again. And the next time,

you might not be so lucky to survive. It could be the same criminals or different ones. They might prey on a different perceived weakness, or they might use the same vulnerability again. Do not let them.

Start with visual identifiers that are seen from a passing car or passerby. Transform your home's curb appeal so that the property no longer looks the same from the street. Paint or re-side the house, and shake up your gardens. Redecorate the porch or stoop, and try swapping out the wattage of your light bulbs. If you used low watt bulbs before, go with a higher wattage. Simultaneously, increase your visual deterrents such as security system signs and Beware of Dog posts.

Up the number of security walks you take around the property. Scope out the perimeter at different times of day and make note of any strange findings. Even if something seems too subtle to warrant a second glance, take the time to look into it. Vigilance is the only way to prevent a second home invasion from unfolding.

Next, shake up your own routine. Avoid leaving lights on during the day, which makes it look like you're not home. Get to know your neighbors and start observing their routines to get inspiration for changing your own daily chores and paths.

If you think you might come across as predictable, others probably feel the same way. Break patterns. Don't always leave your house, get in the car, drive to the same place for coffee and take the same path to work. Instead, once every few days, walk around your house. Dawdle on the lawn for a few minutes, or take a call on the porch. Some days, make a left out of the driveway; other days, take a right. Go to one café every other day, but try new places on the days in between. You're not just changing your family's defenses, you're changing your family's lifestyle to protect them from ever enduring that horrific crime again.

Use the Internet more frequently to add a proactive element to your safety. Understand what's happening around you by reading local news stories focused on burglaries, thefts and home invasions. Look for similarities to the crime you survived. Even if it's a few years after your ordeal, report any striking similarities to the police. It may be enough to link the new attacks to the one you survived.

The absolute worst thing you can do after a home invasion is to lose hope. Do not allow yourself to become desperate, paranoid or scared. Don't settle into the lifestyle of a hermit who stays inside and never leaves, thinking that you can protect your home from future attacks. This is no way to live, and worse, it will not do anything to protect you in the future. Become safety-minded, and know what you need to do to survive. Even if others around you do not understand, remain confident in your own knowledge of what could happen. Be prepared for home invasion situations and danger, but don't let your apprehension rule your life. The best you can do is to prepare for as many what-if scenarios as possible.

With the right mindset, planning and dedication, you can and will survive a home invasion. Approach every action and decision with the knowledge that it may have benefits—or consequences—later. Remember that there is a difference between paranoia and preparedness. Paranoia is thinking that everything is going to happen and that you will not be ready for it. Preparedness, on the other hand, means that anything can happen, but you're ready for it.

I don't live in a world where I'm scared. I live in a world where I strive to always be aware. Being ready to take action is different than being hopeful you won't ever have to. As you prepare your family to survive a home invasion I implore you to follow the advice in this book, listen to your gut and stick to your plans.

PRACTICE EXERCISE 10: DIAL DOWN DANGER

In this final exercise, get ready to report a mock home invasion to an emergency services operator. Have a family member sit in a room in one side of your house while you move to an opposite wing. Let the family member call your cell phone, and answer as though you are an emergency services operator.

Use canned dialogue and realistic prompts to get information from your family member, testing their ability to succinctly request assistance. Start by asking if this is an emergency, then prompting for their name and location. Ask about the nature of the emergency. Sample dialogue is available earlier in this chapter to guide your discussion.

To add a realistic angle, abruptly hang up your phone after a set number of seconds pass. Vary the amount of time you stay on the line for each family member, ranging from ten seconds all the way up to one minute. This will mirror the possibility of having the phone wires cut or tampered with by an intruder. The goal is to get as much of the key information over to the operator as quickly as possible.

After everyone has had a turn calling the mock emergency services number, regroup in the family room and discuss your findings. Highlight calls that went particularly well. Suggest improvements for reporting the emergency in the future. This exercise is for home invasion scenarios, but keep in mind that you can extend it to apply to any household emergency such as a fire or acute medical condition.

Jot down notes in a journal entry and store it—along with any scripts you used—in your family action plan dossier. By now, your collection should be quite full. Encourage your family members to review the materials often, and challenge children and spouses to add to the dossier whenever they think up something new for the family action plan. Every three or six months, sit down and recap additions or evolutions to the plan.

Remember that your dossier is the physical embodiment of your family action plan. It's an ever-growing, ever-changing toolbox that is meant to be accessed, utilized and edited over time. Don't be afraid to change elements to better suit your family's survival needs. Let it serve you as the living document it's meant to be.

CONCLUSION

Thank you for reading the survival and preparation strategies covered in this book. It may sound strange, but as a member of the greater police community, I am grateful to you for taking the time to learn about ways to protect your family during a home invasion. The fewer successful home invasions that happen, the less enthusiastic criminals will be to attempt them. Eventually, this may lead to a decrease in criminal attempts, making our country safer and reducing the danger facing our citizens and law enforcement officers.

I want you to survive when the odds are against you. I wrote this book for every man and woman who wants to feel safe and equipped to defend their families at all costs without using a conventional weapon like a gun or switchblade. Now, I hope you'll have a better understanding of the saying that you are your own best weapon, and sometimes, your only weapon. By now, I think you've probably figured out that defending your family and home without a conventional weapon isn't about brawn, it's about brains. You need to be smart in how you plan, position and practice.

As I wrap up, I'd like to remind you that all skills are perishable. What you knew last year is no longer entirely relevant to today, and what you know now might not help you survive a home invasion next year. Evolve your patterns and monitor trends to stay as far ahead of the survival chain as you possibly can. Let the dossier you assembled grow, and never stop rehearsing, practicing and thinking ahead of the curve.

I'm an expert in the field, but I always welcome your comments, input and suggestions. The same goes for questions. I'm all ears. Please reach out to me via my websites. Check out www.yourfamilydefense.com for more details about protecting your family and home, www.armatraining.com for my courses, www.usfightingsystems.com for self-defense and www.vistelar.com for more information. I'd love to hear from you.

Finally, the home invasion survival strategies I've outlined in this book are just the tip of the iceberg. Please dive deeper on any of the subjects you've read about to learn other ways to keep you and your family safe. There are a tremendous number of resources available, and I strongly encourage you to check out my websites for links to leading industry articles, publications and other insightful media.

Once again, thank you. I wish you and your family all the very best.

ACKNOWLEDGMENTS

While writing this book, I've thought about a number of family members, friends and professional mentors who have shaped how I look at family safety and readiness.

Starting at the beginning, my childhood prepared me for many of the career choices I have made. To that aim, thank you to my mother Mary Rose and my father David. Even though the decisions you made in my early life were not always ideal, I believe in my heart that you did the best you could with what you had. Thank you also to my brother Shawn for being the type of brother who allowed me to protect him even when he felt he didn't need any protection.

I also wanted to give thanks to my wife, Lisette, for the unconditional love and support she continues to give me each and every day to do what I do around the country. I also want to give thanks to Gary T. Klugiewicz, director of Verbal Defense and Influence and developer of the POSC® program, for his friendship and mentorship over the last twenty years. If it weren't for you, I would not be me.

I have been blessed by God to have the right guidance, coaching and mentors in my life. Without God in my life, I would be nothing.

Throughout the process of writing this book, many individuals have encouraged me, inspired me and educated me along the way. I am grateful for their time, friendship and shared knowledge and experiences. A tremendous thank you to all of the following individuals, listed alphabetically:

- Roy Bedard, president RRB Systems and Use of Force Expert

- Pete Bludworth, assistant warden, Coffee Correctional Facility

- Harry Dolan, retired police chief, Raleigh Police Department

- David Griffin, editor, *Police Magazine*

- Dave Grossi, retired lieutenant, Lead Instructor for the Calibre Press, Inc.

- Lt Col Dave Grossman, retired US Army, author, Speaker, Trainer

- John E Foy, Law Enforcement Training Officer (Retired), Ohio Peace Officer Training Academy

- Master Jay Kuk Lee, President and CEO, US Taekwondo Center

- Grandmaster Jae Kyu Lee, JK Lee Blackbelt Academy

- Master Chan Lee, JK Lee Blackbelt Academy

- Master Jim Nam, Master Victorville Taekwondo Academy

- Master Sammy Pejo, Technical Director, US Taekwondo Center

- Grandmaster Young-Hak Lee, U.S. Martial Arts Center

- Master Angie Lee, Master U.S. Martial Arts Center

- Master Jason Lee, Master U.S. Martial Arts Center

- Grandmaster Sang Chul Lee, Founding President and Chairman, US Taekwondo Center

- Dr. Bill Lewinsky, Founder and President, Force Science Institute

- "Coach" Bob Lindsey, Master Police Trainer

- Leslie Maris, Publisher, *Police Magazine*

- Fred Maulson, Chief Warden, Great Lakes Indian Fish and Wildlife Commission

- John Nebl, Police Sergeant (Ret.), Schaumburg Police Department

- Lt Col. Barry Neulen, Director, Department of Defense, Task Force

- Allen Oelschlaeger, CEO, Vistelar

- Leslie Pfeiffer, Publisher, *Police Magazine*

- Chuck Remsburg, Writer and Author of Caliber Press Series

- Kati Tillema, Operations Manager, Vistelar

- Bill Singleton, VP Sales, Vistelar

- Larry Smith, Larry Smith Enterprises

- Bob Willis, Master Police Trainer

- Jerry Zacharias, SWAT and Police Veteran and Master Firearms Instructor

Finally, I'd like to take a moment to thank the whole team at Page Street Publishing, including Will, Sarah, Alex, Lauren, Robert, Laura, Meg B., Meg P. and everyone else who had a hand in producing this book. I'm truly appreciative of all your work to share this book with the world. I'm confident that it will help many families learn how to protect themselves during a home invasion, and it has been an honor writing it.

ABOUT THE AUTHOR

Dave Young is the founder and director of Arma Training and cofounder of Vistelar, organizations that conduct training and certification for personal safety and the use of non-lethal and lethal weapons for law enforcement, corrections and security personnel and the United States military.

Recognized as one of the nation's leading defensive tactics experts specializing in physical encounters and home defense skills, Dave's areas of expertise include counter-combatives, crowd management, non-lethal weaponry, firearms and edged weapons. He developed a training DVD series for the U.S. Concealed Carry Association on carrying and using a firearm, improving firearm skills and techniques for winning a gun fight. In addition, Dave serves as the chairman of the policeone.com advisory board. He is a member of the *Police Magazine* advisory board and a technical advisory board member for the Force Science Research Center. He is an active member of several professional organizations including the International Law Enforcement Educators and Trainers Association (ILEETA) and the National Rifle Association (NRA), and he is an International Association of Law Enforcement Firearms Instructor (IALEFI).

Throughout his career, Dave has been featured in national publications and magazines for his expertise related to officer survival, personal safety and awareness. He has appeared as a consultant on CNN and Fox News, providing insights into officer tactics, survival and safety. Additionally, he has hosted several television programs for the National Geographic Channel on police technology and safety.

Dave has more than 30 years of combined civilian and military law enforcement experience. He has served as a sworn corrections and law enforcement officer in the state of Florida, and he is a veteran of the United States Marine Corps with several deployments around the world. He has trained and certified thousands of police, corrections, security and military instructors and trainers around the world on how to survive force-on-force attacks. This includes surviving and responding to home invasion and active shooter attacks. Dave continues to work with city, county, state and federal agencies to help prepare them to respond to life and death situations.

He is married with six children and four grandchildren.

ENDNOTES

This section contains resource links for all statistics and outside information contained within the book.

1 "24 Surprising Home Invasion and Robbery Statistics," by Brandon Gaille, 2 November 2014 - http://brandongaille.com/24-surprising-home-invasion-robbery-statistics/

2 "Are you safer owning a gun for home protection?" by James Causey, *Milwaukee Journal Sentinel*, 18 May 2013 - http://archive.jsonline.com/news/opinion/are-you-safer-owning-a-gun-for-home-protection-b9912440z1-207958831.html

3 "Man, woman terrorized during early-morning home invasion," by Joyce Lupiani and Mahsa Saeidi, KTNV ABC 13 Action News, 06 July 2016 - http://www.ktnv.com/news/crime/man-woman-tied-up-during-early-morning-home-invasion

4 FBI Uniform Crime Report, 2014 - https://ucr.fbi.gov/crime-in-the-u.s/2014/crime-in-the-u.s.-2014/offenses-known-to-law-enforcement/robbery

5 SafeWise – 8 Surprising Home Invasion & Burglary Statistics - http://www.safewise.com/blog/8-surprising-home-burglary-statistics/

6 FBI – UCR 2014, Robbery, Location - https://ucr.fbi.gov/crime-in-the-u.s/2014/crime-in-the-u.s.-2014/tables/robbery/robbery_table_2_robbery_location_percent_distribution_within_population_group_2014.xls

7 US DOJ national Crime Victimization Survey - http://www.bjs.gov/content/pub/ascii/vdhb.txt

8 US DOJ National Crime Victimization Survey - http://www.bjs.gov/content/pub/ascii/vdhb.txt

9 US DOJ National Crime Victimization Survey - http://www.bjs.gov/content/pub/ascii/vdhb.txt

10 "24 Surprising Home Invasion and Robbery Statistics," by Brandon Gaille, 2 November 2014 - http://brandongaille.com/24-surprising-home-invasion-robbery-statistics/

11 FBI – UCR 2014, Crime Trends, Table 15 - https://ucr.fbi.gov/crime-in-the-u.s/2014/crime-in-the-u.s.-2014/tables/table-15

12 "24 Surprising Home Invasion and Robbery Statistics," by Brandon Gaille, 2 November 2014 - http://brandongaille.com/24-surprising-home-invasion-robbery-statistics/

13 "Think Like a Burglar: When Do Burglars Strike?" by Kelley, Simplisafe, 11 July 2014 - http://simplisafe.com/blog/break-in-times#

14 "Security Statistics," from Safeguard the World - http://www.safeguardtheworld.com/statistics.html

15 SafeWise – 8 Surprising Home Invasion & Burglary Statistics - http://www.safewise.com/blog/8-surprising-home-burglary-statistics/

16 "24 Surprising Home Invasion and Robbery Statistics," by Brandon Gaille, 2 November 2014 - http://brandongaille.com/24-surprising-home-invasion-robbery-statistics/

17 "Dad: Having a plan saved my kids during home invasion," by CNN, on Fox 2 Now St. Louis, 24 August 2015 - http://fox2now.com/2015/08/24/dad-having-a-plan-saved-my-kids-during-home-invasion/

18 "Table 107. Personal and property crimes, 2008: Recent distribution of incidents where police came to the victim, by type of crime and police response time," from Criminal Victimization in the United States, 2008 - Statistical Tables, by the Bureau of Justice Statistics, May 2011. http://www.bjs.gov/content/pub/pdf/cvus/current/cv08107.pdf

19 "Average-Police-Response-Time to a 911 call?," by Angie M. Tarighi, Women's Self-Defense Institute - http://www.self-defense-mind-body-spirit.com/average-police-response-time.html

20 "Using Body Language to Show Dominance and Submissiveness," by Sinay Tarakanov. Study Body Language - http://www.study-body-language.com/using-body-language.html

21 "Three of the Easiest Ways to Manipulate People Into Doing What You Want," by Melanie Pinola. Lifehacker, 19 October 2012 - http://lifehacker.com/5953183/three-of-the-most-evil-ways-to-manipulate-people-into-doing-what-you-want

22 "Police: Victim's doorbell security system scares off would-be burglary suspect," by Kimberly Querry, NBC News Channel KFOR, 17 June 2016 - http://kfor.com/2016/06/17/police-victims-doorbell-security-system-scares-off-would-be-burglary-suspect/

23 "National Crime Victimization Survey – Victimization During Household Burglary," by Shannan Catalano / Bureau of Justice Statistics, September 2010 - http://www.bjs.gov/content/pub/ascii/vdhb.txt

24 "Victim foiled home invasion attempt in Carlisle, police say," by Matt Miller, Penn Live, 08 June 2010 - http://www.pennlive.com/midstate/index.ssf/2010/06/victim_foiled_home_invasion_at.html

25 "24 Surprising Home Invasion and Robbery Statistics," by Brandon Gaille, 2 November 2014 - http://brandongaille.com/24-surprising-home-invasion-robbery-statistics/

26 "24 Surprising Home Invasion and Robbery Statistics," by Brandon Gaille, 2 November 2014 - http://brandongaille.com/24-surprising-home-invasion-robbery-statistics/

27 "Building Strong Shapes with Triangles," by Roger's Connection - http://www.rogersconnection.com/triangles/

28 "Police: Mom, sons thwart home invasion," by Trace Christenson, *Battle Creek Enquirer*, 25 August 2016 - http://www.battlecreekenquirer.com/story/news/local/2016/08/25/police-mom-sons-thwart-home-invasion/89359374/

29 "Basic Hand to Hand Self Defense," by Tres Tew, ExpertVillage, 18 January 2008 - https://www.youtube.com/watch?v=vsYIxgGKGq8

30 "911 tape: 'Shoot him again!' husband tells wife hiding from home intruder," by Jeff Black, NBC News, 10 January 2013 - http://usnews.nbcnews.com/_news/2013/01/10/16449815-911-tape-shoot-him-again-husband-tells-wife-hiding-from-home-intruder

31 "5 top tips from self-defense experts," by Alison Bowen, *Chicago Tribune*, 11 December 2015 - http://www.chicagotribune.com/lifestyles/health/sc-self-defense-health-1216-20151210-story.html

32 "Does Eye Gouging Really Work?" by AttackProof.com - http://attackproof.com/does-eye-gouging-work-in-real-sel-defense-fights.html

33 "Violent Home Invasion," the FBI UCR News Blog, FBI, 22 April 2016 - https://ucr.fbi.gov/news/stories/2016/april/violent-home-invasion

34 "What is Mental Conditioning?" by Dr. Lauren Tashman, Inspire Performance Consulting - http://www.getting-u-inspired.com/mental-conditioning.html

35 "A Mindful Difference: Respond vs. React," by Jon Mertz, Thin Difference, 07 March 2013 - https://www.thindifference.com/2013/03/a-mindful-difference-respond-vs-react/

36 Second death report in Polk home invasion, one released from hospital," by Kera Mashek, WFTS ABC Action News, 10 July 2016 - http://www.abcactionnews.com/news/region-polk/one-dead-two-seriously-injured-following-polk-co-home-invasion

37 "80 percent of Americans prefer single-family homeownership," by Charlotte O'Malley, *Builder Magazine*, 13 August 2013 - http://www.builderonline.com/money/economics/80-percent-of-americans-prefer-single-family-homeownership_o

38 "After Brutal Home Invasion, Some Scars Never Heal," by Juju Chang and Candace Smith, ABC News, 17 July 2014, http://abcnews.go.com/US/brutal-home-invasion-scars-heal/story?id=24588314

39 "Home invasion suspect tied up with belt during citizen's arrest," by Nafeesa Karim, CTV Vancouver, 28 July 2016 - http://bc.ctvnews.ca/home-invasion-suspect-tied-up-with-belt-during-citizen-s-arrest-1.3006958

40 Field Manual FM 21-150 Combatives, 1992 - http://www.angelfire.com/art/enchanter/fmrope.html

41 "Fairburn woman shot when crooks find her hiding in closet," by Rebekka Schramm, CBS46, 04 January 2013 - http://www.cbs46.com/story/20500750/woman-shot-during-violent-home-invasion

42 "Robbery victim shot 14 times tells survival story," CBS46, 13 March 2014 - http://www.cbs46.com/story/24970113/exclusive-burglary-victim-shot-14-times-tells-survival-story

43 "National Crime Victimization Survey – Victimization During Household Burglary," by Shannan Catalano/Bureau of Justice Statistics, September 2010 - http://www.bjs.gov/content/pub/ascii/vdhb.txt

INDEX